TO HUNT
A KILLER

JULIE MACKAY AND ROBERT MURPHY

HARPER
element

HarperElement
An imprint of HarperCollins*Publishers*
1 London Bridge Street
London SE1 9GF

www.harpercollins.co.uk

HarperCollins*Publishers*
1st Floor, Watermarque Building, Ringsend Road
Dublin 4, Ireland

First published by HarperElement 2022

1 3 5 7 9 10 8 6 4 2

© Julie Mackay and Robert Murphy 2022

Julie Mackay and Robert Murphy assert the moral right to
be identified as the authors of this work

A catalogue record of this book is
available from the British Library

ISBN 978-0-00-850747-3

Printed and bound in the UK using 100% renewable electricity at
CPI Group (UK) Ltd

MIX
Paper from
responsible sources
FSC **FSC™ C007454**
www.fsc.org

This book is produced from independently certified FSC™ paper
to ensure responsible forest management.

For more information visit: www.harpercollins.co.uk/green

This book is dedicated to Melanie, who never deserved to die.

To Jean, who has shown me such strength and resilience along with kindness, despite over thirty years of trauma.

To Adrian and Karen, who should never have had to suffer.

And to my children, Callum, Connie and Toby, for whom having a murder detective as a mum was really difficult. I love and admire you for the people you have become.

ACKNOWLEDGEMENTS

Julie Mackay and Robert Murphy would like to thank: Gary Mason, for all his contributions, and our agent, Clare Hulton. At HarperCollins we'd like to thank Kelly Ellis, Holly Blood, Ajda Vucicevic and Jane Donovan.

Julie Mackay:

I would like to recognise the unwavering work and dedication of all who are involved in the investigation of murder. Some are named here but there are so many more who contributed to this investigation over thirty-one years. Without their diligence from day one to the final court appearance Melanie would never have got justice.

The statement below was passed to me when I became a Senior Investigating Officer and I have in turn passed it on to those who followed me. Every word rings true.

'No greater honour will ever be bestowed on an officer, or a more profound duty imposed on him, than when he is entrusted with the investigation of the death of another human being.'

I'd like to thank Rob, for listening to weeks and weeks of me, and then writing such a brilliant book.

Robert Murphy:

I would like to thank my wife Ellie and my sons for their help and support. Everyone at ITV News. And Julie for being so brave, open-hearted and searingly honest.

PROLOGUE

It was later, years later, when Jean Road told me about that summer's morning in 1984. Jean didn't tell me in a single sitting. She'd just drop bits in, here and there, at our many meetings over the long years when I was hunting for her daughter Melanie's killer.

We had moved past that polite, early stage when I was a murder detective and she was the victim's mother. We were becoming friends. Jean said she trusted me. We were both mums, both had three children.

If she were alive, Melanie and I would have been the same age: forty-one.

Perhaps it was because I'm a woman. Perhaps it was a shared sense of humour. To her, I was good company, a refreshing change from the male detectives who'd sat in her lounge, drunk her tea, insisted they would bring Jean justice and then got promoted away.

To me, Jean was dignity personified. We laughed in each other's company.

We still do.

But sometimes we didn't joke. And we didn't catch each other's news. Instead, Jean would sit and tell me about that summer's morning.

Few could have understood the pure brutality of that instant when life, for Jean, went from one existence to another.

That moment was seared in her mind. Twenty-five years old, yet fresh as if it were that morning. And for Jean, what struck her most was that 9 June 1984 had begun so normally.

She had awoken. Then thought the questions you ask yourself in the fog of first consciousness:

'What day is it?'

'Saturday.'

'What do I have to do today?'

Then: 'Is Melanie home?'

Jean got up, walked along the hallway and looked into Melanie's room. The bed was made. Melanie's desk was covered in textbooks: maths, geography and chemistry. Melanie's A levels started on Monday.

Pinned to the walls were posters of boy bands pouting. Jean recognised their names: Wham!, Duran Duran, Dexys Midnight Runners. Next to the posters were photos of Melanie with friends. Teenagers laughing. Her daughter was blonde, wide-eyed and had a broad, carefree grin. In the background of the pictures were Bath's highlights: the Royal Crescent, the Roman Baths, Pulteney Bridge. She had only lived in the city two years, but she'd made it her home.

Melanie stayed out overnight with friends occasionally. Not often, just sometimes. And she always called first thing to say she was okay.

Jean went downstairs.

'Tony? Have you heard from Melanie?'

Jean's husband was in the kitchen having breakfast.

'Has she called?' Jean asked again.

'No.'

Jean and Tony spent the next two hours talking, passing time, doing the kinds of things middle-aged parents do when their children no longer need ferrying to clubs, groups or parties on a Saturday morning. They also looked at the clock, checked the phone, reassured each other and tried to remain calm.

Then the sound started.

It was distant at first, but still audible over the birdsong and gentle rumble of lazy Saturday traffic.

Alien, penetrating and distinct.

Three syllables.

It repeated.

Jean and Tony looked at each other.

The sound grew nearer and louder. Jean frowned. She couldn't quite make out what it was saying, but the rhythm of the word was so familiar. To Jean, it was primal.

'Melanie … Melanie …' The sound from outside had become clearer, repetitive.

Metallic and echoing.

Jean leapt to the window, looked beyond the close-cut lawn and well-tended garden. She saw a police car driving along the little side road, outside her house. The patrol car had a loudspeaker on its roof, shrieking the words, 'Melanie … MELANIE …'

Jean didn't recall what happened next; she just found herself outside, running along the street, trying to chase the police car, that loudspeaker calling, 'Melanie.'

The police car was about to pull from their cul-de-sac on to the main road, but Jean reached it, banging on the boot. The car stopped. Jean ran to the side. Even though it was early, the morning was hot. The windows were wound down. A police officer in short sleeves sat with a microphone to his mouth.

'We have a Melanie. She hasn't come home,' Jean cried.

Jean Road describes *this* as the moment when all hell broke loose.

The moment when she knew that her daughter was never coming back.

CHAPTER 1

SEPTEMBER 2009

'The doors won't budge,' I said.

The metal shutters of the police warehouse loomed over at me. What were they? Ten feet high? I grabbed the handle again and tried dragging them apart. They refused to move.

If Gary was laughing, he did it silently, but I'm sure he was amused.

He's quite deadpan, Gary. Gives nothing away. But I'm sure seeing me struggle with the warehouse doors tickled something deep inside.

'Go the other way, Julie,' he shouted from behind the steering wheel. Even his shouting is measured.

'I'm *trying*.'

I started pushing instead of pulling. The big metal shutters didn't move. I mean, not at all. Not even a little wiggle.

'Try pulling.'

'I *was* pulling.'

There was a creak and a rumble. And the doors started to grind open. Then they stopped. I swore. Gary got out of the car and came over, his shirt hanging out of his trousers, as ever.

'They're getting worse. They should have fixed them years ago,' he said.

He pulled and the shutters started moving slowly. His face reddened.

We worked at a twin-assault: Gary pulling the large handle, me pushing the side of the warehouse door.

'Is that enough?' I asked.

'It'll have to be.'

'I'll drive her in,' I said. 'How many times have you scraped the cars this month? Twice?'

'Once. And the wall jumped out at me.'

I got into the car and manoeuvred it through the half-opened door into the darkness of the warehouse. The only light inside was from the shaft of grey sunlight which peeked through that gap we'd made between the warehouse doors. I could see shelves going up, floor-to-ceiling. How tall was the room? Three storeys? Some of the shelves were buckling under the weight of large green crates stacked up.

'It's freezing,' I shuddered.

'You're a cold case officer now,' Gary chuckled. 'You got too comfy in Professional Standards. You'll get your hands dirty here … And cold.'

He wandered off, muttering something about light switches.

I could see my breath, grey and misty in the half-light. I made my way to one of the shelves and looked up at the boxes. My eyes were adjusting. It reminded me of that last scene in *Citizen Kane*. But these were not the belongings of a lonely millionaire hoarder.

This was a storehouse for the force's unsolved murders.

The crates were labelled with codenames. Some I knew, like the murder of a nurse in Bristol in 1976. I was sure we had a DNA sample on that case. Others meant nothing to me.

To the right was a crate, the lid splayed open and a brown paper bag with plastic windows sticking through the top.

An alarm started. Lights came on and the warehouse was suddenly ablaze in an orange glow of sodium strip-lights.

'You okay?' Gary was shouting over the siren.

'What's the alarm?' I yelled.

'It's always going off.'

A door opened to the side and a large traffic officer in a high visibility jacket came in.

'Oh, it's you again, Mason,' he said, looking at Gary.

'Can you turn the alarm off?' I shouted.

He turned to me, his eyes narrowed. Then he spun around and left, wiping his mouth as he went. I was sure he was dusting off doughnut sugar. Moments later, the alarm stopped.

'Why's it so cold?'

'It's the freezers,' Gary said. 'To preserve the samples.'

'You mean, one power cut and bang goes fifty years of evidence?'

He nodded.

Part of the warehouse looked like something you might find under a forensic officer's Christmas tree. A pile of packages, each wrapped in a brown paper bag with the words

'Avon and Somerset Police' in bold, black letters. Orange tags at the neck of each sack with the scrawled details of the package's innards and the murder to which the evidence related.

'What's the killer's name?' I asked.

'The suspect,' Gary replied, correcting me, Mr Fastidious.

'The suspect?'

'Gallagher.'

'Where do you keep the G-cards?'

'Hopefully not under that,' said Gary, nodding to the giant pile.

'And Motty's sure he's the murderer?'

'Said he'd put his mortgage on it.'

I looked at the pile of packages, then glanced at the shelves buckling under storage boxes.

'The cards will be in a shoebox,' said Gary. 'That's probably in a green crate.'

I started looking along the shelves at the green boxes with their labelled codenames: Operation Arrow, Operation Sussex. One was the first murder I'd worked on. The stabbing of a gay man in Bristol in '89. I had been a probationer and had been told the team needed a female officer to help with what they loosely called 'women's things'.

'Julie, you can be the gofer,' they'd said. 'Go for this, go for that.'

Twenty years later, that murder was unsolved, as was the killing of Melanie Road. And that was why we were here.

Melanie's murder inquiry was codenamed Operation Rhodium and I found myself mouthing the words as I walked beside the shelving. 'Rhodium, Rhodium,' I muttered. 'How many boxes are there?' I shouted to Gary.

CHAPTER 1

'We don't really know. It's a paper case. There were 30,000 documents. It was the last murder before they brought in computers.'

I groaned.

'Here's one.'

The box was green and stuck under a pile of four other crates. I tried pulling it, but it didn't shift. Gary came to help. Together, we lifted the boxes up, off and away. Then we slid out the box labelled Rhodium.

'How old was Melanie?' I puffed.

'Seventeen,' Gary replied.

'And it was 1985?'

'Eighty-four. June 1984.'

I worked out my age. Nineteen eighty-four … I had been about to move to Bath then, I was sixteen. Melanie's age, nearly. Just a few months younger.

I opened the crate. Inside were files with names and actions. And a shoebox.

Gary pulled it up, sliding off the lid. His eyes widened, then frowned.

'Cs.' He groaned. 'But it'll be in a box that looks like this.'

He passed the box over. Inside were hundreds of index cards. Six by four inches. With printed sections labelled Surname, Maiden Name, Forenames, Address, Home Tel, DOB, Occupation, Height, Build, Hair. The cards also had boxes for Car Details and on the flip-side were two columns: Ref No and Information. The sections were filled in by hand. Some of the cards boasted neat handwriting, others bore illegible scrawls. Some were filled in fully, others had just a few details.

Cs were no good to us. The killer – sorry, the *suspect* – was Gallagher. We needed the box with the Gs in.

Gary put the shoebox back in the green crate, then dragged it towards the car.

'So, someone really did call into *Crimewatch UK*?'

He nodded.

I knew a bit about Melanie's unsolved murder. Sketchy details, not much more. Back in 2001, I had moved to Bath's CID and a couple of wily old detectives were reviewing the case. They had big hopes and told me it would be solved with science. But despite their experience and shrewdness, they had been unable to find her killer.

Seven years on, now another team was in charge of the case, using the twenty-fifth anniversary and a national television show, BBC's *Crimewatch UK*, to appeal for help. Avon and Somerset Police had appeared in a short film for the programme. It had aired a few months earlier, so I had sat at home and watched it on TV.

The studio presenter read a link with the broad details. It was the twenty-fifth anniversary of the murder of the Bath schoolgirl Melanie Road. She'd been stabbed and raped as she walked home from a night out with friends.

The presenter then introduced a film. A reconstruction showed a pretty, blonde teenage girl, smiling, running out from home, playing tennis with a friend. Slow, sensitive piano music underscored the images.

'She had so many friends, she was taking her A levels, the world was her oyster …'

CHAPTER 1

On screen appeared a woman who looked like Melanie, but older. The name-strap read 'Karen Road, Melanie's sister'.

A man's voice now: 'She wanted to go to university, she'd applied to a number. She was never sad, she was always happy.' This interviewee came into vision. 'Adrian Road, Melanie's brother,' read his name-strap.

The reconstruction continued, with actresses playing Melanie and a younger version of Karen. Her sister described going into Bath city centre, buying flowers for their parents and visiting a travel agent. Melanie had had a Greek boyfriend in Bath and had wanted to book a holiday to travel there with him over the summer.

'I remember dropping her by the hotel, her kissing me on the cheek and that was the last time I saw her,' said Karen, her voice quivering now.

The reconstruction cut to some night-time shots and a new voice was heard, a voice I knew well: 'It was June 8th 1984, the last day of the Bath Festival. Thousands of people were starting to leave the city.'

The camera panned from a night-time cityscape of Bath to find my boss, Detective Chief Inspector Mike Carter. He sounded even more 'Somerset' on TV: long vowels, lilting intonation.

He continued: 'Schoolkids were planning their future, just like seventeen-year-old Melanie Road. But this day would be the last day of her life.'

The reconstruction continued with the actress playing Melanie in a nightclub, dancing to Culture Club's 'Karma Chameleon', chatting to her boyfriend, trying out on him the

7

Greek words she'd been learning. Behind them, two men started squaring up to each other. Melanie pulled her boyfriend from the club, then they emerged outside with two male friends. After Melanie had said goodbye to her boyfriend, he'd offered to get her a cab, she said 'no' and they parted.

DCI Mike Carter picked up the voiceover as a reconstruction played out with Melanie walking through elegant streets, grand buildings of golden stone and black iron railings. Then the roads became narrower, less ornate, more suburban. The reconstruction showed Melanie walking up a hill, Mike Carter saying she was nearly home. Then, in the film, a street-level shot showing Melanie walking in the distance. A man's feet, obscure and out of focus appeared close to the lens. Then he started following her.

The film cut to Melanie, walking at speed, smiling.

Then the hand grabbed her.

Another low shot, the figures of the actors now out of frame, but their shadows remaining on a stone wall as Melanie screamed and a drone sound accentuated the ferocity of the attack, as if it needed to. Melanie fled from the scene, gasping, panting, hiding low down behind a wall.

Then the figure appeared again.

Then they showed the knife: long and serrated, according to this reconstruction.

The film had jump-edits and fast focus-pulls. It was harrowing. I thought of my eleven-year-old daughter upstairs, doing her homework. In a few years she would be going out, perhaps walking home alone, like Melanie.

Then the film showed the actress playing Melanie lying on the ground.

'It was my little sister, I should have taken care of her …' It was Karen now. She'd kept it together so far, but now she was breaking down, the camera lingering on her as she held her face in her hands.

'Melanie's murder kicked off a massive police investigation,' more voiceover from Mike Carter. 'We made 6,000 separate inquiries and arrested 94 men.'

Then it cut to Mike by a garage. I guessed this was spot where Melanie's body was found.

'Twenty-five years later and Melanie's killer is still out there. This case remains open. Now we have brand new evidence.

'DNA left at the scene.

'We believe it belongs to the killer. We need your help to find him.

'You might be worried about putting an innocent man in the frame. Don't be. The DNA belongs to one person only. So give us the name and let the science tell us if it's Melanie's murderer.'

'It's like a space, an empty hole. She should be here …' Karen again, looking distraught.

'Melanie's with me because she's my guardian angel. She's always there, giving me guidance.' This was her brother, Adrian. He continued: 'Over the past twenty-five years it's been a living nightmare to know that someone is out there that killed my sister. This person took Melanie away from me. I want to know why, and who.'

The film ended with Karen: 'I want somebody to be caught. Melanie's at rest, but they could do it again. I don't want anyone else to go through this.'

I found the film heartbreaking and brutal. Karen and Adrian were desperate. It was clear the passing of the decades had done nothing to quell their anger and grief.

When the *Crimewatch UK* film went out, I had been in Professional Standards but I knew the Cold Case team would be busy thanks to the national publicity. And I knew that when I made it across to my new role in a few weeks' time, we would be following up the leads. But the team couldn't have predicted the development which broke days later: a phone call which was at the same time a breakthrough and a mystery in itself.

A woman called the *Crimewatch UK* hotline. She said she was a cancer nurse and had treated a patient. Before dying, he'd admitted to her that he had killed Melanie Road.

But the nurse hadn't left her name. And she hadn't said who her patient was.

And the hotline was anonymous. She could be anywhere in the country.

Gary Mason and the Cold Case team (known as 'cold case' because the case has been left for a while) spent weeks trying to locate the nurse and, more importantly, the name of her former patient. The team called cancer charities and hospices, tried everything they could think of.

Then bingo!

They found the nurse in a hospice in Northamptonshire. And they persuaded her to give the man's name: Donald Gallagher. But by then he'd been dead for two months, his body cremated, and the team had little chance of confirming Gallagher's identity as Melanie's killer. In came the forensic coordinator Andy Mott ('Motty') – a genius of a scientist attached to the Cold Case team, who rarely uttered a word in his crisp, quiet, northern accent that he hadn't thought about at least three times beforehand.

Andy and Gary had gone to Northamptonshire. Gary had spoken with Gallagher's grieving wife and son and had explained that their loved one was our prime suspect.

Gary said he needed to be sure, though – police needed what he described as 'forensic opportunities to eliminate' Gallagher.

The poor woman. Her husband had just died from a painful illness and now police were calling him a killer. What kind of double life had he been living?

Mrs Gallagher consented. And Andy Mott looked around the family home, visited Gallagher's care home and called his hospital.

In medical storage were some paraffin blocks containing Gallagher's body tissue. They had been meant for experimental research into cancer. Andy Mott seized these and sent them to the lab. The tissues in these blocks could be compared with the perfect DNA sample left by the killer at the scene of Melanie's murder. Motty also saw a blood pressure kit lying in the family home. He told Gary that he could get skin cells from the inside of the cuff. That would be enough. A tough job to achieve, scientifically, but it would prove if Gallagher was the killer of Melanie Road.

Weeks later, the DNA results came back from the hospital tissue samples. Motty, Mr Cautious, was beside himself with excitement. The chances that Donald Gallagher was Melanie's killer were 97.5 per cent, according to the scientists and statisticians – the sample was too small to be 100 per cent certain. Motty was still awaiting the results from the skin cells from the blood pressure cuff.

But 97.5 per cent sure.

Everyone in the force was talking about it.

A hit on the Melanie Road inquiry after a quarter of a century. One of the oldest cold case murders to be solved in British history.

I'd been at police headquarters in Portishead when I bumped into Mike Carter.

'Well done, sir,' I said. 'A great result on Melanie Road.'

He smiled back and said they were still awaiting the final science to confirm.

I'll be honest, I felt a pang of envy.

Imagine solving a murder which had baffled generations of detectives.

Imagine being able to sit down with Melanie's family and say 'we've found him'. To go some way towards ending that nightmare Karen Road spoke of.

I was pleased for Mike Carter. A great detective and a lovely man.

But I couldn't help wishing I was in his position.

What would it be like to hunt a killer?

And that's what had brought Gary and me here. To the police's cold case storeroom on an industrial estate in Weston-super-Mare.

'When are we expecting the blood pressure cuff results?' I asked.*

---

* The samples are sent to an external provider of forensic services. The work is meticulous and can take many weeks or months depending on the quality of the sample.

'Any day,' Gary replied.

It took us three hours to find the shoebox with the list of people whose name began with G. They were in a green crate at the bottom of a heavy stack, so heavy that even Gary nearly swore.

Gary never swears.

We opened the shoebox and flicked through the hundreds of names on index cards. Each card related to someone who had featured in the Operation Rhodium inquiry at some point.

'Can you see a Gallagher?' I asked.

He nodded, then groaned.

'There are three, but no Donald Gallaghers. Doesn't mean he's not the killer. He doesn't have to be in the system to be the murderer.'

I looked at the mess around us. Crates we'd thrown to one side, sacks of evidence. Weapons in bags.

'Has anyone ever thought about organising the inquiry properly?' I asked.

'Yes, we need to do that,' said Gary, taking the box with the G cards to his car. 'But not today.'

CHAPTER 2

'On your best behaviour. Here's the Rubberheel Squad.'

The accent was sharp and Irish, and although he was trying to be funny, I detected an edge beneath the gag.

I had just walked into the Major Crime Review Team. Or the Cold Case Squad as most people call it. The unit reviewed both recent and historic unsolved rapes and murders.

It was my first day in the office and Alan Andrews was making a point. He was sitting behind a mountain of old papers which balanced on his desk. His skew-whiff grin highlighted a missing tooth. I had known Alan for years. He was a former CID detective sergeant and a really good one. He'd retired and had returned as a civilian investigator in the Review Team.

'You'd be surprised what they know about you in Professional Standards, Alan.'

'Good to have you on board, Rubberheeler,' he grinned, then looked back to his papers.

The Rubberheel nickname had been attached to the country's first Professional Standards unit, in the Metropolitan

14

Police in the 1970s. And it had spread as forces set up their own squads to weed out corrupt cops.

The last two years had seen me stuck behind two double-locked doors in Avon and Somerset Police's most secretive department. To many officers, Professional Standards (PS) was the enemy. If a bent cop was the subject of our investigations, he would hate us. If we made inquiries with his colleagues, they'd think we were calling their judgement into question.

I'd been successful in PS: there had been a police receptionist stealing lost-and-found money, which had been handed in by the public; a family liaison officer who had wheedled his way into the affections of a young widow; and a firearms officer we successfully convicted for misconduct in public office. I had spent a lot of my time looking at the seedier side of policing. The dark things a small minority of officers get up to. Professional Standards had been very quiet and a little lonely, but I had been proud of my work there. It had helped reinforce that it was important to do the right thing. And the hours had been regular: 8 a.m. to 4 p.m. This meant I could keep my career going, balancing a full-time job with my three children. I would have preferred to be in another department, but it was a good position to have after my divorce, while I took stock of my life.

This wasn't where I had intended to be in my early forties.

When I had joined the force as a twenty-year-old, tiptoeing to scrape past the 5'4" height restriction, I had been singled out. They had said three things about me:

'Julie doesn't suffer fools.' This was in my report. And it was true: I didn't and I don't.

'She's a high-flier. We'll get her on the Accelerated Development Programme. She'll go far.' That was a senior manager at Avon and Somerset Police. This was so exciting to hear. And I believed him.

'You'll have babies within two years and you'll go off on maternity. You'll end up working part-time in child protection. In fact, you probably won't last in the force more than five years. Women don't.' That had been my superintendent. I'd been furious. Who was he to tell me what I could and couldn't do? I told him I didn't suffer fools, even those with a crown on their epaulettes.

His attitude was typical of the top brass in the early 1990s. They were all men. There were few female detectives, just one on each team, no women above the rank of inspector. And none of these was my boss. Few role models for a young, go-getting female officer. The guys I worked with directly were always really supportive on a personal level but it was that male, stale top brass who couldn't bring themselves to congratulate me when I passed probation, couldn't say 'well done' when I'd arrested a thief we'd been trying to catch for months.

I'd show them.

Then came marriage and three children. My husband was in the military and out of the country most of the time. He was around so rarely, and I became so worn down trying to get him to engage, I felt it would be easier to go it alone as a single parent, so after fourteen years I filed for divorce.

I spent late nights parenting alone, revising for detectives' exams in bed as at least one of my babies lay next to me, refusing to sleep. Year after year, I failed those exams. And through the nights were the long hours of insomnia: worrying guiltily about au pairs and where to find them; money and where to find that; my career, and how could I provide for my children unless I got promoted and paid better?

Monday nights were my children's swimming lessons. Poolside, I'd look enviously at the other school mums, not feeling part of their group chatting about the PTA, coffee mornings and school-gate gossip. They always smiled and said 'hello', but I never felt part of them. Instead, as I kept one eye on my children splashing around, I'd be reading papers about police procedure.

I became a detective but it was another three years before I passed my sergeant's exams. Then it was another eleven years, count them – eleven years – before I could get promoted because of my commitments at home. But I had built rich experience as a constable.

I was half of the first female double crew in Avon and Somerset Police's history.

'What'll you do if you find a robber? His ironing?' some sergeant chuckled as we left.

Two hours later, we presented him with a man-mountain of a burglar we had caught red-handed. And over the years I learnt so much at the coalface: undercover work, a historic abuse inquiry, burglary squads and murders. Then came that step up to sergeant. Then Professional Standards: regular hours, 8 a.m. to 4 p.m., as good as it could get for a full-time single mother-of-three. But now, in 2009, I was desperate to start investigating criminals who didn't wear a police uniform.

This was day one for me as a detective sergeant in the Cold Case team. And I was super-excited. If Professional Standards had been Avon and Somerset's watered-down equivalent of

Line of Duty, I'd just walked into an episode from *New Tricks*. The Review Team was made up of mostly retired former officers, such as Alan Andrews. Or Gary Mason. Civilian investigators. I was one of only three warrant-carrying police officers. The room had desks laid out to form a rectangle. Well, I guessed there were desks, because I couldn't see them, they were loaded so deeply with piles of files, crates, boxes, index cards and papers. Except for one at the end of the room: empty, with an empty in-tray and a seat pushed in behind.

'That's you,' said Gary, sitting down at the adjacent desk.

'Oh no, I'm not next to you, am I, Gary?' I said.

'He bored our last DS (detective sergeant) into retirement.' Alan Andrews again.

If you were to see Gary in the street, you'd notice a tall, slim man in his sixties with receding grey hair, glasses and a goatee beard. He looks like a slightly scruffy bank manager, but behind his quiet, calm, fastidious manner is one of the most ferocious investigators I've ever met. When I had been a young cop, he had been my sergeant and he'd helped to teach me how to be a thief-taker. I'd learnt a lot from Gary, but I'd never tell him that – his ego's big enough. When it comes to doggedness and determination, he is quietly inspiring.

Gary had set up the Cold Case unit half a decade earlier. Now he had retired and had returned as a civilian investigator. I was new to his Cold Case team and was his sergeant. Rank made no difference to either of us; we were both hungry to solve cold cases.

'If I'm sitting next to you, will you tuck your shirt in?'

Gary was looking at a file, shaking his head, smiling.

'Or wear a tie?'

'Once Professional Standards, always Professional Standards.' Alan again.

The other members of the team were well known for their meticulousness. Most of all, DC Kath Synott. I had worked with Kath before. She also had piles of papers on her desk but they had a beautiful sense of order, neat towers of bureaucracy. No one was allowed to touch anything on her desk. She joked that it was obsessive compulsive disorder. Kath was fastidious about her appearance, with short hair and glasses. And she didn't shake hands – she wasn't rude, she just didn't like that physical touch.

DC Liz Cousins was particular and completely victim-focused. In the past, she had taken senior officers by surprise when she'd felt they weren't taking a case seriously enough. 'What the fuck are you talking about?' she would say to a chief inspector, not caring about the implications of her rudeness on her career.

Carrie Garrett was a civilian investigator, in her early fifties, at least a decade older than me. Very bohemian, with heavy make-up and coal-black eyes. She had been an investigator for the Department for Work and Pensions (DWP).

I felt a little bit scruffy next to these immaculate investigators. While I dressed smartly, my hair was unruly and I often came to the office from mucking out my horses. I couldn't imagine any of the other officers doing that.

'Is the whole team working on Melanie Road?' I asked Gary.

'Mostly,' he replied. 'But we're fitting it in around everything else.'

I looked around the room.

'How many unsolved murders are there?'

'Thirty-three. And we look at all the unsolved rapes too.'

'Any successes?'

'A couple. Rhodium would be the first murder we've solved, but we've had rape convictions.'

'Any really old cases?'

'Oh, that'd be the cinema shooting.' Gary again. 'Nineteen forty-seven, Bristol city centre. A cinema manager was shot dead during a gunfight scene in the film. No one heard the trigger being pulled for real. That's still unsolved.'

'Is there any update on Gallagher?'

Gary shook his head. 'Have you read the book?'

'The book? No, what's the book?'

'Alan, do you have a copy?'

Alan grunted and I felt a whoosh in the air as a small file of papers flew through the air, landing on my empty desk.

I looked down at a stapled bundle of A4 papers and flicked through it. It was forty-seven pages long, filled with dense blocks of old-fashioned type. No images, just words. There were headings like Boyfriend and Associates, Outstanding Actions and Reported as Green Blood and Alibied.

Green Blood?

'It was written on the first anniversary of the murder, when the case was parked,' said Gary.

The front page read:

AVON AND SOMERSET CONSTABULARY
MURDER OF MELANIE ANNE ROAD
AGED 17 YEARS AT ST STEPHEN'S COURT,
LANDSOWN,
BATH ON FRIDAY/SATURDAY 8TH/9TH JUNE 1984.
CRIME REPORT.

I turned the first couple of pages, giving details about where the incident room had been and where exhibits were held. The main body of the text started on page four:

The Scene

At about 5.35am on the morning of Saturday 9th June 1984, Mr Anthony NOONAN, a milkman, and his son, Ian NOONAN, were in the process of delivering milk in the St Stephen's area of Lansdown when they discovered the body of Melanie Anne ROAD in St Stephen's Court. Mr NOONAN went to a nearby house, from where he telephoned the police.

It had the names of the first officers at the scene before continuing:

At the time the body was discovered there was nothing to indicate the identity of the deceased. Above the body, resting on a wall, was a key fob and keys bearing the Christian name 'Melanie'.

As a result of this, inquiries were commenced in the area both by house-to-house and the use of a police patrol car using the Tannoy system.

Christ! Did Melanie's parents find out about her murder by loudspeaker?

There were background details about Melanie: the youngest daughter of Anthony and Jean Road, born in September 1966. Her elder siblings were Karen and Adrian. Her family had moved to Bath two years earlier with her dad's job. She had studied at Bath High School for Girls:

Her home surroundings are described as very good. Her social circle was confined mainly to her own age group of both sexes. She was a regular visitor to clubs and public houses in Bath.

However, the club which she visited immediately prior to her death, the Beau Nash Club, was not a normal haunt of hers.

I remembered the Beau Nash Club. I'd gone there with friends. It was dark-red and stylish. This was an evocative time for a teenage girl: eighties pop, hairspray and rara skirts. Smoke-filled dance floors, men drinking cans of Hofmeister.

The book continued with a passage about boyfriends. Melanie had had a couple of boyfriends in the past:

Her longest and last relationship was with the boyfriend in whose company she spent her last hours, namely Sebastian CHARALAMBOUS, the deceased and he having been going out together for about six months.

The report stated that Melanie and Charalambous were in a sexual relationship, although they had refrained for the previous two weeks because of Melanie's studies for her exams. It continued:

Throughout this inquiry it has become apparent that the deceased was not a heavy drinker, occasionally having a glass of white wine or the odd lager. She has on rare occasions been a little tipsy but never drunk.

'She seems like such a nice girl,' I said. I realised my voice was cutting through a silence in the cold case room. Alan looked out from behind his pile of papers, grunted and went back to his files.

The report outlined Melanie's final day. She got up at 9 a.m., relaxed at home with her father and mother. Her elder sister Karen was also there, down from the Midlands with her newborn daughter. Melanie and Karen went out at 11.30 a.m., walking the mile or so into Bath city centre. They visited shops and the library. Melanie popped into a travel agent to find out the cost of a summer holiday to Greece.

The sisters returned home. Melanie sunbathed in the garden in the afternoon, then she got changed into sportswear, telling her family she would be playing tennis with Charalambous later that day

Anthony Road returned home from work at 4.30 p.m.:

He, together with the rest of his family, left the house shortly after 5.30pm in order to convey their eldest daughter Karen to Bristol so that she could catch the coach home to Birmingham. Melanie accompanied them as far as Queen Square, Bath, when she left the family car outside the Francis Hotel. She stated it was her intention to walk from there to her boyfriend's flat.

This was the last the family saw of the deceased.

Anthony and Jean Road stayed out in Bristol, calling Karen at 9 p.m. to check she had returned home safely. Karen said Melanie had just called her from home 'and appeared to be excited as her boyfriend's brother, Theo, had arrived unexpectedly from London. They were going out in Bath to celebrate.'

Anthony and Jean Road got home soon after midnight. They found a note written by Melanie, saying she'd be home late, they shouldn't wait up.

Melanie met up with Charalambous and his brother at Clarets Wine Bar at 10.30 p.m. They went back to Charalambous's apartment, where they met his flatmate, Dennis Costas, then left for the Beau Nash nightclub at 11.05 p.m.:

Melanie spent most of the time with COSTAS as her boyfriend Sebastian was talking for most of the evening with his brother Theo.

> The four left the club at 0130am, shortly after an incident in which they were not involved, but in which some water was spilled on the floor.

Costas went to get a burger from a van while Melanie and the Charalambous brothers walked to Broad Street:

> The deceased parted company with her boyfriend, who states that he offered to get a taxi but she declined, stating she would be all right walking.

> She walked in the opposite direction to them along Bridge Street and they crossed Pulteney Bridge. Halfway across the bridge CHARALAMBOUS looked behind but could not see her.

> She was never seen alive again by any person at present on record.

'Poor Melanie.' It was me again, in the silence of the cold case room.

The door opened.

'Hi Julie!'

It was Claire Nelson. I knew Claire a little. She was just as neatly presented as all the other women in the Cold Case team: petite, with big brown eyes that always seemed to look at you in wonder.

'Well done on Rhodium,' I said.

'Thanks, Julie. We had so many names come in, we didn't expect quite that reaction from a TV show.'

Claire explained that after the broadcast, viewers had been calling in with names of suspects: Gallagher and seventy-one others.

'You're reading the book? It's fascinating. Have you got to the Green Blood yet?'

'Green Blood?'

I skipped past the pathologist's examination, seeing words like 'stab' and 'blade':

<u>**Forensic Scientist**</u>

**Mr Michael ROGERS, of the South Western Forensic
Science Laboratory, Chepstow, visited the scene at
10am on the 9th June 1984, where he also examined
the body of the deceased.**

The report said there were seventy-four blood spots, starting near Melanie's body, heading on to the main road, down some stone steps, across Camden Crescent and away. Each spot was numbered. The next page got into the science:

Laboratory Examination of samples taken from the scene.

Blood samples of the deceased

Vaginal swab

Oral swab

'Human semen was found on each of these swabs.

'She was raped twice?'

No one said anything. Gary offered a nod.

They didn't have DNA back in 1984, it was all blood science. I understood this a little. The report said Melanie's blood was group A. Same as 40 per cent of people in Britain, but a protein test narrowed things further.

The technical readout of Melanie's blood was PGM 1+1-. But there was another sample of blood at the scene. It had a different profile: PGM 2-1+.

The bloodspots nearest to where Melanie was found were hers but fourteen bloodspots from the getaway route were from this second profile. And this protein makeup was rare, only 3 per cent of the population had it:

Although not 100% conclusive, it would indicate that the assailant or someone connected to the incident was cut somewhere in St Stephen's Road and then made off down the road, whereas the deceased somehow managed to travel or was carried to the point where her body was found.

For ease of reference, the blood group NOT of the deceased and carrying the grouping PGM 2-1+ is hereon referred to as Green Blood.

'Green Blood?' I said. It sounded like something from science fiction.

'Rogers drew a map of the scene,' Gary explained. 'Not sure it's in that file. He coloured Melanie's blood in orange and the other blood spots in green: Green Blood. The green just refers to the crayon colour he used, but the name stuck.'

'And only 3 per cent of the population has it?'

'Yes. It was a great head start in the days before DNA. They could say quickly if someone was the murderer or not. And if you look at the post-mortem, you'll notice most of the stab wounds were to the right side of Melanie's body. Looks like a left-handed attacker.'

I flicked back and skimmed the autopsy summary.

'Twenty-six stab wounds? Poor girl.'

I had been a member of many murder inquiries over the years. Few homicides had that kind of ferocity. One, maybe two others.

That could be any one of us, I thought to myself. *How have her parents lived with this for all these years?*

Melanie was stabbed twenty-one times to her front, five times in her back. As Gary said, the report confirmed that most of the wounds were to the right side of her chest.

'Who the fuck goes out in the night with a knife and rapes a girl twice, stabs her like that and just disappears? Was Gallagher left-handed? Did he have Green Blood?'

'We're waiting to find out.'

'How hard can it be to solve this? A left-handed man with a rare blood type. He was injured himself. Now we've developed a full DNA profile.'

'He could be anywhere,' said Alan. 'He could be dead, he could be abroad. How many tourists roll into Bath every day? He could be anywhere on the planet.'

'He could be in prison,' noted Claire Nelson.

I carried on looking at the file. There were details of house-to-house inquiries and police operations held the following night and the following week.

'It says here they compiled a list of every hotel guest staying in the city?'

'It was a proper job. No stone unturned, they deserved to catch him.' Alan again.

Then the report began describing Melanie's boyfriend. He was nineteen years old at the time and they had met before Christmas the previous year. There was no sign or history of violence in their relationship:

The CHARALAMBOUS family would appear to be of considerable standing in Greece and are very wealthy. Although there are niggles about his attitude and behaviour, for him to have been responsible for the murder, two other people would

> **have to be telling lies, namely his brother Theo and
> Dennis COSTAS.**

'We took Charalambous's DNA, along with his friends in a review in 2001. No match,' said Gary.

The report looked at the Beau Nash nightclub:

> **Two incidents occurred shortly before the deceased left, one
> being an ice bucket being thrown across the floor and another
> involving the debagging of a male person.**
>
> **Both incidents are believed to be connected but despite
> extensive inquiries the persons involved have never
> been traced or identified.**
>
> **The Greeks all refer in their statements to the deceased being
> seen in deep conversation with a male person described as white,
> 5'8/9", mousey brown short hair.**

The report stated that police had photographed every man known to have been in the club. The images were shown to the Greeks and they had both independently selected number 118, 'namely Nigel WESTON'.

Weston was a civil servant who 'admitted to having visited the Beau Nash nightclub on the night in question'. He said he had talked to and then danced with a girl – she had been identified as someone else. He'd left the club with friends and they all corroborated his story.

'He admitted to having visited the Beau Nash club?' I repeated. 'How suspicious were they?'

'The pressure was on,' said Gary.

'I know, but we wouldn't write that now.'

I read the next heading:

Arab Inquiry

During the early stages of the inquiry, various reports were received concerning an Arab seen to be acting in a suspicious manner, trying to pick up females. This, together with the statement of Jan Webb, a seventeen-year-old friend of the deceased who described an Arab-looking person being a bit pushy with the deceased at a party three weeks prior to the murder, had caused extensive inquiries to be made at various colleges in the city.

The report said police had checked two colleges in Bath: Bailbrook College, which had been run by British Airways as a training school for air traffic controllers from the Arab states, and the Bell School of Languages. Detectives had had to do this quickly before any suspect flew home, moving beyond the reach of British law.

Three women, the report said, 'saw the man at about 11 p.m. in the Broad Street area and in a club known as Harriet's.'

Two different women 'also refer to a similarly described Arab being in the Beau Nash Club at around 1 a.m. acting in a strange manner'.

Two further witnesses saw a man matching the description 'in the Lansdown area of the city at about 1.35 a.m. on the morning of the 9th June 1984'.

Melanie had been at all three of those locations: first, the Beau Nash nightclub, then she had walked along Broad Street towards her home in the Lansdown area of the city. Investigators had designed a drawing, an Electronic Facial Identification Technique – or e-fit – of the man and had held ID parades with students from the colleges. There was, however, a but:

One group of Arabs came to special notice and having been identified have not been eliminated or interviewed as they have returned to their own country.

The report listed five men:
Hazim Ismat
Amir Al-badawi
Fazil Shariq
Jamil Qadir
Mansour Akram

All five stayed in Bath for the weekend. The only one who can be accounted for is Fazil Shariq, who met a girl at the Beau Nash Club, namely Sarah SUTTON, in whose company he remained until 5am.

All five Arabs are employed by the Pan-Arabian Petrol Co. Arrangements were being made by Mr JAMESON, the treasurer of the company, with a view to having these persons flown to the United Kingdom for interview. Unfortunately, Mr JAMESON was arrested shortly afterwards by the Saudis for political reasons and interviews have never been carried out.

'What?' I said. 'Have we ever spoken to these five?'

'No,' said Claire.

'So there was an Arab guy wandering around the route of Melanie's walk home. We have the names of five men, they fly home and are beyond our reach?'

She nodded.

'And the poor guy who tries to help us with this gets locked up?'

'He was in prison for nine months.'

'Fuck.'

'Yes, and there's another report around here.' Claire gestured to one of the filing cabinets behind her. 'We spoke with him in the 1996 review. He'd been banged up, he'd lost his job and he told us he would have done it all again because he thought it was the right thing to do.'

'Did we take any samples from them? Are they Green Blood?'

'No. They could have orange blood, green blood, yellow blood with silver speckles, we just don't know.'

I got a pad of paper and wrote Arab Inquiry.

'But those are just five men,' Claire said. 'There are hundreds in the system. Thousands.'

'Thank God you've got Gallagher. You'd be at this for years.'

'We've been at this for years,' said Alan.

The next section read like something from an Agatha Christie novel:

Other Major Lines of Inquiry:

Man sitting on steps on St Stephen's Church

At about 5.20am on 9th June 1984, Adam DILLAN was going on an organised fishing trip when he passed a milk float on Lansdown Hill. As he approached St Stephen's Church his attention was drawn to a man sitting on the steps. He described this man as 25 years of age, 11 stone, 5'9", with long, shoulder-length mousy-coloured hair. He was sitting with his arms outstretched down by his legs. Extensive inquiries and media appeals have been made to trace this man, with a negative result.

Man cycling up hill by St Stephen's Church

At about 2.10am Rachel GLYNANE was a passenger in a Mercedes car driven by her husband up Lansdown Hill. They were passing St Stephen's Church when they became aware of a man riding a pedal cycle. The cycle is described as an elderly person's cycle with upright handlebars.

On 3rd August 1984 a reconstruction was held at the scene and despite extensive media inquiries, we have been unable to identify this man.

<u>Man running in Fairfield Road area</u>

At about 3.40am on 9th June 1984 Mr Frank SAMUELS, 27, a cleaning contractor, was cleaning in the Rising Sun public house on Camden Row when he heard the sound of running steps. He then saw a man running past. He describes this man as aged 20–22, six feet tall, thin build, dark hair, wearing a grey jacket and dark trousers.

'Have we found these men since? The guy on the church steps or the cyclist or the jogger?' I asked.

'No,' said Gary.

I skimmed through the rest of the report.

'Arrests' was the next heading:

In addition to the main lines of inquiry, a total of 94 persons have been arrested in the inquiry. A complete alphabetical list is at the rear of this report as Appendix 'A'. The main persons to come to light are obviously those who have the Green Blood grouping.

'Ninety-four arrests?' I said.

'It was before the Police and Criminal Evidence Act,' said Alan. 'Life was easier then.'

I could imagine the arrested men dragged by a team of cops to a police station, questioned, left, questioned again. There would have been no 'we're going to hold you for twenty-four hours, get a twelve-hour extension and pop to the magistrates to apply for another thirty-six hours'. It would have been brutal. This had been before my time, but only by a couple of years, and when I started, a few of the older coppers had struggled with the new ways of working.

'But we have a full DNA profile of the killer, we have the science. Have we checked all these names against the science?'

'We're working our way through.'

'How many names have you checked?'

'About three hundred.'

There were two big points at the end of the report:

There is the possibility the victim was picked up from a car, either voluntarily or involuntarily, and then taken to another spot before being dumped near to where her body was found.

It is suspected by a number of officers that two persons may have been involved in the offence, and at least one of them was known to the deceased.

I read these sentences again, out loud.

'Why do they say that?' I asked.

'Well, there is no obvious place where the attack actually happened,' said Gary. 'And Melanie was raped twice. It was such a short time, just a few minutes. They thought one man wouldn't have been able to do what he did.'

'What does the science say now?'

'I think you should speak to Motty, he describes it better than we do,' said Claire.

'What are we going to do if it's not Gallagher?' I asked. 'There are hundreds of names here, thousands in the system.'

'We'll carry on. We've got that report,' said Claire. 'That's just one file, there are many others. That's the problem with them being so good, back in 1984. There are so many suspects.

'If you want the best list, that's in the Green Blood Book.'

CHAPTER 3

I looked at Claire in confusion.

'The Green Blood Book?'

'Yes,' she replied. 'That's what we call it. It doesn't have an official name. No one really knows where it came from, we just found it in the stores. It's probably one from the reviews in the 1990s or early 2000s. But it's a list of names. Suspects who were in Bath with Green Blood. Some had alibis, some didn't.'

Claire spun around in her chair and opened the filing cabinet behind. She harrumphed and opened the door beneath.

'Bingo!' she said, pulling a folded A3 file from the drawer.

She carried it over to my desk and put it next to the 1985 bundle I'd been reading.

'Some of the names are in both files, but some of the names are different.'

It had a green front with the words 'Green Blood Suspects'. I opened it and saw charts going across the large pages. Inside the boxes were names, details, biographies of each suspect and details of their movements – or the movements they

34

claimed to have made – on the night and early morning of
8/9 June 1984.

'Fifty-two men,' said Claire. 'Some are dead, some are
alive.'

'Is Gallagher in here?'

She shook her head.

'Have we pulled out their index cards?' I asked, flicking
through the pages.

I read one of the names out quietly to myself. 'Barry
Walsh, DoB 17/02/1961. He would have been twenty-three
at the time,' I muttered. 'Precons (previous convictions) for
theft, assisting an offender and fraud. I'm sure he loves his
mum. He said he was with his girlfriend the entire night on
the 8/9 June 1984. They went to the cinema to watch *Indiana
Jones and the Temple of Doom*, which ended around
10.30 p.m., and went straight home to his girlfriend's home
in Odd Down. They went to bed just after midnight. His
girlfriend is named Sally Wilson. She provided an alibi.
They were seen by friends at the cinema. But that doesn't
mean anything as that was at least three hours before Melanie was murdered.'

I looked up.

'Have you swabbed this bloke?'

Claire said she couldn't remember.

'Have we got the W cards here, or are they in stores?'

There was a little flurry as Gary, Alan and Claire shuffled papers around and looked at their desks. Then Gary
remembered that they had a good suspect called Whitely a
few months earlier. He got up, went to a cabinet at the far
end of the room, opened the drawer and shouted, 'Yes.'

He carried the shoebox over to me.

'Thanks, Gary. Tuck your shirt in,' I said.

I opened the box, flicking through the names. It took a few minutes but Barry Walsh was there. I looked at the index card: it listed his home address in 1984, his occupation (courier), his date of birth, his previous convictions and car details. Then I flipped over.

'Swabbed for Operation Eagle,' it said. Negative sample for both Operation Rhodium and Operation Eagle.

Operation Eagle.

It had been an evening in September 1996. I had been in the force for nearly ten years. My female colleagues on the Fast-Track Accelerated Development course were sprinting up the career ladder. I had one child at that stage; Callum was nearly two. And I was still on the bottom rung, a police constable based in Kingswood, east of Bristol. I had moved to intelligence but often went out with the plain clothes teams on operations.

After the long summer holiday, the schools had gone back. The roads were busy. It was about 5 p.m. when I turned my car off the street and slinked down the warren of back lanes and alleys behind the terraced Victorian homes in Kingswood. Often, you'd see a burglary in action here. A hooded man running away, or a couple of guys weighed down with hi-fi gear or a TV set. Tech was much heavier then and robbers easier to catch.

But that night I saw nothing.

I'd returned to the station and dealt with the usual run of paperwork and complaints, leaving for home at 2 a.m. When I'd returned to work the next day, the station had been busy: the Eagle rapist had struck again.

The girl had only been young, just eighteen. The man had jumped into her car, dragged her across to the passenger seat, snapped a hairband over her eyes and driven her to Mangotsfield Common, where he'd raped her.

I'd looked at the map on the wall, where the abduction had happened and where the sex attack had been carried out.

'I drove along that lane just beforehand,' I said. 'I was on my little burglary operation in that exact spot.'

'Did you see anything?' someone asked.

'Not at all.'

And this had not been a one-off. It had all the hallmarks of an attacker who had assaulted at least five other women on and off between 1991 and 2000. Operation Eagle, as it became known, was one of the biggest sex assault inquiries in British history.

In one of the later attacks, he had dropped a cap with the *Batman Forever* logo on it. The press had called him the Batman rapist. That name stuck in public.

And he had never been caught.

'Are there any links between Melanie's killer and Operation Eagle?' I asked.

'We don't know. When we swab for Eagle, it's in the consent form that the DNA sample will be used on Rhodium,' said Claire.

'The rapist used a knife, didn't he?'

She nodded.

'And we're still swabbing for Eagle now?'

'Yes. The Eagle rapes have stopped, though. There hasn't been an attack since 2000,' she said.

'The Bath rapist knew his way around the city really well, didn't he? All the back alleys and places where he could take women and not be interrupted. Good local knowledge.

'And Melanie's killer, why'd he attack in Landsdown? There's no reason to go there unless you live or work there. And at 2 a.m.? Surely not a tourist passing through. Must be someone local, or someone who knew Bath really well?'

Were there ties between Avon and Somerset's number one cold case murder and its biggest-ever string of sex attacks?

'We've never formally linked the cases,' said Claire. 'But Bath is a small city. Tiny, isn't it? How many men would go out with a knife to rape and murder or go out repeatedly to rape again and again over years? Could be the same man.'

Had we just had the biggest double-hit in the force's history?

Could he have solved not just the Melanie Road murder but also the Operation Eagle rapist mystery at the same time?

It was so exciting to even be on the coat-tails of the inquiry.

We just needed the science to confirm it.

'It's amazing you're so close to solving this,' I said.

'We're not home and dry yet, but it's looking good.' Andy Mott's chirpy, happy northern accent hid his ferocious talent as a forensics coordinator. 'We haven't got a full DNA profile from Gallagher yet, but the partial we have all matches.'

'Would you really stake your mortgage on it?'

'I was misquoted.'

'Have you done any forensics works on the exhibits yet?'

'A little, but not a full review. The key exhibit you need to know about is MR8. The forensic scientist was Mike Rogers; it was the eighth sample he took at the scene: MR8. It was a semen mark found at the scene; we got our DNA profile from that.'

'I read in the book that they thought it might be two attackers as semen was found in two locations.'

'Yes, they thought that for years. How could one man rape twice so quickly? I did quite a bit of work about that just recently, comparing the swabs. They were always so similar that the original investigators wondered if there were two attackers with Green Blood, perhaps brothers. But I checked them both, they're from the same man.'

'Just one offender.'

'There's semen from one man. Who knows how many men were there who didn't take part in anything sexually?'

'And MR8 has been on the National DNA Database since 1996 and there's never been a match, obviously.'

'Well …' Andy went quiet.

'What?'

He was obviously wondering about the most precise but diplomatic way to say something difficult.

'There was a change to the DNA Database systems a few years ago. And lots of the samples dropped off. Thing was, no one realised it.'

'Christ! For how long?'

'Four years.'

'So if our man was arrested for something and had a DNA sample loaded on over a four-year period, he wouldn't have pinged up for the murder of Melanie Road?'

'That's right.'

'When was this?'

'Between 2004 and last year. Thing was, we loaded it back on and there were no hits anywhere. We'd have found him. But it was a lesson to check everything. We had no way of knowing. Loads of samples fell off. In fact, we had a few more DNA samples to load back on and we caught a rapist that way.'

'So, double-check everything we know?'

'Every single thing.'

CHAPTER 4

OCTOBER 2009

I knew Bath well but I'd had little reason to come to this part of the city in the years when I had worked here – crime was rare in the Lansdown suburb.

Jean Road lived on a quiet, well-kept cul-de-sac in the north of the city, a mile from the centre. The lawns were tidy, the pavements were clear, and the acers in the gardens were bursting with autumnal reds and ambers.

'Tony Road isn't here any more,' Mike Carter explained as he led me to the base of a tall flight of steps leading to a detached house. We started climbing. 'He's had dementia for years, he's in a home now. Jean's here by herself. Adrian will probably be around. He found the *Crimewatch* filming difficult so he might be a bit testy. It's nothing personal. He's the nicest man in the world but this has been with him a long time.'

I was puffing by the time we reached the top of the steps and the white doorway of a Bath stone seventies-style home.

Mike rang the bell.

What's she going to be like? I wondered to myself. I had met the families of murder victims before, but only when they'd come into the Inquiry Room, and it had always been humbling. On the first visit I'd learnt they didn't want to be treated with pity or shock, just professional understanding. But this was the first time I had gone into the home of the mother of a murdered girl.

What will Jean Road think of me? What am I going to do? How am I going to change things for her and make them better? How am I going to do anything that hasn't been done over the last twenty-five years? How many other detectives have gone through this door before? How should I behave?

Just be yourself, Julie. Just be Julie.

There was a short wait, the turn of a lock and a man appeared at the door. I recognised Adrian Road from the TV campaign.

'Mike.'

'Adrian, how are you?'

He didn't answer.

I smiled at Adrian as he ushered Mike and me into a hall-way and into a lounge on the left. A bay window stretched across the width of one wall, giving the lounge a bright glow on its green carpets. The feel was well-kept and cosy.

Jean Road was sitting on a chair to the right. She said hello. A short lady, in her mid-seventies with short, grey hair and glasses, she was immaculately presented: dark trousers, a jumper and slippers. And she had an easy, natural smile, which was at the same time warm and welcoming.

'Jean, this is Julie Mackay,' Mike said.

'Hello, Julie.'

Mike sat down on a sofa which matched Jean's chair and I took a place next to him.

'Julie's our new detective sergeant in the Review Team, she's in charge of the rabble.'

Adrian had followed us into the room and sat on a chair on the other side of our sofa.

Jean looked at him, then at us.

'I've just come to update you about our prime suspect really, Jean,' Mike said. 'We've located him. He is deceased, but the really exciting news is we've been able to find two sets of biological samples from him. You know that the first set is looking very encouraging and we are awaiting the results from the second set.'

'Well, that's good news.'

Jean was speaking as if it were an everyday occurrence, talking about the possibility that her daughter's murderer was a lab report away from being identified. She was calm, very calm. Some murder victims' families wear their anger on the surface but Jean Road sat there: polite, interested and measured.

But Adrian was starting to lose his cool.

'We've been here before,' he said. 'How many times have we had police turn up here, saying they've had a break-through? I'll believe it when I see it.'

There was a silence.

Adrian looked as if he was struggling: that he didn't want to be rude to us, or discourteous. That being blunt went against every grain in his body. But he had to be frank. I had been told to fuck off so many times as a police officer that his words, so loaded with frustration, didn't insult me.

But I was starting to understand where he was coming from.

I looked around the room. There was a large painting above the fireplace, a rural scene. There were photos in frames on a glass cabinet and on the mantlepiece. One was an old studio-portrait photograph: three young people. It looked like Adrian years before, with a head full of hair – he must have been twenty. He sat between two young women, looking directly at the camera. To his right was a woman in her early twenties, a young Karen. To his left was Melanie. Melanie had a wide grin, her shoulder-length blonde hair was blow-dried, the same style I'd tried in the early eighties. She had a look about her, like she was clever, really clever. Not bookish, but smart.

There were other pictures in frames. Karen in her thirties with two young girls. Adrian with a child. Melanie in a school uniform.

'Adrian, I know you found the *Crimewatch* filming really hard, but the results have been beyond our wildest dreams,' said Mike. 'For the first time, we've got this close to a suspect and the science'll tell us for sure if it's him. We'll know in a week or so.'

Adrian looked away; he couldn't shake the look of disbelief.

'And we have more leads too,' I found myself saying. 'There's this lead, which is amazing. But he's one of seventy-two names that have been phoned in. Seventy-two names. If it's not him, we'll go through each of them.'

Adrian was looking at me.

'We're going to find Melanie's killer. You know that, we will find her killer. This case is so solvable.'

'Yes, but it's not been solved for twenty-five years. And Melanie was my sister. And until I know for sure you have arrested her killer, I won't believe you.'

Mike smiled politely.

'We appreciate everything you're doing.' It was Jean now. 'It's nice to know the police haven't forgotten about Melanie.'

'It's just …' continued Adrian, 'It's been twenty-five years and you're still looking.'

Well, I'm just starting to look, Adrian. This is just the beginning. I said this to myself. Adrian had heard these words before, from generations of detectives. They would have meant nothing to him.

But I made a silent vow: *I will find Melanie's killer.*

We said our goodbyes and made our way down the steep stone steps to the road.

'I might look at the scene,' I said.

'There's a little alleyway down there.' Mike pointed to a gap between two houses. 'It'll take you there. She really was just two minutes from home.'

We said goodbye. After opening my blue book, I pulled out the diagram of the scene. I made my way through the alleyway which slid down, bringing me out on to St Stephen's Road. At the top stood a church, looking down on the narrow road. Double yellow lines one side, residents' parking bays the other. Steep walls and green bushes both sides, hiding detached suburban Bath stone homes. Houses which were firmly twentieth century, unlike the Georgian mansions of the city centre.

I looked at the map and headed about thirty yards downhill until I found, on my right, a little road with a sign which said 'St Stephen's Court, Private, residents only'. The diagram showed me that Melanie's body had been found a short distance down. There was the set of garages I recognised from the scene photos. The low wall where Melanie's keys and eyeliner must have been found.

There were flats on the left just across from the garages. Homes just ten metres away from where Melanie died. Melanie was stabbed twenty-six times. Surely someone must have heard *something*? The early hours of a hot, sticky summer's night. Windows open, people awake, how could a man silently rape and murder a poor teenage girl just metres away, just a scream away, from where people were trying to sleep?

I tried to look at the scene. What was it telling me? What were the silent signs? Why would anything happen here? It made little sense.

I looked again at the map.

Back in 1984, most of the Orange Blood – Melanie's – was found where I was standing. Bloodspots 1 to 24 started here outside the garage, where her body was discovered, running out to St Stephen's Road. Had she fled in here, bleeding, to hide? Had she been attacked elsewhere, escaped and sought sanctuary crouched by the garages?

I followed the route of the blood and went on to St Stephen's Road.

One of the things that the original investigators couldn't understand was why Melanie's pants had been found in the opposite direction to the getaway. I looked at the map and yes, up to the left, about fifty yards away, was that location.

Why were they there, nowhere near Melanie's body?

But the blood trail went in the opposite direction, to the right.

I turned right, looking at the map and looking at the pavement.

About five metres down, scientists found three more bloodspots – numbered 40, 43 and 45. Numbers 43 and 45 were still Melanie's Orange Blood. But spot 40 was the first place where Green Blood had been found.

So had the killer started bleeding here? How and why was he injured? Had Melanie put up a fight? Had he stabbed himself? Had he been injured earlier, elsewhere, but evidence of that cut became apparent here?

I carried on down the sloping pavement. The map showed that nothing of interest was found as the killer crossed the junction with another residential road, Lansdown Grove. But on the other side, on the pavement, a solitary spot – 47 – was discovered. Green Blood again. According to the plan, there were no other blood spots nearby. The pavement veered down and round to the left. There was a triangle of grass; the map showed no blood here. Then the pathway headed into some bushes and an old set of stone steps appeared to the right. Tight, curling clockwise.

These steps had been covered in blood spots, the crime-scene plan said.

Green Blood.

The killer's.

He'd somehow managed to stop bleeding as he fled down the pavement, but as he descended the old stone steps, his bleeding had really started.

Why was that?

Scientists labelled the blood spots on the map: 49, 51, 52, 53, 54, 55 and 58.

Why this cluster here?

Even in the daylight the stones were steep, uneven, coiled in a hairpin. They must have been treacherous as a night-time getaway route.

I went to the bottom of the steps where the alleyway broadened out on to Camden Crescent. Not one of Bath's better-known crescents, but a glorious street on which to live. The kind of road that, were it in another city, it would be the prime address. Here, in Bath, it's just another grand, opulent street: Georgian and gorgeous.

The pavement here was wide, spreading out from the railings of the large homes. And according to the map, more spots of Green Blood were found here. Two more at this section of the road, by a lamp post. Then they crossed the street and headed along the eastern side of the pavement. The blood trail stopped at the end of Camden Crescent. If the Green Blood Trail truly was an indicator of how the killer had fled, then what did it mean?

Had Melanie's killer got into a car near here and driven away? Had he gone to his hotel if he were a tourist?

If Gallagher was Melanie's killer, which hotel was he staying in that night? Or had he crashed with friends?

He had been sixty-eight when he had died a few months earlier. That would have made him forty-three at the time of the attack. What was he doing out by himself with a knife in his hand and murder on his mind?

How had he lived with himself? Had he put the killing in a vault in his heart and carried on living, smiling to the world around him? He had blood on his hands. He'd left his own blood on the streets. What kind of man could function with this on his conscience?

I picked out the forty-seven-page report and read the last paragraph:

The main mystery of the entire inquiry is that from the time she left the company of the CHARALAMBOUS brothers until she was found by the milkman NOONAN there is not one positive sighting of the deceased. No matter which route she took, she would have to walk through parts of the city which were full of life. The clubs were turning out and the night was very warm. This, in my opinion, adds credence to the possibility of her having been picked up by someone in a car.

Down the hill was the city centre, from where Melanie must have come. On foot? In a car?

I retraced my steps, walking up the stone staircase. Had this been Melanie's route? She had walked up these steps on her way home; could this be the point of attack? It would have been dark and even though she hadn't drunk much alcohol, she may have been disorientated. Vulnerable, certainly.

At the top of the steps I passed the triangle of grass, the junction of Lansdown Grove and the corner of St Stephen's Court. I looked back down towards the garages where Melanie had perished.

The scene was still keeping its signs secret after a quarter of a century.

I left St Stephen's Road, got into my car and drove the short distance to my home village. As I opened the front door, I stumbled over a pile of cardboard boxes packed with our belongings in the hallway, ready for the move. I had been so absorbed in Jean, Adrian and the murder scene that the sale of my house had been pushed to the back of my mind.

Connie, my middle child, was looking at the pile. 'Mum, do we really have to move in with Matt?' she said.

'Yes, it'll be great. We'll have a bit more room, his house is nicer and I'll be happier. It'll do you good to have a bit more stability too. We've been winging it a bit since your dad and I divorced.'

I thought back and shuddered at the long list of au pairs I'd hired and sometimes fired. Now Connie was eleven, Callum was fourteen and Toby was nine; moving us in with my partner and his two children was the right thing to do. We'd been together a couple of years, we shared a love of the countryside. He was a nice, decent man. He lived in the same village, my children would keep their roots.

'Tell you what, let's go for a hack around the fields.'

My children are fearless around horses. I couldn't afford a saddle for Connie, so she had learnt to ride bareback and now she was a formidable competitor. Toby would mortify me with his feats of daring on his pony. And Callum was also a brave rider.

As they flew around the field, wearing out their ponies, the questions kept coming: 'Will we each have our own bedroom?', 'Will we really have a bit more money?', 'Could we go on holiday?', 'What if we don't get on with his kids?', 'Does this mean he'll be our dad?'

'Yes, hopefully soon. Hopefully … hopefully … They are brilliant children, I'm sure you will get on. No, your dad is your dad and I guess Matt will be your stepdad.'

CHAPTER 4

Matt was also a police officer. We had worked together in the past and had always got on really well. We'd got together not through work, but because we'd been the single friends that couples would invite to parties.

Matt's children lived with him, not his ex-wife. She wanted her money out of the property. I had sold my home and was to buy in to his. It would have made more sense to buy somewhere completely new together, but if we didn't do this now, it would never happen and we'd carry on drifting.

And I'm not a drifter.

CHAPTER 5

OCTOBER 2009

The weeks were passing and we were still awaiting the return of the 'science': confirmation that Donald Gallagher was the killer of Melanie Road. My desk had now grown its own collection of files, papers, books and index cards and looked like all the others – apart from Kath's, whose workspace was maintained in, as she described it, 'OCD perfection'.

I pored over my files, fascinated, looking at the names of men who had been at some point a suspect in the inquiry. Some of them had PDFs – Personal Description Forms – from 1984. Some of these had images attached.

You didn't need a date-stamp underneath to prove the photos had been taken years before. Just looking at the pictures was enough. Their haircuts were generally larger, curlier, long at the back. Their tops were sometimes pastel T-shirts or New Romantic-style shirts and ties. People seemed slimmer.

What had become of these men? Had they grown to have successful careers or had they ended up penniless? Did they have families? Were they alive or dead?

CHAPTER 5

Melanie Road's was one of thirty-three unsolved murders in the force. Over the years I had worked on some in the feverish early days when they were live cases. I had been an undercover officer following the disappearance of Melanie Hall in Bath in 1996. A chilling coincidence: two Melanies killed in the same small city.

Melanie Hall had gone out into Bath city centre with her boyfriend, a German doctor called Philip Karlbaum. It was the first night of Euro 96 and the pubs had been packed with football fans. The couple had ended up in Cadillacs night-club and had an argument. Karlbaum had left. Friends had later seen Melanie sitting on a stool by the dance floor, her last confirmed sighting.

That was probably the best-known cold case in the force. Back in 1996, as a new mother and still a police constable, I had been sent into Cadillacs undercover to gather intelligence on the club. What was its vibe? What was its reputation? Were the bouncers rough? What were the bar staff like? What happened in the office space upstairs?

Melanie Hall had just disappeared.

Her parents had made public pleas; there was a large reward for information. She had been declared dead in 2004. But still, thirteen years after her disappearance, we had no idea of Melanie's fate. Her body had never been found.

The Review Team was looking at other cases, all apparently separate from Melanie Road: Philip Green was an eleven-year-old boy who'd been collecting balls on a golf course in Bristol in March 1970. He'd been bludgeoned to death, his body spread out on a bed of beech leaves. Winifred Locke, an eighty-year-old with Parkinson's disease, was found in her sheltered

53

accommodation in Somerset in October 1983; she'd been sexually assaulted and asphyxiated. Back in Bath, there was the 1978 fatal stabbing of a welfare worker, Beryl Culverwell – her body had been found tied up in her garage as the dinner she had been cooking burnt in the oven. And Glenis Carruthers, a twenty-year-old who had been strangled as she walked near Bristol Zoo in January 1974. These were just four of the thirty-three unsolved murders which had baffled investigators at the time and left the families of the poor victims with a long list of questions and no justice.

Then there were the undetected rapes. More numerous than the murders, some were filed in big, fat folders bursting with papers. Others were in the system in the office on just one or two sheets of A4.

As the Review Team's detective sergeant, I read through all the cases, writing a list of actions on the front of the files, handing them to the investigators to carry out. And as the weeks progressed further, I noticed the calm efficiency with which the team worked. There was banter – something I hadn't really experienced for two years in Professional Standards – but there was no need for me to chase any of the investigators to do their jobs.

They just got on with it.

I set up a spreadsheet of jobs, actions and progress and it started to fill out. Basic stuff, simple and methodical, but after my time in Professional Standards, I realised that most good policing really is simple and methodical. It's when you don't do the basics that mistakes are made.

I started making a few changes to the unit. Partial DNA samples were the bane of our lives. The science we used at the time looked at twenty points of a person's DNA. These twenty points were unique to each person. If we had DNA from a scene, we would need the suspect's sample to match those twenty points exactly. Some forensic samples were too poor to be a full DNA sample and scientists could only identify some of the twenty points. We had a full sample from the Melanie Road murder scene, but several other rapes and murders produced only a partial sample.

The UK government wouldn't allow these lower-grade samples to be stored on the National DNA Database so I introduced a policy of checking them every two years to see if any matches had emerged since they were last on the database. I also started to organise the room in as methodical a way as possible. The old, grey filing cabinets had drawers which stuck, seeming to open only when they felt like it. There were roller shutter cabinets which were newer, but once those doors were open and the old papers spilled out, you were back decades in time. The papers for Operation Rhodium were chaotic, stored in that jumbled mass of green crates at the warehouse in Weston-super-Mare. And there were piles of files, scattered index cards and the folders left on the floors and cupboards of the Review Team.

'Gary, you'll have to help me get a grip on this,' I said. 'When we get the science back for Gallagher, we'll need to write a closing report to say why it's him. And if it isn't, we can't carry on with the inquiry like this.'

One morning when I was sitting at my desk, Gary silently on my right, the rest of the team quietly working away at their cold cases, DCI Mike Carter burst through the door.

'Denmark,' he said.

'What? Melanie Hall?'

Operation Denmark was the codename for the murder of Melanie Hall.

'Yes, she's been found.'

'Where?'

'By a motorway junction near Thornbury. Julie, they want you in the MCIT. They need a receiver.'

MCIT was the Major Crime Investigation Team, the murder squad which covered three forces: Avon and Somerset, Wiltshire and Gloucestershire.

I packed up and within thirty minutes I was in the car, driving to MCIT's base at Kenneth Steele House in Bristol. I'd only worked there once before, as a receiver for a murder inquiry in South Bristol.

What will happen? I asked myself as I walked up the stairs in the modernistic office block. *Will people notice me? Will they not notice me? Which is worse? Can I do the job?*

I opened the door.

MCIT was in a large room, filled with six banks of desks on each side. Phones ringing, the low hum of chatter punctuated by an occasional shout. Some of the desks were filled with detectives, others had indexers writing up details on Holmes, the national police computer system. To the left were two rooms with glass walls which had writing on them and maps stuck to them. A couple of officers I knew who worked in intelligence were gathered round, pointing at a computer screen.

Mike Courtiour, a detective superintendent, was in the other office, a phone clamped to his ear.

'Aaah, Julie, you're receiving. Sit there.'

An inspector I vaguely knew pointed to the back of the room.

After two years behind the two locked doors in the silence of Professional Standards, it was like being in a cauldron. And to be part of a team who might find the killer of Melanie Hall was such a privilege.

'There are two receivers. You and Jenny …' The DS was head-down in a small mountain of papers, but looked up occasionally to glance at her computer screen.

Observing a well-run, high-profile murder inquiry in action is a bit like sitting in the audience watching a symphony orchestra. The Senior Investigating Officer (SIO) is the conductor of the orchestra, setting the pace, tone and direction, the detectives bringing in information and carrying out actions, often playing in concert, sometimes performing solo; the indexers filing information and leads tapping away, providing the rat-a-tat-tat rhythm. A beating heart.

And the receiver. How did I fit in?

I knew what to do; I'd done it before, but only once and a long time ago. How would I play my part and how could I do it without cocking things up?

Jenny smiled as I sat next to her: 'Hi Julie, you're receiving for the archive, for the original inquiry in '96. I'm doing it for the new information coming in.'

I nodded, started logging on to the computer and asked for some of the files.

Christ, I thought to myself, *I haven't even used Holmes in years*.

Jenny was deep in her folders, looking at the information, prioritising actions, writing these up to send to the SIO.

I looked across the room and saw Barbara, an indexer I knew. I popped over and asked her for a quick refresh on how to upload to Holmes. Then I started reading through the notes. Melanie Hall had been found by workmen clearing a motorway verge at a stretch of the M5 at Junction 14, near Thornbury. Her remains had been found in five black bin liners. On the finger of one hand was a ring. Scene of crime officers had photographed the ring and detectives had shown it to Melanie's parents – they confirmed that Melanie used to wear it.

How long had Melanie been lying here? Since she vanished in 1996? And what new leads were there? She was found bound in a blue rope. Were there forensic opportunities with that? Who had owned rope like that in 1996?

Why there? Who would have been driving north? Were there security cameras? ANPR (automatic number plate recognition) cameras? They would have monitored all the registration plates which passed before them. How far back did those records go? We had made two arrests in 2003. Was there any new evidence here which linked us with those former suspects? How about people who had been in Cadillacs nightclub? Was there anything there?

Was there stuff we already knew?

I looked through the files:

Disappearance/presumed murder of Melanie Hall
Aged 25 years.
Last seen: Cadillacs Nightclub, Bath, June 9th 1996.

I looked at the front cover again: that date, 9 June.
I picked up my phone and dialled.

'Yes, Julie?'

'Gary, what date was Melanie Road murdered?'

'Ninth of June.'

'You do know that Melanie Hall vanished on the same day?'

'Er … yes, I think we did.'

'Were they ever linked?'

'Same name, same city … same date?'

'Yes.'

'Well, when Melanie Hall disappeared, we looked at possible connections. But there wasn't much – apart from that. Have they said how Melanie Hall died? Was she stabbed?'

'Don't know. They've just started the forensics.'

'Well, that'll tell us something.'

'What was Gallagher doing in '96? Was he living in Bath?'

'He never lived in Bath. His wife couldn't remember him ever even going.'

I hung up, wondering how Gary could remain so calm about things.

The same name, Melanie, on the same date, 9 June, in the same city, Bath. And Bath is tiny. Must be one of the country's smallest cities. What were the chances of that being a coincidence?

I carried on reading through the reports, looking at the names of the workmen who had found Melanie Hall. Who were they? Could one of them be the killer? Did they have a pang of conscience and want some answers to be given to Melanie's mother and father?

What had they been doing in 1984?

And what about the Bath rapist? Operation Eagle. I looked at Holmes to refresh myself.

There it was.

Two weeks before Melanie Hall vanished, the Eagle rapist had attacked a woman as she returned to her car, throwing a black bin bag over her head. His attack on that poor teenage girl in the lane in Kingswood, the lane I had driven along just an hour beforehand, that had happened in the September of 1996.

And in October of that year a sixteen-year-old girl had been grabbed by the rapist in a southern suburb of the city.

Had the Bath rapist gone a step further? Had Melanie Hall been attacked by the Bath rapist? Had she seen his face or even recognised him? Had he murdered her so he could not be identified?

The Operation Denmark inquiry continued. After several days, the post-mortem results were shared: it appeared that Melanie Hall had died from a head injury, possibly blunt force trauma. The pathologist looked to see if there were stab marks on her bones. This was a tough ask. Some of her remains had been scattered, possibly through animal activity, but it appeared there were no knife wounds to her ribs.

Melanie Road had suffered twenty-six stab wounds. If this was the same killer, using the same modus operandi, we would have expected there to have been some evidence of cuts to the skeleton.

Perhaps it was the same man who used a different method of murder? Perhaps they were separate killers and the links – the same name on the same date in the same city – were just a dreadful, gruesome coincidence.

CHAPTER 5

I spent a month in the MCIT, looking at the new information coming in, seeing what links existed with the original 1996 inquiry, with the Bath rapist and with Melanie Road. The inquiry started to lose its intensity and I was told I could return to the Cold Case team.

Return back to the day job and the inquiry into the murder of the first Melanie.

But as I was getting ready to go back to things in my work life, my home life had new horizons.

'Come on, this is exciting. A new house, a new start.'

'I was happy with the old one,' said Callum in the passenger seat. In the back seat, Connie at least looked interested. Toby just looked out of the window.

'And we don't have to call him Dad?' she asked.

'You didn't before we moved in, you won't now.'

'When will we get our own rooms? Will we have to share with George and Zoe?'

'You'll have to share until we do the building work. We'll convert that little barn into a couple of rooms.'

'Can we live in there?'

'I'll see what I can do.'

We pulled into the drive. My parents and sister would have described this as a large house, but we had five children between the ages of nine and sixteen between us. It might not be big enough.

Matt opened the door and gave me a smile and a peck on the cheek. Then we started unloading the cardboard boxes from our old life into our new home.

After years of parenting alone, I was finally in a partnership.

CHAPTER 6

DECEMBER 2009

The Review Team, which had seemed so exciting after my move from Professional Standards, felt a bit slow after a dynamic month on the Major Crime Investigation Team. Some of the others had also been transferred to the Melanie Hall inquiry and I wondered what they'd felt about working with the buzz of the live murder.

I was looking at a cold case rape, a 1992 job from Weston-super-Mare, when Mike Carter came in.

'What's up, Mike?'

Normally so smiley, his face seemed gaunt and tired.

'I've got some news on Operation Rhodium.'

I noticed that the room had fallen quiet, even Alan had shut up.

'We've had the scientific report back on Gallagher: it's not him.'

'Fuck.'

That was me.

'Shit.'

That was Alan.

CHAPTER 6

'Oh no,' said Gary.

'How can it not be Gallagher? It was a 97.5 per cent hit,' I said.

'When we had the full profile from his blood pressure cuff, the skin cells, that sample was a better quality than the sample from the hospital. The 2.5 per cent which we didn't have doesn't match. And it's an important 2.5 per cent.'

'Oh, Mike, I'm sorry.'

'If it's not 100 per cent, it means nothing.'

'This is the closest we've ever been to catching Melanie's killer.'

'No, we weren't close at all. Gallagher's nothing to do with it. The science isn't there. I'm going to have to tell the Road family. Julie, can you come with me?' asked Mike.

The drive to Bath was as grim as Mike's mood. Rain pelted the car as traffic crept forward on the A4.

'I can't believe it,' he said.

'How will Jean take it?' I asked.

'She's amazing. She'll be disappointed, but she'll be gracious. She will offer us tea and biscuits and she will take the news with perfect poise.'

'Have you told the Chief Constable?'

He nodded.

'It's not him, he's fine. But the whole force thought we'd got the hit. It doesn't look good for the Review Team, does it?'

'We'll carry on trying.'

'And there's Gallagher's family. We've essentially told them we think their recently dead husband and father was a rapist and murderer. How do we come across? We got it wrong.'

'You were following a lead, you were doing what was right.'

We reached Jean Road's home, got out of the car, climbed the steep steps and as Mike pressed the doorbell, I was sure I heard him let out a gentle sigh.

The sound of the lock, the door was pulled open and Adrian Road's face appeared.

'Hello,' he smiled.

'Hello, Adrian, may we come in?' Mike had a smile, but there was a gravity behind it.

We made our way into the lounge. Jean Road came through with a tray of tea and biscuits. She said hello and told us to sit down.

It was heartbreaking to watch Adrian's face fall as Mike broke the news. Jean, meanwhile, maintained that perfect dignity Mike had talked about.

'You said he was the man,' said Adrian. 'You said there was a, what was it? Ninety-seven per cent chance of him being Melanie's killer. I don't understand it.'

'Well, to be honest, none of us really understands the science like the experts. But they said that the initial DNA sample looked good, but the parts we were missing were really important. It's difficult when you're dealing with a dead suspect, samples are hard to come by. And when we got a good sample, those important missing bits showed us it wasn't him.'

'I'm sick of this.'

Jean put a hand on Adrian's.

'I know this is a big blow,' I said. 'But this case is so solvable.'

'We've had detectives coming here for twenty-five years saying that,' he told me. 'Twenty-five years! Do you know what that feels like? My sister's been dead for a quarter of a century and you're nowhere near finding her killer.'

'Look Adrian, we have a full DNA profile from the scene. Do you know how important that is? So few cold cases have that, particularly murders, particularly from that long ago.'

'What about Chimera?'

'Chimera?'

'I read about it online – it's when a person has two sets of DNA. If you have a bone marrow transplant or some other medical condition. What if you find the killer and you take the wrong set of DNA from him?'

I tried to keep the look of incredulity from my face.

'I don't think so, Adrian. That's all a bit far-fetched.'

'Julie, it might be, but I have no faith in your science. Look it up.'

'Adrian, I will find Melanie's killer.'

'I'm sure you will, Julie. But I don't want to see you again until you do.'

I tried to keep my face as impassive as his voice was calm, matter-of-fact.

'I mean it, Julie. I don't want to see from you or hear from you.'

Jean took her hand off Adrian's, bent forward and poured herself a cup of tea.

'Julie, we understand you're doing your best and we appreciate all your work, but this isn't the first time we've had news like this,' she told me.

'I don't mean to be rude, Julie, but you can't expect to have any idea what it's like. To be me,' said Adrian. 'To live inside here,' he tapped his head. 'For twenty-five years, every man I've seen, I've wondered one thing: did you kill Melanie? Every man I've passed in the street: "Is it you?" That's what I ask myself.

'Every man in a restaurant. Even my friends. I'll be out with them, and I'll see them laughing. And I'll wonder if they are laughing at me, laughing that they killed my sister and got away with it.

'Every single man for *twenty-five years*, Julie. Could you imagine living like that?'

'No.'

I looked across at the glass cabinet behind Jean. On it stood the photo: Adrian in the middle, Karen to his right and Melanie to his left. All smiling, all young, all oblivious to the attack which would rip their family apart.

'We have so many more things to try. You know we have seventy-one other names which have come in through *Crimewatch*? Seventy-one. Melanie's killer could be any one of them.

'We have the man's DNA. And we have boxes, dozens of boxes, full of names.'

Adrian made to say something, but Jean tapped him again on his hand.

'We know, Julie. You are doing your best, thank you.'

'I meant what I said, Julie,' said Adrian. 'Carry on with your inquiries, but I just can't cope with this. I don't want to see you again until you've found Melanie's killer.'

CHAPTER 6

Okay, Adrian, I thought to myself. *That is absolutely your right*.

I would need to stay in touch with Jean. I would have to talk with her directly, unchaperoned. It would be Jean and me, just the two of us.

CHAPTER 7

JANUARY 2010

I looked up at the Royal Crescent and shivered. Grand, golden and sumptuous, no matter what the season, including today. It was a winter's afternoon and a north-easterly wind whipped over the crescent's curves and ran right through me.

I had worked on and off in Bath for nearly twenty years but this was one of the first times I had actually come to the city's most famous street for a job. When I had been a uniformed sergeant here, I had rarely been bothered by crime at the tourist highlights: the Circus, Pulteney Bridge, the Abbey and the Roman Baths. Work for me was tackling burglaries in the suburb of Twerton, drug-dealing in Fox Hill, fences in Snow Hill. Student suicides in their halls of residence and drownings in the River Avon. Sometimes it was low-level, grimy crime. Other times it was heartbreaking. Seldom was it anywhere near the city's architectural highlights, where the hordes of tourists are bussed in for the day.

Kath Synott was with me, my partner for our first swab of the seventy-two men called in as suspects after the *Crimewatch UK* show.

'My hands are freezing,' she said, holding one hand up, the other clutching the bag with the file and the swabbing kit. She'd read through the paperwork in the car on the way over. Gary had prepared the file in his usual, meticulous way.

'Sid Farthing, DoB 17/9/1959.'

It listed his address as a flat on the Royal Crescent.

'Occupation: unemployed/freelance artist. Vehicle: none. Lives alone. No children. Precons: Sex Offences Act 2003 (voyeurism), twelve-month sentence, suspended May 2005. Suspected of theft of alcohol from Oddbins, Bath, August 1998. Cautioned under Sexual Offences Act 1956, Bath, 1988 (lewd act in public toilet).'

'You're single, aren't you, Julie?' said Kath after reading out Farthing's biography.

'No, I have a boyfriend and actually we've just moved in together.' I peered again at the front of the file. 'But if that doesn't work out, I may have to remember this address ... I hope he looks as good as he sounds.'

Even on a biting day, there were still a few hardy tourists. Japanese people listened intently to their tour guide as he delivered his city-guide spiel through chattering teeth. We made our way along the Royal Crescent's sweeping, pristine wide pavement.

'It's down here,' said Kath.

She had stopped. Not by one of the front doors, but at one of the gates above a basement flat.

I looked down at the stone steps which led to a peeling front door. The window paint was cracked, the flagstone patio was muddy and covered in leaves. I looked back at Kath, we made eye contact, I raised a brow and started down.

I rang the bell.

Nothing.

I rang the bell again.

'Who is it?' A man's voice from behind the front door.

'The police,' I said.

More silence.

'The police?'

'Yes.'

'What do you want?'

'Can you open the door?'

Another silence.

'Mr Farthing, can you open the door, please?'

There was the sound of a lock turning and the door opened on a pale, thin face.

'Mr Farthing?'

'Is it about that thing in the toilets?' he said. He had a high-pitched voice. A local accent. He wore a pair of glasses on the top of his head and squinted at me. His hair was dark, lank, greasy. He wore an old-fashioned jumper and a pair of what I assumed to be Marks & Spencer trousers.

'Can we come in, please? It is Mr Farthing, is it?'

'Yes.'

He pulled away from the door, creating a space for me to enter and Kath to follow behind. I didn't see Kath shudder, but I knew that coming into a property as grimy as this would be sending her OCD sensors haywire.

The only light was a bulb which hung with no lampshade from the middle of the room. Its pathetic glow showed a small pile of broken, wooden furniture across a wall. There was what could loosely be described as a kitchen in the same room. A Belfast sink with exposed pipework leading to a single tap. I couldn't quite place the smell. Mould, for sure. But it was mixed with old cooking fat, out-of-date deodorant and something unidentifiable.

'We've come here about a murder, Mr Farthing.'

'A murder?'

'Yes, the murder of Melanie Road. She was killed back in 1984.'

'Why are you investigating that now? What's that got to do with me?'

'Probably nothing, Mr Farthing. It's just we've been given a list of names and you're on it. It's a long list. And we're just going through everyone to eliminate them.'

'I've got nothing to do with a murder. Never even heard of Melanie Road.'

'We're sure you don't, but we just need to take a mouth swab from you to check the DNA …'

'I'm not giving you a mouth swab.'

'Mr Farthing,' Kath said, 'we have just had the twenty-fifth anniversary of Melanie's murder so we're looking again at the inquiry.'

'Yes, for twenty-five years her family haven't known who her killer is. It's heartbreaking,' I added. 'How would you feel if it were your sister or daughter?'

'Don't have a sister or daughter. What if you use my DNA to look at other things?'

'We're using your DNA just to look at this case. I'm sure you're not the killer. If you are, your DNA will match. If you're not, you'll be fine. Nothing to worry about.'

'Well, your people got very funny about that thing with the toilets. It was just a call of nature, it just looked odd when your officer walked in the gents. Do I need a solicitor?'

'You don't need a solicitor, we're not looking at other offences. It's here on the consent form.' Kath opened her bag and pulled out the swabbing kit and the consent form. She passed it over. He moved to the centre of the room, positioning himself under the dull glow of the naked bulb, poking his glasses down on to his nose, and squinted at the form.

'It'll take five minutes, Mr Farthing,' I said.

He continued to ask questions: how long would the swab stay on file? Where would it go? How could we assure him it wouldn't end up on any national database forever? What was her name? Melanie Hall? Hadn't they just found her a few weeks ago?

'It wouldn't stay on file, it would go to an independent laboratory where the scientists would check it against the DNA from the murder scene. Her name was Melanie Road, you've got the wrong murder. Yes, it is a coincidence they had the same name.'

He shrugged, lifted his smeared glasses from his nose on to his greasy forehead and I opened the swabbing kit. Perhaps I just imagined it, but he seemed to take a lot of notice of me putting the nitrile gloves on my hands. We had to prevent any of our DNA appearing on the swab, though. I opened the bag and pulled out the plastic box. From inside, I pulled the long, thin brush.

'Could you just stand by the light please, Mr Farthing?' I asked.

He moved back to the lamp.

'Open wide.'

He opened his mouth and I pushed the end of the swab on to the inside of his mouth, my free hand holding the outside of his cheek for resistance as I rotated the stick around. I pulled out the swab and pushed it into a plastic tub before repeating the process with the backup swab.

The second swab refused to go back into its tub, so I found myself making small talk with him as I worked to click it back in.

Eventually 'snap'.

I gave Kath a pleading stare.

She picked up the conversation while I filled in the paperwork, bagged the swabs and peeled the barcode from the kit and stuck it in my pocket notebook. I wasn't really listening to what they were saying, but I heard a smattering of words: 'Lived here fifteen years', 'Still play sometimes', 'People don't like folk music like they used to', 'I have a collection, would you like to see it?'

I looked up.

'Thank you, Mr Farthing. Would you like to know when we get the results?'

'Yes, please.'

I took his number and we went to leave.

He opened the door and we said goodbye, sucking in the fresh, freezing air from the Royal Crescent. I was sure I saw Kath's face relax in relief.

'Mum, I think Ben's going as Harry Potter. I bet he's got the proper costume.'

I was kneeling in front of Toby in our kitchen, fastening a dog blanket around his neck.

'Well, I think Ben's mum may have a bit more time to get an outfit sorted than I do. I think you look great.'

Toby smiled.

'Do I really look like Captain Underpants?'

'Yes, you do.'

'Ben says he stopped reading Captain Underpants books when he was seven. He says Harry Potter is for big boys.'

'Well, they are big books. But do you like Captain Underpants?'

He nodded.

'That's all that matters. Now, could you wear a scarf, please?'

Toby shrugged and I put a scarf over his T-shirt and blanket combo. After saying goodbye to Matt, we walked out of the house, past the builders who were starting to convert the barn, got into the car and drove off. We passed Callum and Connie, in their secondary school uniforms, waiting at the bus stop. Toby had seen them ahead and wound down his window.

'I'm Captain Underpants,' he screamed at them as we sped past.

I dropped him at school. The car's clock said 07.56.

'Please don't take off that scarf, Toby.'

He opened the door with a 'No, Mum' and scampered from the car, clutching his schoolbag and lunchbox.

It took me fifty-three minutes to reach Portishead and I walked in to a tutting from Alan Andrews.

'Was there a problem with your shoes? Were those Rubberheels holding you back this morning?'

'Sorry, Alan. The kids had to dress up as a book character. I would have suggested the Fat Controller, but you'd
already taken it.'

He gave me a grin and there was a twinkle in his eye.

'What are you up to? Alan?'

He grinned again and placed a file on my desk.

'Fat Controller or Sherlock Holmes? I'll let you
decide.'

I sat down and picked up the file.

'It was in the folders,' he said as he returned to his
seat.

I looked at the report:

Operation RHODIUM, Suspect Report
Luis Fernandez.
DoB: 07/02/1964, Address: 17 St Etienne Court, Bath.
Occupation: chef.
Fernandez did not come to notice until September 17th 1985,
more than a year after the murder.

A telephone message was received from Bradford-on-Avon
Police Station, saying two young girls claiming to be friends of
the deceased wished to see someone as a result of their attending
a seance with a Ouija board.

Stacey HITCHINS and Sara ACHESON were duly
interviewed. They claimed that at the seance the deceased had
indicated a person named as 'Luce' was responsible for Melanie's
death. Inquiries were made and the above-named was traced.
In addition to being a chef, he works as a waiter for his parents,
running a restaurant in Bath.

FERNANDEZ readily admitted knowing the deceased and
had done so ever since her arrival in Bath from Scotland. He
also stated he liked her and he had attempted to arrange a

> date with her, which she declined. He was unable to
> account for his movements on the night in question
> and blood samples were taken, which eventually proved
> to be of the Green Blood Type.

The report went on:

> Due to the length of time before he came to notice, nothing
> further can be done at this stage to connect him.

'What do you think?' asked Alan.

'Have we tried him since 1985?' I asked.

He shook his head: 'His name's been sitting on this file ever since. We've not touched him.'

'A chef? He used knives.'

'Exactly.'

'Does he have any form now?'

'He's clean, but we've never taken DNA from him. He lives just in Frome.'

'I like him.'

'Thought you would.'

'Could you get a swab?'

'I've an appointment with him tomorrow.'

My phone rang. I saw the number and my heart sank.

'Mrs Mackay?'

'Yes, Mrs Northey.'

'It's Toby.'

'What's he doing?'

'Well, he's dressed up as a book character.'

'I know, I made the costume.'

'Well, he's sort of dressed down now.'

'What?'

'He's taken off the blanket and all of his clothes. Except for his pants.'

'He's just wearing pants?'

'Yes. And he's been running around the school shouting, "I'm Captain Underpants."'

'Could you put the clothes back on him?'

'He's refusing. And it's very cold. And actually, he's being quite disruptive to the rest of the class. Miss Terry says she can't get any of them to concentrate because they keep laughing at Toby.'

There was a pause. I knew what was coming next.

'Would you mind collecting him?'

I said I would, turned off my phone and swore.

'Whose wearing pants, Julie?' It was Gary.

'Toby. He's gone berserk, he's running around on the coldest day of the year half-naked.'

Even Gary smiled.

I screamed silently, went back to my car and drove back to my village.

Toby was in the headteacher's office.

'What are you doing, Toby?'

'I'm Captain Underpants, Mum.'

'I told you to wear your trousers.'

'I needed to be in the spirit of the character.'

'And your top and scarf.'

'Mrs Mackay?'

'Mrs Northey. Sorry about this.'

Mrs Northey offered a small smile. Surely she would see the funny side?

'Mrs Mackay, we do need to speak with you about Toby. Thing is, today isn't the only time he's been disruptive. He has been getting increasingly agitated in class, refusing to listen, his work is very poor and he's unruly.'

'He's nine.'

'Please, we know there are a lot of changes at home. We think he could do with some more help with his work with you after school.'

I said I'd try, and led my semi-naked youngest son by the hand from the school.

'Toby, could you just try a bit harder?'

'I can't see the board, Mum.'

'I thought Captain Underpants had special powers. Surely he can see a blackboard? I'll get you an eye test.'

I felt like a coin. On one side I was a mum, on the other I was a detective. Sometimes, the mum face was showing and I was at the school gates, looking out for my children, but I didn't feel like I was doing that properly. Not truly. On the reverse, I was a professional law enforcer. But when that side was showing, when I was at work, I was always thinking about the other part of me: my young family. And I loved both. I was permanently flipping between both sides and neither seemed to be working.

How can I do this? I thought. *How can I be a full-time detective and a mum at the same time?*

CHAPTER 8

FEBRUARY 2010

I seem to have spent my life being talked down to by middle-aged white men in positions of power who are coasting in the final moments of their careers.

And it was happening again.

But I was sitting next to a true ally: Nigel Rock. Round-faced, with sleepy eyes and a Brummie drawl which disguised the ferocity of his intelligence, he was a brilliant Avon and Somerset detective superintendent, ex Serious and Organised Crime, who knew I would need some help with this all-male crew.

Opposite us were four men, the aforementioned middle-aged white men, who appeared to be career-coasting at the College of Policing.

'So why do you want to make a bid for a familial DNA run?' said Number One.

'Because we have a DNA profile and we haven't caught the killer yet, after twenty-five years.'

'But why now?' It was Number Two, clearly irritated that Number One had asked the first question.

'Well, we last made a familial run in 2001 and there will be millions more names on the system.'

'You realise it's expensive?'

'Yes,' I replied.

'About twenty thousand pounds?'

'Yes, but the government has money for it and we think it's a straightforward case. Also, Melanie's family hasn't had justice for twenty-five years. We think it's the best way to solve it.'

I think Number Three was asleep, but Number Four perked up now: 'You know, it's very clever, this familial DNA. Finding DNA which is so similar to the offender's that it has to be that of a close relative.'

'Yes, I know what familial DNA is, that's why we're here.'

'Look, gents …' Nigel took over in his gentle, non-confrontational but steely Brummie voice. 'It's a great case, Julie's done a brilliant job getting it in order. We think there's a good chance that familial DNA will be the tool that solves it and we need your help to get the government funding.'

'I agree with Nigel,' said Number Two. 'It looks appropriate on the face of it.'

'Have any of those guys done anything in years?' I asked as we left the room.

'No, but they hold the purse strings,' Nigel replied. 'Can you write up a business case for a familial run and we'll get it in?'

'You've been hurt before, you've been in pain.'

Barbara Bradley stood before me in the Review Team room, hand on my forehead, whispering in her soothing Scottish accent.

She was right. After years of agony, I'd recently been diagnosed with fibroids. The pain they caused felt like period pains on performance-enhancing steroids but now wasn't the time for the cold case squad to know.

'Listen, Barbara, no one gets to my age, has three kids, goes through a divorce and sits next to Gary Mason every day without feeling pain.'

'Did you know she was a white witch?' said Alan.

I'd heard something about Barbara's mystical powers, but I'd never seen her in action. I wanted an indexer, not a clairvoyant. For weeks I'd been badgering the MCIT to get one. One of the Bristol indexers had been due to start weeks earlier, but she'd refused to travel to Portishead. It had taken another seven phone calls, two weeks, three false starts and then finally, Barbara Bradley arrived. And she stood before me in all her white witch glory.

'Actually, if you have these powers, Barbara, can you just tell me who the killer is, please? It'd save us a lot of trouble.'

Barbara had heard that one before. She found a seat with a computer terminal and I gave her a box of index cards listing people whose surname began with A.

'How many names do you have to load on the system?'

'Twelve thousand.'

She looked at me.

'Give or take a few hundred.'

The College of Policing had approved the funds for the familial DNA run. I told her we needed to be up and running.

'When this comes back, it'll almost certainly have the name of someone related to Melanie's killer,' I said. 'We'll need to go through the list, find things out about them quickly and go off to swab their fathers, sons or brothers. We need to be ready to go.'

I was feeling confident about the familial DNA testing. The College of Policing had given approval and three days earlier, Gary and I had visited a detective inspector who had solved a rape case using the technique.

'We all have lots of similarities in our DNA sequence,' the DI told us in his Bournemouth conference room. Next to him was a folder. 'Even though you're a blonde woman and I'm a brown-haired man, we share about 90 per cent of our DNA, probably more.

'This is about identifying the points in the DNA sequence which are specific to you.

'Currently, we use 20 points on the sequence which offer us the chance to see how you are different from other people. It used to be 12, it'll be 34 in a few years' time. At the moment it's 20 points. Not all of those 20 points will be completely unique. Some you might share with a sibling, a parent or a child, others will be just yours. We don't know which ones until we do the test.

'Familial DNA is brilliant. It solves loads of cases. We were looking for a man who used a date-rape drug on a teenage boy he met in a club. We got DNA from the offender's semen. There was no direct match to the National Database.

'We went for a familial run. The list came back like this.'

He pulled open the folder and there was a list of names and numbers next to them. Those were the names of people who had DNA similar to the attacker. And next to that was a likelihood ratio.

'The top man here, we call him "the Screamer" – he's screaming out to be eliminated.'

I looked at the name: 'Luke Savage'.

'Yes, so Luke here has a likelihood ratio of 51,000. This means he's 51,000 times more likely to be the offender than any other man or woman.'

'And it's always in the top ten?' I asked.

The DI covered the numbers from eleven downwards.

'They are always in the top ten. This man here, number two, Jasper Hughes. He was swabbed after a really minor motoring offence but the officer thought for some reason to take a swab. His likelihood ratio was 21,000. He was 21,000 times more likely to be related to the attacker than most people, but that's still less than Luke at 51,000.

'We went through the top ten, swabbed the family members who could be the offender. We found Jasper had a brother. We swabbed him. Got our hit.'

'That's brilliant,' I said.

'It is brilliant.'

'Is it really worth just keeping it to the top ten?'

'Go to fifteen if you like, but it's always the top ten. Do you have a full DNA sample in your case?'

I nodded.

'Then you'll get your hit. I bet the relative will be in the top five.'

'Do you use Y-STR?' asked Gary.

'Yes.'

'What's Y-STR?' I wanted to know.

The DI flipped the familial list over and pulled out a pen. He drew a circle: 'In this circle is your DNA; it has twenty numbers.'

He drew another circle above: 'This is your mum's DNA; let's call her Janet.'

He drew a third circle next to the mum's: 'This is your biological dad. We'll call him John. Put Janet and John together and that's you. The twenty numbers in your circle are ten random points from your mum and ten from your dad. Now, your brother and sister will have similar DNA, but it's never quite the same. But some will be similar, particularly from the male line. So if you have a male killer you can't find, often you can get enough from a brother, father or a son to eliminate your suspect.'

There was something so calm, kind and measured about DCI Mike Carter that even when he was delivering bad news, there was a softness to the blow.

'The government's got cold feet on familial DNA,' he said. 'We can't go ahead.'

'Jesus fuck! Why?' I'd long since stopped caring if people of a Christian disposition might be offended by my language and this seemed like an appropriate time for blasphemy.

'They're discussing the rights and wrongs of it,' said Mike.

'So we've applied for a list. At the top of that will be the name of Melanie's killer and we won't get it?'

'It's worse than that, Julie. They've sent me the list, I've got it in my inbox.'

CHAPTER 8

'Well, can't you just open the attachment and have a little look?'

He shook his head.

'Could I?'

'There's a password, Julie. They won't send it until we're "go". Hopefully they'll see sense after a few months.'

I swore at the politicians and went back to my inquiry. We were just a few clicks away from finding the name of Melanie's killer.

The letter was handwritten on old, crumpled paper which had once been white. Black ink in a curling left-slanting hand. I sniffed it and was sure I could detect a whiff of pot.

I was in the Review Team room with Gary, Kath and Alan when the post delivery had brought through the small envelope addressed to Melanie Rhodes Team, Avon & Somerset Police.

I'd ripped open the envelope and held the scruffy, weed-infused note.

'Here we go, gang …' I started reading:

> I was watching the TV and saw the appeal over Melanie Rhodes. Have you thought about Francisco Arce Montes?
>
> I was in Devon in the 80s. And so was he. But he was in Bath beforehand. He's a killer. He killed a girl in France. They've got him in a prison, I think.
>
> He's Spanish. Nasty bastard. But he was in your area when it happened.

The letter was unsigned and there was no address. I noticed that Kath and Alan had stopped working and Gary was tapping away at his computer.

85

'Are you checking with detective inspector Google?' I asked.

'Montes?' said Gary.

I could see the results page scrolling up in the reflection in his glasses.

'Francisco Arce Montes.' He clicked.

'He's got his own page on Wikipedia,' continued Gary. 'Born 1950, described as being "a serial abuser and murderer." He's known to have committed assaults in Germany, Spain, France, the Netherlands and the United States.'

'He's a nasty bastard,' I said.

'Murdered Caroline Dickinson, a thirteen-year-old school-girl who was on a class trip to France in July 1996. Sentenced to thirty years in prison in 2004.'

Gary swung his computer screen round. The image on the screen was of a white man with a deep tan, a slim face, his forehead lined, a dusting of stubble on his chin. He boasted a full head of dark hair, which was greying by his ears.

Are you him? I asked silently.

'He's in a French nick?' said Alan. He had his hand out, beckoning for me to pass him the letter. 'I'll take this one. I might need to go and take a swab from him myself.' He gave a gappy grin. 'A little overnight in the Dordogne would be a lovely break from seeing Gary's face.'

He picked up the phone and started growling into it.

'Sergeant Davies? Yeah, it's Alan here in the Major Crime Review Team. We've got a man down here, his name's come in. He's in a prison in France for murdering a schoolgirl. We need to get his DNA for one of our inquiries. What do you boys need for an Interpol application these days?'

He put down the phone and smiled. 'You know what? I think today our Force Intelligence Bureau is living up to its name. It'll be no bother, just a form. Hey presto!'

The envelope arrived the following day and landed moments before a 'fuck me' spilled from Alan's lips.

'Is this an application form or a phone book?'

He flicked through it.

'Six fucking forms for a DNA profile? Interpol has gone and exceeded its own low expectations.'

'How are you getting on with the indexing, Barbara?'

'I've done thirty-five names.'

'Great work,' I said, then muttered, 'only 12,400 to go.'

I looked at the Inquiry Room. Barbara with her boxes of index cards, Alan filling out a bible-sized application form for a foreign DNA profile, Gary, who had just received a fixed penalty notice for driving in a bus lane in Trowbridge.

Would we ever find Melanie's killer?

Operation Rhodium was one of thirty-three unsolved murders we were working on and I was reviewing, but it was when I was looking at the papers for another killing that I saw the word Melanie and my heart stopped.

The heading of the report read Broadmoor Hospital and it was dated December 1984. The recipient had been a detective I didn't recognise: Lew Clarke.

And it was about the murder of another woman: Shelley Morgan.

I knew a little about Shelley's killing. She had been a thirty-three-year-old mother, an American living in Bristol, who dropped off her young children at primary school, was spotted catching a bus and was never seen alive again, except by her killer. When she failed to pick up her children at the end of the day, teachers raised the alarm, but Shelley was gone. Four months later, her remains were found in a copse in Backwell, a village about eight miles from Bristol. Shelley had been stabbed and sexually assaulted.

Then I looked at the date of her disappearance: 11 June 1984. Two days after Melanie Road had been killed.

This report from a Broadmoor psychiatrist seemed to be linking the murders of Melanie and Shelley. At the end of paragraph two: 'Given the low incidence of sexually motivated homicides, which at least in part we must assume both to have been, and given the low incidence of these in the area, it is extremely improbable that two such events would occur so closely together other than as the result of the actions of one man.'

The psychiatrist didn't seem to have much science in his report, but he made a few other conclusions. He said the shape of the knife and the pattern of the wounds were the same: 'Another similarity between the killings, although it may not be beyond dispute, is that the responsible party would seem to have had some knowledge of the area ...'

And he went on, focusing on the Bath killing: 'I have a hunch that Melanie met her killer earlier on, perhaps at the disco, for it is notable that she was unable to make the short distance from where she was left by her three male chaperones to her own home and it may well have been the assailant was at the disco and was alert to her movements and plans.

CHAPTER 8

'It is difficult to speculate on how the homicides started. Did the assailant regularly carry a knife? In my experience the severely mentally ill, with persecutory delusions, for example, may carry a knife to protect themselves against their imagined persecutors ...

'With little to back up this speculation it seems more likely to me that the offender here is somebody with marked ambivalence about women, both idealising yet fearing them. He has a very low opinion of himself and little faith in his capacity to satisfy or please women, either sexually or in any other aspect of the relationship.

'But why did the homicides stop? Clearly the offender might have left the area or the country. Or alternatively have been admitted to hospital or jail, perhaps on some minor matter. Spontaneous remission is also possible, but given the savagery of the attacks and the closeness of them together in time it seems more likely that some sort of incapacitation (hospital or prison) intervened and perhaps nipped the continuation of the process in the bud.'

'What do you think of this, Gary?' I asked.

Gary shrugged. 'He's the expert.'

'But he's not basing this on any science, is he? There are no figures or data behind what he says. It's just an opinion.'

'He was based in Broadmoor; he saw killers every day. He knew how their minds worked.'

'Was anyone ever arrested for killing Shelley Morgan?'

'No,' he replied. 'We had some good suspects but the evidence was a struggle.'

Was the man who murdered Melanie Road also behind the rape-killing of another woman two days later? Was he also the Bath Rapist? Could he have taken Melanie Hall? There were too many coincidences going on here. Each of these offences was depraved and violent. For a man to commit any of these attacks and then live with himself would take a certain kind of mind. A compartmentalised brain. A sex-driven, knife-wielding killer without a conscience. Could there really be several of these men out there?

Or just one?

Casework Results Report

My heart skipped a beat when I saw the email appear.

'Here we go, team …' I shouted. Alan was behind his pile of papers, filling in forms about Montes in France. Gary was building a family tree of a suspect who died in July 1984. Claire was writing a report. But they stopped what they were doing and looked across.

I clicked on the message and up popped a box. It had the laboratory logo and I scrolled down:

Sidney FARTHING
Luis FERNANDEZ
These DNA profiles have been compared to the unknown DNA profile obtained in Operation RHODIUM (MR8). These profiles do not match therefore these individuals can be excluded as potential contributors.

'They'd have called if it were a hit,' said Alan.

I exhaled.

'I thought your Ouija board guy was a good shout,' I said. 'The Royal Crescent man was just a fucking deviant.'

'Welcome to cold case work, Julie,' said Claire. 'It's a long slog, lots of wrong turns. It'd have been solved if it were easy. We're the last roll of the dice.'

Right. Let's be positive, I thought.

We still had some good leads from the Green Blood Book. An undergraduate who had been to a couple of parties with Melanie and lived in a flat on her route home, a coach driver who had been ferrying Canadian tourists around Britain and had stopped in Bath that night. He'd cut himself shaving. His blood was green. And a patient who should never have been let out of his psychiatric hospital before his medication took hold. He'd been arrested stealing underwear from washing lines two weeks later. There was just so much to this investigation.

I had been in the Cold Case team for ten months now and I was enjoying the work. It felt a privilege to be able to pick a file from the shelf and read old reports and documents about an unsolved rape from the seventies or a murder from the sixties and to think that I might be the person who could finally get justice for the victim.

Each individual case was fascinating in its own way, with its own characteristics and quirks. Some had been dogged by bad forensics, others investigated poorly. Other rare inquiries had been a good job but the prime suspect really had got away with murder. And while it might be easy to see these mysteries as an academic challenge or an abstract puzzle, when I read an autopsy report or a victim's statement or a witness's account of the horror of what had happened, it was a reminder of just how important this work was: people had lived with the traumatic consequence of these crimes for decades.

People like lovely Jean Road.

CHAPTER 9

SEPTEMBER 2010

It started with an email. A ping in the inbox. The title was
Melanie Road from Bath Police:

> To: the Major Crime Review Team. We've received
> a call from a man who believes he was a witness to
> the Melanie Road attack. He thinks he saw Melanie
> on the night she was killed. He would like you to call
> him back, he believes he has information which might
> help you.

A witness? After twenty-six years?

The email had his name. Ben Schwarzkopf. And his
phone number.

I read the message out to Alan, Gary, Kath, Claire and
Barbara.

'What do you think?'

Their faces were a mixture of surprise and incredulity.

'Why now?' Alan.

'He could be mad.' Claire.

'We should see him, but what use will he be after twenty-six
years?' Kath.

'He could be the killer.' Claire again. 'Wanting to confess
but not able to bring himself to go through with it.'

Gary was busy typing away on his computer, looking up people called Ben Schwarzkopf, I assumed.

'Barbara?' I asked. 'What does your karma tell you?'

Barbara was holding a small pile of index cards and smiled. 'Do you have any choice? You've got to see him.'

The questions continued. If he had witnessed the attack, or something before the attack, why now? I knew sometimes people come forward hoping to be told that their information was of no value whatsoever. Hoping they'd been wrong for all these years.

'He could describe the killer.' Claire.

'He might have seen him running away.' Kath.

'He might be full of shit.' Alan.

'I've found a Ben Schwarzkopf,' said Gary. 'He's an architect now, down in the New Forest. But there was someone of that age who used to live in Bath in 1984. In Camden Road.'

Just by the murder scene.

'You haven't got his mental health history there, have you?' said Alan, picking up his phone and dialling.

From across the room, I could hear the distant ringtone through Alan's mobile, a pickup and a 'hello?' Alan introduced himself. Then I watched him fall silent as the distant, tinny voice at the end of the line talked.

And talked.

I saw Alan sitting back, his eyes widening, but he was also trying to stifle a yawn.

The man was still talking.

Eventually, Alan managed to get a word in and arranged to meet Ben Schwarzkopf the following week. He ended the call.

'Christ, he speaks more than Gary,' said Alan.

'What did he say?' I asked.

'Reckons he saw Melanie before she was stabbed. Thinks he saw the killer running away.'

'Why's he come forward now?'

'Fuck knows.'

'What did he sound like?'

'Talkative.'

It was surprising how quiet the Review Team was without Alan and Gary. Kath, Claire, Barbara and I were working in silence while they were out talking to Ben.

Gary and Alan had met Ben at 10 a.m. I had assumed they'd be back by 2 p.m. at the very latest. Earlier, if he were a crank. But now the clock was nudging a quarter to four. We clocked off on the hour and Wednesday evenings were the most challenging: my children's homework deadline and Pony Club.

The door burst open at 4.05 p.m. Gary came in.

'What was he like?'

There was a sparkle in his eyes. Even Mr Cautious couldn't contain his excitement.

'Well, it was a very informative meeting. He is talkative. Hard to get a statement from. He goes off at tangents. But it was very ...'

'Fuck me ...' Alan followed in. 'He saw the whole fucking thing. Everything. Gold dust. Fucking gold dust.'

'He saw the killer?' I asked incredulously.

'He knew the killer. Kind of.' Alan.

'Well, he would be able to identify him. He didn't know the killer's name, but …'

'He saw Melanie and her killer before the attack. He went away, then he heard it and saw the murderer fucking off across Camden Crescent.'

'Fuck.'

Alan was nodding. He added another 'Gold dust'.

'Why's he only come forward now?'

'He hasn't. He's tried before. Three times. Police have always turned him away,' said Gary.

It was like a wave coming over me. That feeling of a breakthrough.

'Take it from the beginning,' I asked.

Gary started: 'It was an unusual account, wasn't it?'

Alan nodded.

'He talks in the present tense as if he's recounting what happened live.'

'I think he's autistic,' said Alan. 'Or he's on the spectrum. He remembers things by putting them in boxes, compartmentalises things, but his memory is so fricking vivid. Photographic.'

Gary picked up: 'Ben says he's just bought a camper van in June 1984. A left-hand drive. It's new, he's really proud of it.'

'Really proud,' interjected Alan. 'Didn't stop talking about the feckin' thing.'

'He's coming back from a night out, it's about 1.45 a.m.,' continued Gary. 'And he's looking for a space to park. He finds a spot, tries to park and can't because of the left-hand drive thing, he can't get the right angle to reverse in. So, he drives around the block so he can park in the space from the opposite direction. He drives up St Stephen's Road and he sees two people on that triangle of grass, between St Stephen's Court and the old stone steps.

'A young woman and an older man. They're arguing. Shouting.'

I was focused on every word Gary said.

'Ben drives up, turns round and returns down to park. Now he sees the young woman again and she's walking ahead of the man. She's silent now.

'She's ashen, that's how Ben described it, looks terrified.'

'Poor Melanie,' I said.

'But they aren't arguing any more, so Ben just carries on and parks in his spot,' continues Gary. 'He gets out, starts walking to his house, he's about to go in the front door, then he hears a scream.'

'It's not just a scream,' Alan added. 'It's a chilling, heart-breaking wail. Piercing. Awful.'

'So, Ben wonders what to do,' said Gary. 'He says he's concerned. Not about the couple but because of the radio in his car. There's been a load of thefts of stereos and he loves his camper van.'

'So he fucks off back to his van and it's near the green triangle of grass,' said Alan. 'His van's fine, but he sees the man coming down St Stephen's Road. Not flat-out running, but fast. He shouts to your man, something like, "Had a row with yer girlfriend?" The guy says yes and goes down the steps and away.'

'Christ,' I said. 'And he saw the killer?'

Gary nodded. 'A white man, early thirties. And he'd seen him before in Bath.'

'Where had he seen him before?'

'The cricket ground. And the snooker club.'

'The Red House Snooker Club?' I found myself asking.

'Yes,' said Gary, surprised that I knew it.

I swore under my breath. I'd read about that when reviewing the Melanie Hall inquiry.

'Could he identify him?'

Alan nodded. 'He's on the spectrum. He's like … a genius.'

'And he's known this for all these years? Why now?'

'This is the thing …' began Gary. 'He came forward on the day of the murder, 9 June. He wanted to get his camper van, but it was behind the police cordon. He said to the policeman at the tape, "I think I saw something …" and the police officer asked where he lived. Ben pointed to his house and the cop said he'd be picked up on house-to-house inquiries.'

'But he never got the knock,' added Alan. 'He says house-to-house never called. And he tried twice again. Once, he calls up and the operator says the case had been solved. The last time they took his number and no one phoned back.

'He saw the twenty-fifth anniversary publicity and has been having sleepless nights. Said the reconstruction had been preying on his mind.'

'That was months ago,' I said.

Alan shrugged.

'Okay, let's start corroborating his story. We'll need records of his address in '84, the house-to-house files from the time, a full description of the killer. Could he do an e-fit?'

Alan said yes.

'And can we go to the scene so you can walk us through it?'

The dull drizzle seemed to have sucked all the vibrancy from Bath's golden buildings. A gentle rain tapped on the windscreen as we struggled through the city's snaking traffic. We were in two cars, the whole crew. I was in the passenger seat next to Gary, who was driving. In the back was Claire. Alan, Kath and Barbara were in the car ahead.

We parked our cars on Camden Road. Alan had a long coat on and started waving his umbrella around like a tour guide.

'Okay, class?' he began.

We assembled outside one of the yellow terraced homes.

Alan jabbed the air with his umbrella in the direction of a house with a purple door.

'Ben …' he said with a dramatic flourish, 'lived there in June 1984. He was a designer back in those days, twenty-two years old and fresh out of college. A young man with a new job and a camper van he loves. Follow me …'

We sauntered after Alan in the rain.

'Here …' he turned his folded umbrella upside down and tapped the road next to a kerbside, '… was the spot where he wanted to park. But he couldn't get the van in. It was a squeeze and he loves his van. He wants to treat it like his first girlfriend. Gentle, like. So, he spins off to come back in the opposite direction. This way …'

We started walking along the narrowing road. Uphill. High Bath-stone walls peered down from either side of the lane.

'It's tight along here and he remembers concentrating because he didn't want to scrape his camper van,' said Gary.

The road then spun hard left in a hairpin bend.

'And he remembers worrying about this turn.'

We carried on walking up.

Alan slowed to catch his breath. 'Feck me,' he muttered.

'Then he gets to this triangle of grass. This is where he sees a young woman, who he recognises, arguing with a man – who he's also seen before. They're shouting.'

'Does he remember what they were saying? Could he make it out?' I asked.

Gary shook his head.

'He just heard them arguing.'

'If he's sure this is Melanie, this is the first time we have a confirmed sighting of her alive since she left her boyfriend in the city centre.'

'Exactly,' said Alan, 'so they're arguing here to his left and he drives off up the street and turns round, and comes back down.'

Alan waved his umbrella around, beckoning us further up St Stephen's Road. By now he had pulled a map out of his pocket and was looking down at it.

'Here …' he frowned, shook his head, then brolly-pointed at a higher stretch of pavement, 'sorry, there was where he sees them again.

'She's walking in front. Pale. Ashen. The man's directly behind.'

'Melanie's post-mortem showed she had puncture wounds in her back,' I said. 'Do you think he was jabbing a knife behind her as she walked up? It'd explain those cuts.'

Alan nodded, then continued: 'Your man drives back down to his house and he parks.'

He fell silent, holding a hand up.

'Then he hears a scream. He's walking into his home, he's worried. He's got a car stereo in his camper van. Could it be a thief? So he goes out to check. But his van's okay, not a scratch. Something makes him carry on. Follow me ...'

Alan waved his umbrella around and we started back to the green triangle of grass. He stood at one of the three corners.

'Ben gets here and sees the killer half-walking, half-running down the pavement we've just come down. The same route as the Green Blood Trail. But there's something funny about it. When you run, you usually have both your arms out.'

Alan started swinging his arms.

'One of the suspect's hands was in his pocket,' added Gary. 'If he's injured his arm, that could explain why the trail stops between that junction and here. Between blood spot 40, which is the first evidence of Green Blood, up near the deposition site, spot 47, which is the only trace of Green Blood halfway down, and here, where spot 49 is the first of many down the steps.

'Ben shouts, "Had a row with yer girlfriend?" and the guy says yes. And he takes his hand out of his pocket to steady himself down the steps. It's dark, the steps are steep.'

Alan nodded and darted to the top of the grey stone, spiral staircase and we followed him down, careful not to slip.

'The killer comes down here, arm out, bleeding, dropping his Green Blood everywhere ...'

'Blood spots 49 to 58 ...' interjected Gary.

'And Ben follows him down. He can't say why, just follows him. And he watches as the killer stops by this lamp post …' Alan pointed his umbrella at the light.

'That's where blood spots 65 and 67 fall,' added Gary. 'And the killer fucks off across Camden Crescent. A straight line. Same as the Green Blood Trail. It's fucking perfect.'

'Who knows about the Green Blood Trail?' I asked.

'All the investigators,' said Alan.

'I mean,' I said, 'we told the media about blood spots. But have we ever given the specific details out about the route of the trail?

'If he's a fantasist or an attention-seeker, he could have read it and be having a bit of a laugh with us. Kath, could you check that, please?'

She nodded.

'Or, he could be the killer,' I added.

'I took a swab from him,' said Gary. 'We'll know soon enough.'

CHAPTER 10

NOVEMBER 2010

When there are two of you in a team and one of you swears a lot and the other never offers a profanity, it accentuates how awful the first person's language is.

When I say 'first person', I mean me.

I'm sure people thought my language was rougher and readier than it actually was because Gary refused to swear. And here I was again, struggling with the big metal gates of the Weston-super-Mare police storage unit, rolling out F-words as if they were going out of fashion.

Gary sauntered over from the car, his shirt hanging out of his trousers.

'Nice of you to help.'

He pulled and I pushed, and eventually we dragged the metal doors open.

The next five minutes followed the usual routine: drive in the car, find the light switch, alarm goes off, traffic officer comes in and complains, realise I've left my coat in the office in Portishead and it's freezing.

Or 'fucking freezing' as I described it at the time.

'Will you stop effin' and jeffin'?' asked Gary.

I told him where to go.

With an eff, not a jeff.

Did Ben's story check out? How could we prove whether we were dealing with a real-life silent witness or a jumped-up fantasist?

We made our way through piles of exhibits, past the freezers, beyond the shelves buckling under green crates to the dedicated space I had organised. Operation Rhodium was now in a semblance of order. Our green crates were stacked together neatly, away from the other cold cases.

'House-to-house inquiries should be in that box there,' I said, looking at a crate which was at the bottom of a stack of five.

Gary and I started lifting the upper crates off.

'So, do you think he could be the killer?' I asked him.

Gary shook his head. 'He's too talkative. He would have had to tell someone, it would have come out.'

'How could someone just murder anyone and keep it a secret?' I asked. 'Who goes out in the middle of the night with a knife, wanting to rape and murder someone?'

He nodded.

'What were those three leads from the forty-seven-page book?' I asked between breaths as we carried on lifting crates. 'The man on the church steps, the cyclist and …'

'The jogger?' Gary said. 'No, we asked him, but he knew nothing about those.'

We got to the bottom crate and opened the lid.

I pulled out a box of house-to-house forms and started rummaging through.

'Camden Road, Camden Road, Camden Road …' I muttered under my breath. 'What number was he?'

Gary told me.

I carried on flicking. It took me twenty minutes to work it out, check, double-check and get Gary to triple-check.

'One more knock …' I said.

Police house-to-house inquiries went as far as Ben Schwarzkopf's next-door neighbour. If they had gone one house further, they would have found this witness in the hours after the murder.

At the time the killer was injured. He was at his most vulnerable. The investigation could have had a description of the prime suspect, they could have publicised this in the golden hours after the crime.

One more knock.

'He's telling the truth,' I said.

Gary looked at the map of the house-to-house parameters.

'One of the hypotheses in '84 was that the offender ran along Camden Crescent, into Hedgemead Park, on to Walcot Street and across the river.

'That's where the Bath rapist attacked.'

'Yes, they were all that side of the river, weren't they? Apart from the Kingswood rape.'

I left Gary putting the Operation Rhodium files back together and went off to find Operation Denmark: the inquiry into Melanie Hall. This was also well-organised since the discovery of Melanie Hall's body next to the motorway, ten months earlier.

It took a little while to find what I was after.

CHAPTER 10

I opened the crate and there it was: The Red House Snooker Club.

When Melanie Hall disappeared in 1996, I had been sent in as an undercover officer to Cadillacs nightclub. This had been where she was last seen alive. Detectives wanted to know who visited the club regularly, what the vibe was.

In 2009, when Melanie's body had been found by the side of the motorway, I'd reviewed the case and had read that all of the Cadillacs' ledgers had been seized back in 1996. This included all the paperwork from its previous incarnation: The Red House Snooker Club.

Ben Schwarzkopf had said he'd seen Melanie Road's killer in that same snooker club.

From snooker club to nightclub. Melanie Road to Melanie Hall.

The books in the crate were tatty and scratched, but the register from 1984 was there. I opened the pages, started flicking through. Dates next to names of members and guests. Could the killer be listed here?

Had the murderer been out playing snooker earlier on the evening of Melanie Road's murder?

I got to 8 June.

And I swore.

Again.

Gary came over and asked what was up.

'Ben said he'd seen the killer here but there are no entries on the night of Melanie's murder. Looks like there was a party on or some event, it's just a block booking.'

He sighed.

'It's like he's here somewhere, the murderer, we just can't find him,' I said. 'The clues are telling us something, we just don't understand what.'

Our inquiries into Ben Schwarzkopf's account continued for months. He had also seen the killer in the car park of Bath Cricket Club on a previous occasion.

I visited Jean Road at her home the following week. Juggling Operation Rhodium with the other cases meant I was starting to see her every few months. It was always just the two of us – Adrian knew I was going, but he was never around when I went.

'The bloody gardener, he hasn't shown again,' she said, looking at her overgrown lawn.

'Jean, Tony used to play cricket, didn't he?'

'Yes, he was a member at Lansdown.'

'Did he go to watch at Bath ever? Somerset?'

She said he did.

'And did Melanie ever go with him?'

Yes, again.

'What was that scene like, do you know? Were there any friends there, any people he used to see at Bath Cricket ever?'

'I don't think so.'

I pressed Jean a bit more gently, trying to jog her memory about men who might have been at the cricket in 1984: was there anyone there who had been difficult or edgy or strange?

Nothing.

I finished my cup of tea, grabbed a biscuit, then mowed Jean's lawn.

'Fucking French!'

Between Alan and me, the air in the Review Team office was turning blue.

'What's up?' I asked.

'This Montes chap, in France, they say they have no record of him.'

'What? It's in every news item about Caroline Dickinson's murder. He was sentenced to thirty years in a French prison.'

Alan picked up the phone and gave the Force Intelligence Bureau – our link with Interpol – a piece of his mind.

'They'll try again,' he said.

There was a pause.

Then he picked up the phone: 'Hello there, it's Alan Andrews in the Major Crime Review Team. Yes, I need an e-fit made up.'

There was a distant voice from the end of the line, then: 'No, it's from longer than forty-eight hours ago.'

More distant voice.

Alan's face reddened.

'Twenty-six years – 1984.'

A pause at the end of the line, then more distant voice and Alan said, 'What? That's ludicrous? My man here has a photographic memory.'

The to and fro of the conversation ended with Alan slamming the phone down.

'Would you come with me to make sure I don't kill these boys, Julie?'

I followed as he headed downstairs to the e-fit team.

Sitting at what looked like a little cupboard with a computer were two guys who were building a face on a big screen.

'Listen,' started Alan, 'this is an old murder. For the first time in the inquiry we have a man who can describe what the killer looks like.

'For the first time. Do you understand just how big a deal this is?'

'Yes, I understand what you're saying,' said the first man. 'But we simply can't trust the integrity of a person's memory after forty-eight hours. There's no point. In fact, what he thinks he's remembered has probably changed over the years. We'll produce something which is detrimental to your inquiry.'

'Look, this guy is fucking autistic! He has a brilliant mind, remembers things perfectly. Could have been yesterday, could have been last year, could have been twenty-six years ago. We should take a chance.'

'No, we're not doing it. It's against force policy.'

As we made our way back to the Review Team office, Alan told me where he would like to stick that force policy. We decided that he and Gary would take a written statement from Ben Schwarzkopf and when they saw him, they would ask if he could draw a picture of the killer.

'Kath, can you look at the car radio thefts, please?' I asked.

'From '84?'

'Yes. Ben said there was a spate of car radio thefts in 1984. Was anyone ever caught for that? Could be our killer was the thief. Had he left fingerprints? Is there a link?'

Kath went through the files, but all records of the car radio thefts had been destroyed in 1991.

Another blind alley.

A month had passed. We had swabbed another ten suspects who were on the list of seventy-two names which had phoned in after the *Crimewatch UK* show. Ben Schwarzkopf's DNA swab had come back negative, confirming our belief that he wasn't Melanie Road's killer. I was reviewing Alan's latest attempts to get the DNA chart of Francisco Arce Montes. The French authorities had rejected our paperwork because we had filled his date of birth out as day/month/year instead of month/day/year.

Alan burst in.

'Want to see a killer?'

His eyes were sparkling; he was waving a black A4 folder in his hand. Gary followed behind.

Kath and Barbara looked round.

'He's done it, he's drawn him.'

'Show me.'

Alan opened the folder. Inside were three sheets of paper, each with a different drawing of the same man. They were sketchy, *very* sketchy. A white man with a thin face looking up. He had a full head of dark hair, thin eyebrows, a straight, simple nose and thin lips. His face was blank, emotionless, open. He wore a shirt, the top button undone.

There was something simple, almost childish, about the drawings, but knowing the evil inside this man made the image more haunting.

Ben's account seemed to be checking out. All our corroboration showed he was telling the truth. After a quarter of a century, we now knew so much more about a killer who had arrived one night, murdered, then disappeared.

He was white, lived in Bath at the time, he had a local accent, he was in his early thirties then, probably late fifties now, we knew where he used to go.

And we had a picture of the murderer: just a sketch, just a simple image.

But for the first time, I was face to face with Melanie's killer.

CHAPTER 11

MAY 2011

Some of the swabs were easy to obtain: lots of men were happy and obliging when we'd turn up and ask if we could put a stick in their mouth as part of an inquiry into the historic murder of a schoolgirl. Others took persuasion, some refused. One was downright fraught.

We were still corroborating Ben Schwarzkopf's story. We had worked out that no media releases had ever described the route of the Green Blood Trail – in fact, Green Blood had never been public knowledge. Ben had been telling the truth. And we had also decided not to release to the press the details about Ben's account.

When that information was out, we could never take it back: we would have no control.

The swabbing of the men in the Green Blood Book was continuing.

I wanted to chase the Saudis.

The forty-seven-page book listed five names of men who had been in the city and disappeared the following day back to Saudi Arabia:

Hazim Ismat
Amir Al-badawi
Fazil Shariq
Jamil Qadir
Mansour Akram.

We had never spoken to them. Ben's account said the killer was a Bath man but we had to close off this open lead.

I wanted to get the DNA chart from Melanie Road's murder scene loaded on to the Saudi DNA Database to see if there was a match, but I needed a manager's approval.

'Can't do it, Julie,' the superintendent said.

'Why not?'

'Because it's Saudi Arabia.'

'So? The killer could be there.'

'They have capital punishment in Saudi. This is for an offence of rape and murder. If we get this loaded on the Saudi system, what's to say they won't round up an enemy of the state, say he did it, execute him and effectively end the inquiry? And we, here, don't even know if he's the right man or not.

'I'm not doing it.'

And other leads were dragging on. The French authorities were still refusing to allow us access to Francisco Arce Montes or his DNA.

'Fucking French!' Alan said, not for the first time. 'It'd be easier if I just went there and got him to spit in a cup.'

We resubmitted the form for Montes with further reasons, including that we didn't actually need to see the killer, we just needed his DNA bar chart to compare with Melanie's murderer's.

And it was a Friday morning when I took a call: it was a detective from Bath CID.

'Hi Julie.'

'Hello.'

'We've got this man who died in a car crash last week. Nothing unusual about the death. Sad, you know. But we've received intelligence that he may've been responsible for Melanie Road's murder.'

'What? How do you know?'

'He told a friend.'

'What's his name?'

'Saul Griffiths.'

'Saul Griffiths?'

I saw Gary's face perk up.

'Okay, we'll look at it. When's his funeral?'

'Tomorrow.'

'Tomorrow? Why are you telling me now?'

'We only found out earlier. Thought you'd like to know.'

I got the details of the funeral parlour and hung up.

'Saul Griffiths? He's in our system,' said Gary.

'Look, here. DoB 30 November 1962; job: unemployed, address in Bathwick. He has some minor preconvictions for theft and a long history of treatment by the Avon and Wilt-shire Mental Health Partnership.

'He was on my list to find and swab.'

'He died in a car crash last week. Could you swab him?'

'Sorry, Julie. My flight's at 2.30 p.m. I'm on a half-day.'

Gary was always going on holiday.

'Could you do it, Julie?'

I was horrified at the thought. I'd have done it, but I had a vet's appointment that afternoon.

Caesar was my lifetime horse. I'm a firm believer that if you're into horses, one will connect with you in your lifetime above all the others. And Caesar was mine. He was brilliant, had the most beautiful temperament, did everything I asked of him, but he had a bad illness and the vet said nothing more could be done.

'We can't just rock up and swab a dead man, we need consent,' I said.

We found Griffiths's files and tried to locate his family through the electoral roll, Police National Computer and Facebook searches.

He had a brother and an elderly mother.

We tried the brother's number: no reply.

I tried Bath Police Station.

'Pete,' I asked a uniformed sergeant I knew. 'It's Julie. We've got a man who needs swabbing on Operation Rhodium. A good suspect, but he's dead. He's in a funeral parlour. Could you get someone to do it, please? We're just awaiting consent. He's due to be cremated tomorrow.'

'Swab a dead man? Sorry, I can't find anyone. And we don't really know what we're doing, we haven't swabbed a dead man before.'

'Pete, it's exactly the same procedure as normal. We're trying to get consent from the next of kin. I just need some-one who is free to be able to go and do it.'

'Well, I'm not sure about this, it's not really my job.'

'Look, Pete, we're both sergeants. You know what to do as much as I do, please try and help me out here.'

I put the phone down and rang Bath CID. I got lucky, or so I hoped. Andy answered the phone – he had been on my team when I was at Bath. Once, I'd left him a list of things to do and he'd complained, saying, 'That's the sort of note my mother-in-law leaves me.'

I'd told him I liked the sound of his mother-in-law, both she and I got things done.

Andy said he could see the brother but he had an appointment later. So, much as he would like to help, he couldn't take the swab from the dead man. Colin was in the office, doing nothing – he could do it.

'We'll have to delay the funeral,' I said to Gary, hanging up. 'We can't let it go ahead until we've swabbed him.'

We were a Cold Case unit, not a team of live investigators. We weren't meant to have ticking clocks and scrambles to get results. Our work was meant to be slow and methodical.

When I looked at my watch, I realised I was late. I ran to the car, sped away from headquarters and hit the road home.

Andy called.

'Yes, the brother has consented. He was great.'

I made it home as the vet was turning up. She was a small Dutch lady. Very direct, very professional.

'It's very sad,' she said, 'but it's the right thing to let him go.'

We stood on the grass and she gave Caesar the lethal injection. And my lovely, big horse fell to the floor.

Half an hour later, through tears, I turned my phone on.

There was a voicemail: 'Hi Julie, it's Colin. Yes, I've done that swab. That wasn't the worst thing I've had to do ever, but it wasn't far off. You owe me. I like single malt, by the way.'

The funeral went ahead. Saul Griffiths's mother had no idea of the drama surrounding her son in his chapel of rest. Two weeks later, I received an email from the lab:

DNA Profile
Saul GRIFFITHS (deceased)
This DNA profile has been compared to the unknown profile obtained in operation RHODIUM (MR8). This profile does not match therefore this individual can be excluded as a potential contributor of the sample taken from the scene.

I had other plans. They had been thwarted so far, but the news we had been waiting for was just about to break.

CHAPTER 12

APRIL 2011

For nearly a year, my boss, DCI Mike Carter, had been sitting on an email with an attachment. On that attachment was a list of names and somewhere towards the top of that list was someone related to Melanie's killer.

We were convinced.

We had spoken with other forces, we had spoken with experts around the country. Cold cases were being solved every day through familial DNA hits. But the UK government had put that block on familial DNA investigations; they had concerns about human rights which I understood, but didn't agree with.

We were back in the Review Team. We had eliminated most of the seventy-two names called in following the *Crimewatch UK* programme and we were still working through the intelligence Ben Schwarzkopf had provided. We were also awaiting news from the French authorities about Francisco Arce Montes. And I could persuade no one to let me follow up the Saudi inquiry.

Slow, methodical work.

Andy Mott, the forensic coordinator, came in. 'Great news,' he said, in his chipper northern accent. 'The government's lifting the embargo on familial DNA. We're good to go.'

'Brilliant.'

What do we do? Do we know what we're doing? Are we ready to go? How do we get the list? I thought to myself.

'Mike's got the password,' he added.

Great. Of course I know what I'm doing, I thought to myself, trying to remember all the DNA science from months earlier as I picked up the phone and started dialling DCI Mike Carter.

'Hi Julie, I'm in a meeting.'

'The familial list is on, Mike. You've got the password.'

'Well, it's on an email, but I can't forward it to you, that'd be a breach of security.'

'How are we going to get it?'

'You'll have to wait until I'm in the office.'

'When's that going to be?'

'I'm back-to-back this morning. Mid-afternoon maybe?'

'Mike? The killer's on this bloody list, probably at the top. Get a wiggle on.'

Waiting for mid-afternoon felt like forever. We filled the time rereading our notes about top tens, Screamers and Y-STR eliminations – the scientific method we used to rule out the male line of a suspect's family.

Mike breezed into the office. I think he wanted a cup of tea and a chat first, but Gary and I were having none of it.

'Mike, the password.'

'Oh … oh yes.'

He sent us the link and the password. Then we needed to enter a second password.

And then it appeared …

A long list of names.

There were four columns: Sample ID, Name, Gender and Likelihood ratio. A woman's name was at the top: Trish Blackmore. The likelihood ratio was 44,505. She was 44,505 times more likely to be related to the killer than most people.

The second name was another woman's: Dana Fox. Her likelihood ratio was 17,000. A massive gap between the two. The likelihood ratios plummeted further from third on the list downwards: 12,000, 10,000, 9,400, 7,900.

We had a name at the top of the familial list which stood out from the others.

We had our top suspect. Our 'Screamer', as scientists called him.

Barbara was on to it, looking through the digital indexes she had created from the old card files: 'There's no Trish Blackmore in our system.'

'There wouldn't be,' I said. 'It'd be a male relative. We need to find all the Trish Blackmores in the country to find out who their fathers, sons and brothers are.'

Kath was on Facebook.

Gary was looking at the electoral roll. 'There's actually only one Trish Blackmore in Britain,' he said. 'In Ipswich. Date of birth 17 May 1987.'

I looked at her online.

There she was. Young, slim and pretty. Smiling with her friends on Facebook. Girls together on what looked like a Balearic island.

'Does she live with her dad?' I asked Gary.

'It looks like she's with a boyfriend. Or a man, at least. He's twenty-four. But there's a previous address for her dad …'

Gary clicked away as I looked at Trish's photo – she seemed so carefree.

'Yes, Mark Blackmore,' said Gary.

I went to Gary's screen.

Trish's dad's name was listed on the electoral roll list: Mark Blackmore. DoB: 12/02/1958, Address: 48 St Olave's Crescent, Ipswich. He'd have been twenty-six when Melanie Road was murdered. An older man, as Ben had described.

'Look here, he has a company directorship.'

More clicking.

'Managing Director, East Anglia Paints.'

I loaded the website. It was a cluttered site with bright colours and lots of writing in different fonts. A homemade homepage, I guessed.

'East Anglia Paints,' it said. 'A family business since 1963.'

I scrolled down the images of paint pots and brushes, rollers and ladders. There were lots of words. I caught glimpses of 'company you can trust' and 'first-rate customer service'.

Back at the top of the page, I saw an 'About us' button, which I clicked:

Mark Blackmore, Managing Director.

There was a picture of him. A medium-build, white man with stubble, he wore a short-sleeve stripy formal shirt with a company logo on his breast pocket. He had an easy smile and eyes which sparkled as if to show he didn't mind having his photo taken – he was proud to be on the website, proud of his company:

> Mark took on the family company following the
> retirement of his father, East Anglia Paints' founder
> Ian Blackmore, in 1994. Under his direction, Mark has taken
> EAP from strength to strength, opening depots in Norwich,
> Cambridge and Peterborough. He has exciting plans for new
> branches in Northampton and Bedford.
>
> Mark is married with a daughter and a son. He lists his interests
> as cycling, football, cricket, travelling and motorbikes. He has
> raised more than fifty thousand pounds for charities in Ipswich,
> including Macmillan Cancer Care, drugs outreach work and for
> victims of violent crime.

'No Mark Blackmore on our system,' said Barbara.

'Looking at his electoral roll search, his previous addresses are all in East Anglia. Nothing which says Bath,' said Gary.

'Means nothing,' I said. 'In '84 he could have been working here, could have had a girlfriend here. Maybe he likes cricket and was watching a match. Who knows?'

Blackmore's twinkling eyes looked back at me from the screen. I reread: 'He has raised more than fifty thousand pounds for charities in Ipswich, including Macmillan Cancer Care, drugs outreach work and for victims of violent crime.'

'What about his family?' I asked. 'Does he have brothers? In '84 Mark Blackmore's dad must have been around. It's not beyond the realms of possibility he could be the killer – Trish's grandad?'

'His dad sounds older if he retired in 1994,' said Kath. 'Mark is on Facebook. And there's a Dave Blackmore there too. He looks similar. Could be Mark's brother?'

I looked over Kath's shoulder: the pictures were smaller and I had to lean in to get a better focus. The eyes were similar. Sparkling. But whereas Mark Blackmore was in the formality of a work shirt and office setting, Dave was on a beach wearing shorts, a vest and flip-flops. In his arms were two pairs of young Asian women. I thought Thai. He had a beer in one hand and a cigarette in the other – and he looked as though he were about to explode with pleasure.

The four women were in bikinis and seemed happy enough. His face was more drawn than Mark's. Lined and leathered. I thought I noticed tattoos on what could be seen of his arms.

'I like him ...' I said to Kath.

Gary was looking at the Police National Computer.

'He's got preconvictions. Fraud, theft, assault and something under the Sexual Offences Act. Looks like kerb-crawling.'

'I really like him,' I said.

We continued our research. Through the Department for Work and Pensions we could see that Mark Blackmore, the Screamer's dad, had an impeccable record. Hadn't drawn any benefits ever, everything paid. Dave Blackmore seemed in and out of work all the time.

I looked again at the image of Dave Blackmore on a beach with his Thai teenagers and asked myself: *Are you him?*

We looked down at the other names on the familial list. Dana Fox was the number two, with a likelihood ratio of 17,000. Still a very good number. She also lived in East Anglia, in Cambridge. She was a student. Her father was a teacher: Nathan Fox was head of sixth form at a school in the suburbs of the city. No previous convictions, no links with Bath. Fifty-four years old. He would have been twenty-six at the time of Melanie's murder.

'How are we going to swab them? Just turn up?' Gary asked.

'Yes. We'll see Mark Blackmore at his office and Nathan Fox at home. We can't go into a school sixth form and swab him in front of his students.'

We spent the next two weeks researching everyone in the top ten. None of them had relatives who were in our system.

Gary built family trees for everyone. He gets drunk on research, and spends hours looking at genealogy websites and government services available to the police and social media.

There was a buzz about the Review Team. We had names, we had researched everyone.

And we had our Screamer.

I went to see Jean Road to tell her about our progress a few days later. We were having tea and biscuits in her front room.

'That's a beautiful picture, Jean,' I said, looking at the painting on the wall.

'I did that.'

'You've got hidden talents.'

'I couldn't go back to teaching after Melanie. I couldn't be responsible for other children after what happened. I painted. Not a lot, but I painted.'

'It's amazing.'

'Melanie was artistic. Well, musical. She played the guitar, but didn't have lessons. It was hard for her, really. We'd moved around so many times with Tony's job. She'd had four secondary schools but she was never unsettled.'

I had been to four secondary schools as my parents had moved around the country, running pubs and hotels, before divorcing.

'I used to worry about her,' Jean continued. 'But no, she would just walk into her new school, introduce herself and be off. Sometimes she'd make cakes. She was always baking. And she'd take these cakes into school to help say hello.'

I looked at the photo on the glass cabinet behind: Melanie with a baby on her knee.

'She sounds amazing.'

'She was so popular, she was loved by everybody. She didn't have enemies, I don't know of anyone who'd want to hurt her. And she loved Bath. We'd only been here a year or so, so I was busy, decorating the house. "Mum, stop working," she'd say to me. "Come into Bath, it's the most beautiful city."'

Jean paused.

'Look what Bath did to her.'

I waited. If Jean wanted to say anything more about Melanie, she could. If she didn't, that was up to her. Jean stayed quiet, looking at me.

'Who is that in the photo?' I said, nodding at the picture. 'The baby?'

'That's Karen's daughter. She's twenty-six now. That was the last picture of Melanie. It was taken on the day she was murdered.'

Another silence hung between us as I stared at that photograph.

It was taken on the day she was murdered. Jean's words rang in my ears.

A beautiful teenage girl, so vibrant, so clever. Twelve hours after that picture was taken, her life would be over and the lives of everyone around her would be destroyed.

More silence.

'Do you know my last memory of Melanie? Have I ever told you?'

I shook my head.

Jean smiled with her mouth, but there was a sadness in her eyes.

'It was the day before – the Friday. She'd been in and out of the house, off to the city centre with Karen and then come back. That evening, we were taking Karen and her baby back to the coach station so they could go back to their home. They used to live in the Midlands.

'The coach station was in Bristol – Tony and I were going to go out for a meal afterwards there. But Melanie asked if we could drop her off in Bath centre. She was going to play tennis. So we all got in: Tony was driving, I was in the front and all three girls were squeezed into the back. They were laughing and chatting and it was magical. And we got to Queen Square, you know, in the centre of Bath?'

I did.

'Well, there's a hotel there, the Francis Hotel. And it was laid out for a big event that night. The doormen were waiting outside in uniforms and there was a big red carpet.

'Melanie kissed Karen and the baby and jumped out of the car. Then she noticed the red carpet. And she turned to me. She said, "Look, they knew I was coming. What a way to go!" And those were the last words Melanie said to me.'

'What a way to go?'

Jean nodded and paused.

'And that's right there, all the time,' she said, tapping her head. 'Has been since 1984. The last words she said to me.'

Jean went quiet. She wanted me to know this, wanted me to understand just what had happened to her.

'You know I'm going to find the killer, Jean. I *will* find him,' I told her.

'I believe you, Julie. But like Adrian said, we've heard it before. We've heard it for twenty-six years. Every few years we get a new team, a new detective. They come in and say they'll find Melanie's killer.

'They said it back in the beginning. They said it in 1984: "We're going to find the killer."

'Well, they didn't tell me that. They told Tony. They didn't talk to me, they just sat here in this lounge, they sat there …'

Jean pointed to where I was sitting: 'They sat there, drinking my tea. All these men. They were here for months. They probably thought they were helping. I just wanted them gone. They couldn't bring Melanie back. I wanted to be alone, to be with my other children. I wanted to gather my family and go away. I wanted to grieve in peace. Not be stuck in a house filled with policemen I didn't know.

'You know what happened? On the day Melanie died? They asked *Tony* to identify her. They asked *Tony* to see her in the morgue. Didn't ask me, they wanted me to stay here.'

'What did you do?'

'I told them: "I gave birth to that girl, I'm going to see her in death too. You're not stopping me." I barged in, I made them. Who were they to tell me I couldn't see my daughter? What right did they have to tell me that?

'Men. All men. For twenty-six years, men. Nice men, well-meaning men. Doing their best.

'You're the first one I believe, Julie. Out of all these police I've seen over all these years, you're the first one I believe.'

What an honour, I thought. *What an honour that this clever, inspiring, heartbroken mother could say that.*

'We've got a big day, next week, Jean,' I said. 'We've gone to the scientists and asked for DNA, which looks like it belongs to a family member of Melanie's killer. We've got a day in East Anglia. For some reason, it looks as though the killer has some connection over there.

'And there's a name at the top of the list. He's what we call a Screamer. It's all to do with science and forensics and DNA. But this might be the best lead we've ever had in this inquiry. So keep your hopes realistic, but as a team we're really excited.'

I looked back at the photograph of Melanie and her niece. A photograph taken before anyone outside a laboratory had even heard the term DNA. And I wondered if scientific developments and a link in a family's blood might really lead us to Melanie's killer.

My instinct washed over me. *I'll find him*, I thought. *No idea how, no idea when. But I will find him. I know it, I will find this man.*

CHAPTER 13

'You ready for your Screamer?' Kath asked.

I put my foot on the accelerator, desperate to get to our prime suspect as quickly as possible.

'Thank Christ you're driving, not Gary,' she added.

Kath, in the passenger seat, said what we'd both been thinking.

'I know,' I replied, pulling into the fast lane as the speed-ometer reached a number a police officer probably shouldn't admit to hitting. 'We'd be getting there next month, there's no fast way to Ipswich.'

Alan Andrews and Claire Nelson were in the car behind. I wondered how many Irish swear words Claire would pick up by the time she reached Suffolk.

'What do you think?' said Kath. 'Do you really think it's the Screamer?'

'Well, yeah. If not her dad, her uncle. My money's on the uncle. Or a cousin we don't know about. I mean, we know nothing about her grandad even, the one who set up the paint firm. He could have fathered another son decades ago. *He* could be Melanie's killer. Or it could be Mr Managing Director who we're seeing today. A nice public face and a nasty secret.'

It took nearly five hours to plough our way around the M25 and along the A12 to reach Suffolk.

Alan and Claire had veered off to swab people lower in the list. Later, they'd head up to Cambridge to hang around for the teacher to return home, the father of Dana Fox, the seventeen-thousand-to-one shot who was number two in our familial charts.

Kath and I pulled into an industrial estate and found ourselves confused by one of those impossible to follow maps that show which business is in which unit. East Anglia Paints was housed between a dry ice manufacturer and a precision engineering firm. It was grey, soulless and bleak. We found a visitor parking bay.

We got out of the car, stretched, yawned, checked our swabbing kit and made our way to the reception. Inside, there was a desk with a young woman wearing a headset, taking an order.

'Yes, the Velvet Whistle is still available, but we're discontinuing that range from September …' she said.

'I'd go with an "East Anglia Guaranteed" colour, a Ruby Blossom or a Scimitar Rouge … we'll always make those …'

We waited quietly until she had finished the call.

'Hello there,' she said. 'You want paint?'

'Hello, my name's Julie Mackay, I'm a detective sergeant with Avon and Somerset Police. This is my colleague, Kath Synott. We're looking for Mr Blackmore, Mark Blackmore.'

'Mark?' Her face whitened. 'Just a moment.'

She took off her headset and disappeared into the offices behind.

Kath and I looked at each other. More time passed.

The door opened and a medium-sized man in a short-sleeved stripy shirt with an East Anglia Paints logo came through. I recognised him from his website – he seemed paler, somehow.

'Mr Blackmore …'

'Yes, hello.'

His voice was more high-pitched than I thought it should be.

The receptionist came back in and sat down. She picked up the headset and tried to carry on as normal. She started tapping the phone system. I wasn't sure why.

'I'm Julie Mackay from Avon and Somerset Police, this is Kath. May we have a chat?'

'What's it about?'

I looked at the receptionist and he nodded.

'Come in,' he said.

We walked through the door and into a spacious open-plan office with large pictures on the walls of paint cans, brushes and ladders.

'What do you want?' he half-whispered as we made our way past desks filled with people making calls, looking at computer screens and filing paperwork.

'We'll chat in a second, Mr Blackmore,' I replied as we glided past clerical staff who performed what seemed like a Mexican wave of nods, looking up as we passed.

Mark Blackmore guided us to a glass office in the middle of the large room. He showed us through, motioned to chairs in front of the desk and sat behind it.

It was a tidy, well-kept office. A complete contrast to the Review Team's. And unlike the Review Team's office, where we had images of crime scenes on the wall, he had family pictures on his desk: a son on a beach. Trish on a car-racing circuit.

'Mr Blackmore, we're investigating a historic murder.'

'A murder?'

His face paled.

'Yes, it's an old case, happened twenty-seven years ago in Bath. The victim's name was Melanie Road.'

I opened my A4 file and showed the large photograph I had of Melanie on the inside of the front cover.

Mark Blackmore seemed to breathe out and a little colour returned to his cheeks.

'I've never been to Bath before. And I've never heard of Melanie Road.'

'Okay, well that's good to know,' I said.

Shit, I thought, *are we barking up the wrong tree or is he a high-end liar?*

'We've been looking at the science and DNA results, and we are taking swabs from thousands of people all across the country. If scientists say someone has a similar DNA sample to the one found at the murder scene, then we're duty-bound to eliminate that person.

'One of your relatives has appeared on the National DNA Database and scientists said it's not a direct match, but it's close enough that we should just take a quick sample to make sure it's not you.'

'Who was it? Dave? My brother?'

'We can't say, I'm afraid. We just do the swabs and the eliminations.'

His face was now back to full-colour, if not reddened.

'We've travelled all the way from Bristol to be here today. The science is really clear: if you're the murderer, it will be your DNA. But if, as you say, you've never even been to Bath, the science will clearly say it's nothing to do with you.'

'I'm sorry, it's a bit of a shock. It's not every day you get police turning up at our workplace. This is my firm, it's a bit embarrassing to do this in front of everyone,' he said.

I looked out and could see that most of the staff were watching us in one way or another. Furtive glances from their calls, quick glimpses from their files.

'Would you like some privacy?' I said, pointing at the white venetian blinds which were tied up around the glass of his office.

'No, I've nothing to hide. Do I need to speak with my solicitor?'

'No. We have a consent form, you just sign it. We are looking solely at this case, the DNA won't be loaded on the National Database or compared with any other crimes.'

Mark Blackmore looked out at his office and then back at us.

'Okay,' he sighed.

I opened my bag and took out the kit. Kath started asking gentle questions about his company and his family.

He had a daughter, he said. She wasn't interested in paint or the family business.

'You mentioned your brother, Dave? Do you see him much?' Kath asked. He saw his brother very little. Dave spent a lot of time away – the Far East usually, he said.

I told him I was ready; we both stood up. I held the DNA swab in my nitrile gloves. I talked him through the procedure. He opened his mouth and I stared into it, making little scrapes from the inside of his mouth, my free hand offering resistance on the outside of his cheek.

When that was over, Kath carried on with the small talk.

I tried clipping the head of the swab into the casing, but it refused to go. I swore under my breath.

'You okay?' he asked.

'Yes, fine,' I smiled.

Kath frowned at me.

If I got this wrong, the lab would refuse to take it. If the case wasn't sealed properly it would be put down as a 'fail' and we would have to come back to Ipswich again. Or even worse, Suffolk Police would have to do it and Avon and Somerset would look like a bunch of amateurs.

I reddened as the plastic case refused to click.

Kath was still talking about his family – there was only so much longer that she could do that.

'Click …'

Phew!

'I just need to do the second, back-up swab now, Mr Blackmore,' I said.

'Another?'

I nodded and prepared the swab.

He opened his mouth and I made a second sweep from the inside of his cheek.

'Thank you, Mr Blackmore.'

'Mark, please.'

I took the swab. This time the swab went back into the casing easily but my hand was shaking as I filled out the form. Like a passport application, if your writing so much as touches the box outline, the lab sends it back.

Another way to fail.

I stopped, tried to catch my breath and tried again. I tried to think that I wasn't swabbing the father of our Screamer – the best lead we'd had in twenty-seven years. Slowly the words came from my pen: date and address of swab; name, address and date of birth of person, the gender. I stuck the barcode from the kit into my pocketbook and sealed the bag.

Kath was chatting, but was running out of small talk: she was on to good beaches on the Suffolk Coast.

'All done,' I said.

I looked up. He seemed relieved, nearly as much as Kath was. But out of the three of us, I was sure that I was the one with the fastest heart rate.

Outside the room, I noticed the office was silent. We shook hands and said thank you. As he showed us out, we noticed that phones were ringing without being answered and an office full of people were looking our way.

We said goodbye to the receptionist and got into the car.

'What do you think?' I asked Kath.

The swabbing kit in my bag did not just give us the DNA from the father of the Screamer; it had information, through the Y-chromosome, to eliminate every male member of his family. Or not.

'Not sure. But his brother?' said Kath.

'Yes, his brother sounds really good.'

Kath and I were just about to get a cup of tea from a service station when Gary called from the Review Team office in Portishead.

'Julie, how was the Screamer?'

'A very nice family man, but who knows what he did twenty-odd years ago?'

'The brother?'

'We'll see.'

'Well, I've been looking down the list and there's another man who appears at number 11. And his brother is the right age. Preconvictions. And he's in Suffolk. Could you pop over and swab him?'

'What's his name and where is he?'

'Samuel Gibbons.'

Gary gave me an address in Bury St Edmunds.

It was a flat, grey drive along the A14. We found ourselves slowly circling round what looked like a housing association estate. I was following the sat nav, but it was all a bit confusing because it directed us to a garage, not a house. The property we needed was round the corner.

We got out of the car, grabbed the swab bag and made our way past a broken fence to the front door.

I checked the number.

I could hear a TV on inside and the high chatter of an edgy conversation which had not yet escalated to a full-scale argument.

I rang the bell: it didn't work.

I knocked.

The speed with which the door was opened took me by surprise.

It was a woman in her fifties, dressed in leisurewear, sliders on her feet.

'Hello.' I realised my voice suddenly sounded a bit posh. 'I'm Julie Mackay, I'm a detective with Avon and Somerset Police over in Bristol. This is my colleague, Kath.'

I could see the woman's eyes narrowing. She pulled a cigarette to her mouth and sucked on it.

'Is Samuel Gibbons here?'

'What do you want?'

'Well, we're here about a murder ...'

'A murder?' She cut in. 'I don't know nothing about a fucking murder.'

'I'm sorry, I'm sure you don't. But we are working through a list of names which scientists say may or may not be related to the inquiry. There are thousands of names on the bloody list and it's our job to eliminate them.'

The woman took another tug on her fag, scattering ash on her doorstep.

'We ain't done nothing wrong.'

'We are sure you haven't, but we've got to work through these names.'

'Sam? SAM?' she shouted, her gaze remaining on me.

136

'What is it?'

'Cops. They're here about a murder. Do you know anything about a fucking murder? She's calling you Samuel as well.'

There was a low voice from inside.

'A murder? I don't know nothing about a fucking murder,' it said.

'Can we just come in and see Sam?' I asked. 'We've come all the way from Bristol and this is just one of our stops today. We're doing loads.'

The woman carried on staring at me, then she nodded us in.

We made our way through a hallway piled with boxes of toys, sports equipment, trainers, and found ourselves in a small room with a big television. There was a faux leather sofa. At one end was a dog, at the other end sat Sam Gibbons. In his fifties, he wore a black Adidas tracksuit and box-fresh white trainers. An ashtray was balanced on one of the sofa's arms, into which he tapped a cigarette.

I wondered what this sight was doing to Kath's OCD antennae.

He looked over.

'Police,' said the woman.

'What about?'

I repeated what I'd said on the doorstep.

He lit another cigarette and breathed in the smoke.

'I don't know anything about a fucking murder. When was it?'

'Nineteen eighty-four.'

'Nineteen eighty-four? I know fuck-all about a murder in 1984. Where was it?'

'Bath.'

'Never been there. Why've you got my name?'

I explained.

'Who was it? Who was killed?'

'Her name was Melanie, she was seventeen.' I took out my book and showed him Melanie's photo on the inside of the front cover. There she was, in black and white, an image taken from a passport photo booth. Looking out, looking young and serious.

He looked down at the photo, then up at me.

'How was she killed?'

'She was stabbed. And raped.'

'Fucking bastard! Who the fuck did that?'

'We don't know, we've been looking for twenty-seven years and are trying some new science work. It's very simple. If you didn't do it, you've got nothing to hide.'

He looked at the woman, then at the pile of boxes in the hallway.

'How do I know you won't use my DNA for something else?'

'It's on the consent form here. It says we're comparing the DNA to the one found at the scene. It's not being put on the National DNA Database, see it says that there.'

He nodded, and Kath got out the kit.

'We need ten minutes after a cigarette before we can swab.'

'Oh, oh sorry,' he said, stubbing out his fag.

We chatted. I told him about Melanie, I told him about Jean and Adrian and how they had waited all these years, not knowing who had killed her.

Kath took the swabs. I watched her efficiency with envy. She started filling out the forms.

He lit another cigarette.

We started making our way past the boxes and out of the house.

Before we closed the door, we heard him shout: 'Good luck. You get that fucking murderer!'

CHAPTER 14

Kath Synott and I managed four swabs in East Anglia on that day. Alan Andrews and Claire Nelson got three. We were debriefing the next day, back in the Review Team room.

'How was your teacher? Fox, wasn't it?'

'Shifty fucker,' said Alan. 'Wouldn't let him teach my daughter.'

'Anyone else interesting?'

Claire shook her head.

We fast-tracked all the swabs, packing up the samples from Mark Blackmore, Sam Gibbons and Nathan Fox.

Three days later, I received an email from the laboratories:

These DNA profiles have been compared to the unknown DNA profile obtained in Operation RHODIUM, MR8.
Samuel GIBBONS can be excluded as a potential match.
Nathan FOX can be excluded as a potential match.
Mark BLACKMORE can be excluded as a potential match.
Using the Y-STR profile, we are also able to exclude all the male biological siblings, father and offspring of Mark BLACKMORE.

'Fuck!' I banged the table. 'Can we just get a break?'

There, in two sentences and thirty-one words, the biggest leads featuring the brightest science disappeared in a flash. Everyone had said this was the path to Melanie's killer. And it was a bloody wrong turn.

'Not the brother?' asked Gary.

'None of them. He's a deviant, that brother, a bloody deviant. He's done something horrible along the way. Somewhere. Either here or in Thailand.'

And it was only a few days later that Alan got an email from Interpol. 'Well, look here, it's only taken ten months and we've finally got the DNA code for Montes,' he growled. 'This is international crime fighting at its most dynamic.'

He pulled up the attachment.

By now, Gary and I knew the killer's DNA, the twenty markpoints which differentiated the murderer from other people.

And the killer of the schoolgirl Caroline Dickinson was not the killer of Melanie Road.

The slog continued. We waded through the familial lists, going through the top twenty, then the top thirty.

'Oh my God!' I yelled.

'What?' Gary, Kath, Claire and Barbara replied. Only Alan remained silent, but he couldn't hide the startled look.

'I've done it, I've finally passed.'

I read and reread the email from the HR department at Avon and Somerset Police:

To DS Mackay,
Congratulations on passing the Inspector's exam. You will now be invited to board for a position.

I had tried three times previously to pass the exam. Every summer I would spend weeks revising the rules and regulations, juggling the work with cold cases, three children and horses. And for three autumns running I had sat the exam and failed.

Yes, there was still a board to go, but I was halfway there.

It was now twenty-two years since I had joined the force and twenty years after I had been singled out for fast-track, accelerated development. Since then I had climbed precisely one rung on the policing ladder. I had done lots, I had worked in many different departments and had irreplaceable experience, but I had been unable to move up.

Until now.

I had never doubted my ability, but I was just dreadful at exams. I had sat that bloody test so many times and I wouldn't have to again. What a relief.

Fast-track, accelerated development.

CHAPTER 15

OCTOBER 2011

'Gary, you're in a bus lane.'

'Julie, I know where I'm going.'

'You clearly don't.'

My right foot pushed down on an imaginary accelerator as I sat in the passenger seat.

'Gary, I've been on quicker intercontinental flights. It's only bloody Cardiff.'

He didn't say anything.

'Look, the sign says bus lane.'

'I'm following the sat nav. What's that bus doing up my backside?' Gary was looking in his rear-view mirror at the coach, which was approximately a metre behind us on the approach to Cardiff.

'He's where he should be, a bus lane. Gary, do you have any idea how irritating your driving is to the motoring public?'

'This is the speed limit, Julie.'

'Sod the speed limit, you've just got a bus lane ticket.'

Gary shook his head.

'Look, we're here.'

He pulled up outside the large, art deco-style hotel in one of the many new-build parts of the Welsh capital.

I got out, muttering something like 'finally', before grabbing my suitcase. Gary said he'd park the car and would follow in a minute.

We went into the conference room and made some small talk with officers we recognised from other forces. After a little while the hall lights went down, the stage lit up and a man appeared at the lectern.

'Welcome to the Annual Review Team conference. Some of you may have been to other types of police conferences in the past – the Senior Investigating Officer ones. Wonderful events where we hear about brilliant jobs of incredible police work.

'Well, this is quite different. This is the Review Conference, it's where we hear what went wrong. What stopped police finding the killer or rapist in the first few hours after the crime? What opportunities were missed?

'It's about cock-ups and fuck-ups and bobbies who blunder.

'And how do we stop it happening in the future? What lessons can be learnt?

'Hands up how many of you have had a newly qualified PC put wet-bloody clothes in a plastic bag?'

I looked around. There were hands up everywhere. I gently raised mine too.

'Still to this day ... paper for wet, plastic for dry blood. It's not difficult, it's always been the way.

'How many of you have reviewed a case involving CCTV, only to find the original officer was looking at the wrong day? That the victim wasn't believed because the attack wasn't on camera. Only it was – but the investigating officer and his superiors can't read a calendar. Or that a rape victim wasn't believed because she went out wearing a short skirt and the first police officers to investigate the case had some prejudice that she was "asking for it"?'

He went on, listing severe breaches of police procedure, many of which I had witnessed in my time in Professional Standards and the Review Team.

I wondered about Melanie Road. I thought the original officers had performed a brilliant job, back in 1984. And all the reviews over the years seemed to think so too. Had they? Were we missing something?

The first speaker gave way to a detective inspector from the Metropolitan Police, Nathan Eason: 'We had a series of rapes in London. At first, we thought it was three attacks.'

Behind Nathan, on a screen, was a map of south-east London. There were three pins with dates next to them, denoting the location and timing of each assault: 1990, 1992 and 1997.

'The victims were elderly women in their own homes and we think there may have been lots more than three during this time. People who are of an age where they don't like to bother the police.

'We set up a major inquiry, we called it Operation Minstead. The press gave the attacker a name: the Night Stalker. We had a description of the attacker. We knew he was a light-skinned black man, around six feet tall and had a scar on his right cheek.'

The screen behind him swapped to an e-fit.

'And at first sight, it seemed solvable. We were able to take a semen swab from one of his victims. We had the offender's DNA. The science was so good, we used an ancestral analysis to suggest he originated in the Windward Islands.

'Of course, we tried the National DNA Database and there were no matches.

'We knew his MO: he was a proficient and talented burglar. For the rapes he would disable the fuse box, throw the house into darkness and he'd spend a long time with his victim, chatting and then attacking her.

'And the attacks continued ...'

Behind Nathan, a map appeared showing south-east London with pin marks in Dulwich, Orpington, Norwood, Downham, Lee, West Wickham and Bickley.

'And as well as sex attacks there were burglaries.'

More pins emerged on the map, showing where the burglaries happened.

'But for much of the time, we had the name of the offender in our system. In May 1999, there was a burglary in a house in Bromley. A witness noticed a suspect put on gloves and a balaclava nearby. The witness took the registration plate of the suspect's car and phoned it in.

'We sent a detective to the address where the car was registered. This was where things went wrong. We didn't arrest him, didn't even interview him. And we didn't take a DNA swab either. That would have solved the crimes up until 1999 and would have stopped many, many more victims from being attacked.

'There was some confusion. The suspect's name was Delroy Easton Grant. There was another man in our system called

Delroy Grant. And what you are thinking is correct. Even if we had thought it was just one burglary, it would have been poorly investigated.

'The lead was looked at by Operation Minstead and rejected as a possibility for the Night Stalker. We used false assumptions. Another mistake.

'You'll probably know that we caught Grant in 2009 …'

A custody image of a man appeared on the screen.

'He pleaded not guilty and he was convicted of twenty-nine counts of rape, sexual assault and burglary earlier this year.'

The screen behind him had switched to a simple graphic reading, 'The offender is in the system'.

'But the key thing was: the offender was in the system. And this is the learning I want you to take from today.

'Research shows that in the majority of large-scale, major inquiries, the offender is there, somewhere. He may not be a suspected criminal. He – or she – may be on a house-to-house inquiry form, or a list of witnesses, or have their car parked somewhere nearby. But they are in the system.

'It was the case here and it might be for you.'

I found myself breathing out.

Only 12,500 names to get through.

CHAPTER 16

The conference had been so exciting. And now what we had to do was daunting.

We had to prioritise the list of people. How to do it? How to organise 12,500 names? What if we could put names in different categories and focus on those most likely to be the killer?

I looked around the office. All the investigators had spouses who had ironed their clothes and made them their packed lunch. They had flopped out of bed and rocked into work. As ever, I had slept little, the pains from my fibroids were like red-hot pokers turning inside. I had been up since 5 a.m., ironed all of our shirts for the day, made seven packed lunches, mucked out the horses, driven nearly an hour to work and developed a formula which I was about to describe.

'We need to prioritise these names in some way. We can't swab 12,000 people. We need to work out which are the best bets, the most likely to be our killer.

'So, I'd like us to put them into three groups.'

I turned off the lights and the projector illuminated the wall.

'Group A,' it read.

'Group A will be people who were mentioned in the inquiry but didn't feature. They may have been referred by someone else, they aren't relevant to the night in question.'

I changed the screen.

'Group B are people who were there on the night. So, they probably made a statement. They were maybes, they are people who are less likely to be our killer, but we can't rule them out. They will be lower down our list.'

I changed the slide on the wall.

'Group C,' it said.

'These are the good ones. Cs will have intelligence on them, they were definitely there on the night, they haven't got a good alibi, they might have criminal history. Or they knew Melanie.'

'Who is going to do that work?'

'I'm glad you asked that, Gary.'

And he didn't groan. He never did. Gary Mason was and always will be the ultimate cold case investigation machine.

After the high of passing my Inspector's exam, there was the board. I sat in a glass room in police headquarters in Portishead across from three people: a high-ranking officer, another a rank above me and an HR rep who would have watched many a humiliation.

'Give us an example of when you've managed a critical incident.'

I described responding to a murder on New Year's Eve, managing the community, the victim, not knowing who the offender was and having no staff at the starting point.

'How have you managed a difficult member of staff?'

There's always someone who is hard to manage, trying to find out why is the tough part. I'm known for my honesty so I just start with asking what's wrong, say the person's attitude's making my life difficult – as well as the lives of others around them – so why don't we try and sort it out? If we can't, then we may need to take a different route.

'What innovations would you like to see in neighbour-hood policing?'

I don't know, I'm a career detective. I've never been in neighbourhood policing.

I made something up.

I walked out of the room wishing the ground would swallow me up. I had crashed and burned and waited for the email telling me that I had been unsuccessful. When that arrived, a depressing little message informing me of my failure, I was invited back for feedback.

How could I improve?

'We know you can do it, Julie. You just didn't pass the board. How about some practical experience?'

'Great. What do you mean?'

'Well, we do have an opening in Weston-super-Mare. Not for long, just three months. But there's an inspector's vacancy in CID there. Want to try it?'

'Yes.'

I said the word before even thinking.

I went to see Jean Road to tell her I was leaving the Review Team, at least for a little while. It was hard to believe I had been working on the case and coming to see her for more than two years now.

'I was desperate to get away from Gary,' I joked.

'That's good for you,' Jean giggled – she was well aware of my inability to get promoted.

We were having lunch in the Blathwayt Arms, a pub near her home. Jean said she liked starters and puddings, but didn't really eat main courses any more. I noticed she even sipped soup in a regal manner.

I was thinking of all the previous officers who had been promoted away: 'You know, I'll keep going with Melanie's inquiry. I'm not leaving that, nothing's going to stop.'

'It must be exciting for you, getting such an important job. Doing something new.'

Jean seemed really happy for me.

'It is. I know I can do it, but it's a bit nerve-wracking. I haven't worked in a live CID office for years now. But I want you to know, I won't forget about Melanie.'

My long daily commute had nearly doubled. Some days it took almost an hour and a half to get from our village to the police station in Weston-super-Mare. And the job was busy. If your image of Weston is a pier, ice creams, beaches and donkeys, mine is of thieves, break-ins, Friday night fights and murder. With that came an overwhelming workload for a small team. I was leaving the office late and getting back home to a frosty Matt, whose look said, *You should be here, you have three children; they are yours, not mine.*

Toby, my youngest, had moved to secondary school, where he had been diagnosed with dyslexia within a month. I phoned his old primary school and said: 'All those times you sent him out of class for being disruptive, all those times he said he couldn't see the board. He was dyslexic, he couldn't read it. You failed my son, you failed him.' But even though his new school was working with him through his dyslexia, he found lessons hard. Parents' evenings were more like a non-stop volley of loaded questions about Toby's lack of effort and my abilities as a mother.

Connie was a golden child. Her reports were great. Sometimes even my ex-husband volunteered to cover her parents' evenings. But I went alone to hear about Callum, who was now sixteen, and Toby to hear never-ending stories of how they had upset teachers, refused to work and disrupted class after class.

'Boys, could you just try a bit harder in school. Look, you're not in school for long, just a few years, why not make the best of it?' I would say.

They'd agree with me. And the following week I would be at work, standing in a crack house or at the scene of a ramraid and my phone would ring. It would be the school – Toby had left a teacher in despair and could I collect him from the headteacher's office? He had been suspended again.

And among all of this, I was still thinking of Melanie Road.

Sometimes I would return to police headquarters in Portishead. I would slope off to the Review Team to steal the office biscuits, offer Gary tips about how to improve his personal tidiness and catch up with the latest on Operation Rhodium.

I had been replaced by a detective inspector; it was his job, not mine, to set the vision for Rhodium. And a new investigator, a capable retired detective sergeant, Greg Avis, was working on something which we felt really might solve the case.

After 1994, DNA samples were routinely taken from new prisoners. But if Melanie's killer had been jailed for another offence before that date, he could be sitting in a cell and we would have no idea who he was.

Operation Nutmeg was a government idea. A plan to take DNA samples from all inmates imprisoned before 1994. It would be unusual for a man to rape and kill just once and have never done it before – or never go on to do it again – so surely the chances were high that our man had reoffended and had been caught.

Greg Avis was working through the names which were coming in from Operation Nutmeg. And Gary and Barbara were prioritising the 8,000 male names into my categories: A, B and C. It seemed that although the pace of the inquiry had slowed, we had every chance of finding Melanie's killer through my prioritisation scheme or a government initiative.

My phone rang.

'Hi Julie, Colin Port.'

The Chief Constable.

'Yes, sir?'

'Julie, well done. I'm making you a detective inspector on a permanent basis. You don't need to do a board. You're good, you're doing great work. I'm doing this with you and two others.'

I was elated but I couldn't carry on working in Weston-super-Mare. The months were stretching and so was Matt's patience. Even though Matt was an inspector, he seemed to have little sympathy for the demands of my new job. And when I did get home after an exhausting day I would have fires to fight with one or more of my children.

Then I read about the opening: a detective inspector's position in the Major Crime Investigation Team. The last time I had worked there was for that month in 2009 when I had been a receiver on the Melanie Hall inquiry. As a DI, I would get to do the job I had always wanted: a senior investigating officer in a murder squad. And as hard as I had found progress in the past, this application seemed easy: a simple form to complete and I was in.

At last! The job I had always dreamed of.

CHAPTER 17

MARCH 2013

'I need a murder.'

It was Andy Williams, the superintendent in charge of the Major Crime Investigation Team.

I sat in his glass office. Behind the window, teams of detectives sat at banks of desks, talking on phones or tapping on keyboards, working on rapes and assaults. But no murders were under investigation. Andy Williams was new to his role and wanted his Professionalising Investigations Programme – or PIP accreditation. And for that, he needed a homicide.

'I'm thinking about bringing one of the cold cases into the MCIT. I wondered about Operation Rhodium?'

'Good idea,' I said. 'It's match-fit, we've been working on it for years, the inquiry's in great shape, there's a full DNA profile and I know the case back-to-front. Could we bring Gary Mason over?'

It was that simple. He agreed.

Later that day, I saw Andy's email in my inbox:

I'm bringing Operation Rhodium across to the MCIT. Please express an interest if you want to work on this and if you want to be my deputy.

I replied instantly:

Andy, I know Operation Rhodium inside out. If you
don't appoint me as your deputy, there'll be another
murder. And I'll be asking to leave MCIT even though
I've just arrived.

I got the job.

I had a team of thirty-five detectives. I refused to sit in the
sterile glass offices where inspectors and superintendents
worked. Instead I set my desk up in the middle of my unit.
This was where things happened, including the office banter.

We would be working on live murders as they came in.
And in the quieter moments, we would deal with Operation
Rhodium.

Gary came across with the boxes and filing cabinets. He
would be dedicated just to that job.

As well as Avon and Somerset Police, the MCIT (Major Crime
Investigation Team) covered the Gloucestershire and Wiltshire
police forces. One hundred and eighty detectives and civilian
investigators were at my disposal. And I intended to use them.

But none of them knew anything about the historic murder
of Melanie Road.

At a training day I outlined the case to the entire squad. I
noticed a few detectives stifling yawns as I started talking
about my cold case. Most of these officers had probably
never even worked on a historic murder, I thought. Behind
me, on the wall, a projection of images changed as I moved
from subject to subject:

A photograph of Melanie. Who was this teenage girl?

**Images of the crime scene. What had happened in the early
hours of 9 June 1984?**

**The map of the Green Blood Trail: why had
this killer fled in that direction?**

**Facts and figures: the thousands of names in our system, the
thousands of men we had swabbed.**

**The picture drawn by Ben Schwarzkopf: we knew the murderer
was a white man, he was then in his thirties, probably local.**

The DNA chart: the key to catching Melanie's killer.

Slowly, I saw the penny dropping. Some of the detectives who had been slouching in their chairs, yawning, were sitting upright, focused. Nobody was yawning now. I played a clip from a news report in 1984 when the case was in its feverish early hours. There was a killer on the run, a family was in mourning, a city stunned.

'The killer's still out there. Unless he's dead,' I said. 'He's never faced justice. Melanie's family is still grieving. Nearly thirty years have passed. To Melanie's mum it's like it was yesterday. It's not right, is it? That Melanie should have had her life taken from her, that her family's lives should have been destroyed, while the killer has carried on living his.'

I told the MCIT we would be swabbing men from around the country to eliminate the Group Cs on my list. The highest priority. And we would be approaching the inquiry with a new vigour: we would find the killer.

My team was a mixture of sergeants, detective constables, police staff and indexers. There was Neil Meade – or Meader – a big, rugby-playing detective sergeant who I had known from my days in Bath.

Jon Hook, a short, bald, swarthy-looking Bristolian DC, a fantastic family liaison officer, agreed to be the officer in charge. He was training up Natalie Ace to be a civilian investigator. She was in her twenties, a graduate, and this was something new in the MCIT. These civilian roles were still frowned on back then, but Natalie was meticulous, sorting out exhibits and helping with the running of the case. And Gary was there. Together, we readied the Operation Rhodium inquiry for the MCIT.

We put a picture of Melanie on the wall, the same image I carried on the inside of my detectives' book. There were photos of the garages and streets taken in the hours after the attack; the map showing the Green Blood Trail. There was Ben's drawing of the killer. And on a laminated piece of A4 we wrote out 'Rh' in big letters, the chemical symbol for Rhodium.

'Andy?' I asked the superintendent as we were going through the files. 'Can I ask a favour?'

'What, Julie?'

'Well, there are five suspects who we've never been able to get hold of. They're abroad, they left in a hurry the day after Melanie was murdered. We just need the DNA chart from the murder scene to be loaded on their national database. Simple thing, really.'

'Where?'

'Saudi Arabia.'

'No.'

'Why not?'

'They execute people for rape and murder in Saudi Arabia. If we go sending them proof, they'll hunt down the first man it's convenient to kill and say he's our offender. No way!'

'But we've never done this work. We've spent nearly thirty years looking all around Britain for the killer. He might never be here, he could be anywhere on the planet. And if we don't eliminate these five really good suspects, all our work could be for nothing.'

'I'm not signing someone's death warrant.'

I felt the lorry juggle underneath me as we bumped down the country lane. I was driving, Connie and Toby were in the two front passenger seats, hidden under blankets. Steam rose from their open flasks and I was sure I could see condensation as they exhaled in the freezing cab. In the back of the lorry were their ponies: Wednesday night was Pony Club.

'Mum, why doesn't the heating work?' asked Connie.

'It's the only lorry I could afford, but it does the trick. You've got your coffee?'

Toby smiled, holding up his Thermos.

'Quick, do your homework, we'll be there in twenty minutes.'

Connie pulled out a schoolbook and started filling in some maths answers, tutting as the jolting van made her writing scribble off course.

'Mum ...' she scolded.

'Mum?' asked Toby. I noticed he hadn't bothered with his schoolbooks.

'Yes?'

'What's pot?'

'Pot? Well, it's something we use in the kitchen. Or it's a drug. Why?'

'It's just something Cal's talking about.'

'Do you think he's getting into cooking?' I asked.

'No.'

Great. I had been worried about Cal's increasing unpredictability.

'What's he said?' I asked.

Toby was about to say something, checked himself and kept quiet.

'Why are we late again?' asked Connie, looking up from her maths. 'We should have been there ages ago.'

'Well, I just finished work. Would you rather Matt take you?'

'No,' they both answered at the same time.

You see images on TV adverts of blended families, but while Matt and I had tried to create a nice environment, often the mood in our home was spiky. We had converted the barn next to the house into bedrooms, everyone had their own space. But the boys fought. I thought teenage girls were meant to be difficult, but Connie and Zoe got on well.

It wasn't helping that Matt refused to take my children to their clubs, or come to parents' evenings, or have anything to do with my three. They were very much my children, not his. Sometimes I wondered what the point was of becoming a larger family.

Matt had gone quiet when I told him about joining MCIT. He was a detective, a good one, and he had always wanted to work on the murder squad. He never told me that he was envious of me being an inspector or working in my new unit but when I achieved my dream job, his silence was deafening.

CHAPTER 18

'He's a doctor, but he's not a doctor.' Meader (DS Neil Meade) looked up from the old files.

'What do you mean?' I asked.

'Well, he calls himself a doctor, he has some qualifications, but he only seems to do insurance work. He's not like any medical professional I've seen.'

He passed me the file.

Dr Brent Bowen. He lived in Essex. DoB: 28/1/1961. He would have been twenty-three at the time of Melanie's murder, fifty-two years old now.

'He was in Bath on the night,' continued Hooky (DC Jon Hook). 'He's mentioned by a witness as being in the Beau Nash, he was down visiting his younger brother at Bath University.

'Gary found him in the system. He came up as one of your category Cs.'

'Do we have any guys going out that way soon? Can we swab him?'

Meader shook his head.

'Can you put him on the list for the south-east?'

We had built lists for most of the country. If a detective was going to another region, I'd add a couple of swabs to their workload. This was met with a variety of responses from polite compliance to grudging hostility.

My prioritisation system had thrown up a few more interesting names. Dr Brent Bowen would become known as the Fake Doctor, but we also had the Paedo Nurse in Hull, the Crazed Cobbler in Somerset and the Suicidal Chef.

The Paedo Nurse had died. Simon Tyson had taken his own life after being investigated for a sex assault in the late 1980s. He'd been invited for interview with Humberside Police in 2008, but hadn't shown. A warrant had been issued for his arrest and officers eventually broke into his home. They found a bottle of Scotch, seven empty packets of tablets and no note or confession. Tyson had been cremated. He had no relatives; his house had been cleared and his belongings were gone.

'How are we going to eliminate him?' asked Meader.

'There's got to be a way, there has to.'

'I've been thinking …' said Gary. 'You know I've become a grandad?'

Gary's entry into the world of grandfatherhood had come to dominate his already plentiful conversation.

'Yes, you've mentioned it a couple of thousand times.'

'Well, my daughter told me that they still do the Guthrie heel prick test. You know, get a blood sample after you're born. They've been doing that for decades. I wondered if there was some central register we could use?'

'You're a fucking genius, Gary.'

He didn't disagree.

Gary made some calls. It took a day or two, but eventually he came back with his three favourite words: 'I was right.' He had found that there was a central register, a store in a hospital on the south coast. He'd called them.

No, they couldn't just give us the blood sample if the suspect were still alive, we would have other means of getting it. But if the suspect was dead, then yes, we could have access to the heel prick sample from when the suspect had been born.

The records began in 1965. That would mean we could only link to suspects who were aged nineteen or under at the time of the attack. But it was better than nothing. And the managers at the store were relaxed. No need for a court warrant, just phone up and ask. If we got lucky and found the killer this way, then we would have to go through all the legal channels to use it in evidence. But for an initial intelligence check, that was fine.

Simon Tyson, the Paedo Nurse, had been born in 1965. Gary checked the heel prick records and his blood sample from birth didn't match Melanie's killer.

The Crazed Cobbler had been known to police before Melanie's murder. He was mentioned in the forty-seven-page book, but we had been unable to find him:

Nicholas JACKSON, Born 7/4/1961, a shoe operative of Frome, Somerset. First came to notice as the result of an M.O. suggestion. He had a conviction in 1978 when during the night he climbed through a woman's bedroom window and stabbed her in the chest.

Jackson's statement said that on 8 June 1984 he had driven to his girlfriend's, Susan Simmonds. They went for a drink in the Saracen's Head pub. He'd left her at 11 p.m. and returned home an hour later.

That took a while, I thought.

His alibi was his parents.

'He's also dead, I'm afraid,' said Gary. 'He went on to marry Susan and they had a son. We can get him through his son's Y-STR.'

Jackson's son Eddie was now twenty-three and living in Frome.

A couple of DCs made the mistake of discussing an inquiry in Frome within earshot, so I promptly gave them the swab kit and a 'thank you'. They grumbled. I'm sure I even heard one of them mutter under his breath, 'What's the point of this cold case?' but I let it go. The pair left the inquiry office dragging their heels. They came back towards the end of the day, both of them pale and wide-eyed.

'Bit of a problem with this one, ma'am,' said DC Number One.

I was being called 'ma'am' now.

'What?'

'Well, we went to swab the son,' said DC Number Two. 'He was there, opened the door. We said why we were there. He was fine, said yeah, hated his dad. No problem taking a swab from him. We went into the lounge and his mum's sitting there, watching *Neighbours*.'

'She looks horrified,' DC Number One picked up. 'Asks her boy to make us a cup of tea. He goes to the kitchen. When he's out of the room, she beckons me over, shaking her head.

'"Nick, the bloke you're after," she whispers, "he's not the boy's dad. I've never told him. There's no point doing a DNA swab with him, they're not related."'

'What did you do?' I asked.

'We did the swab anyway, to be polite,' said DC Number Two.

'Well done.'

I formulated a policy quickly. We would never reveal to any child the discovery that their biological father was different from the man they believed him to be. There would be other times when we found out about a person's real biological father. These would be sticky moments, but we would always maintain our discretion.

And then there was the Suicidal Chef.

Gary was looking at my category Cs when he let out a yelp – yelps were not Gary's thing.

'Julie, listen to this! Daniel Baker, he was twenty-three at the time Melanie was killed. He worked in the Great Pulteney Hotel, he was a porter. He had a night off on 9 June, he was seen out in the nightclub. He returned to his room on-site.

'The on-duty porter said he saw Baker coming back, worse for wear. He had blood over his shirt, saying he'd got into a fight, went to bed and was seen throwing the shirt away the following morning. The on-duty porter only reported this to police the following month. By that time Baker had killed himself.'

I found my eyes opening and was about to say something when Gary held up a hand.

'It goes on … He made admissions to a friend that he had killed a woman.'

'Have we ever checked him?'

'Not according to this.'

'Can you do one of your family trees?'

Gary didn't need asking twice. In fact, he didn't need asking in the first place. Within three hours, he had a spidery diagram with names and dates on a piece of A4.

'Eight relatives.'

'Where are they?'

'Well, his mother and father are still alive and in Bath.'

'I'll do it,' I said.

'Gloryhunter.'

'Can you just not take a sip of vodka for six minutes?' I asked Daniel Baker's dad.

It was late morning and he was holding the drink as if it were a cup of tea. The old man wiped his mouth and took a drag from his fag, tipping it out on an overflowing ashtray on his lap.

'And your cigarette, the test won't work.'

'Sorry, sweetheart,' he said.

He carried on holding the glass in his left hand and the ashtray in his right.

We sat there in his brown room in his brown flat while I counted the minutes before asking him to open his mouth and taking the swab. I watched this man, who looked back without realising just how important he was to the inquiry.

Why did your son kill himself? I asked myself. *Could the killer really live so close to Melanie's home? Why would he kill her? And why would he take his own life? Was he a sexual deviant? Will the answers end here, or just begin?*

I had kept in touch with Jean Road, even during my year away in Weston-super-Mare. I hadn't seen her much – the long commutes and longer days had prevented that – but often I would ring to say hello.

I still had no contact with Adrian, that was his wish and I observed that. But I had never met Karen.

I thought informality would be best. And she lived in a village just a short drive from mine, so I gave her a call, arranged to see her that afternoon and popped over.

Both Adrian and Jean had a grief which they kept under a composed exterior. They were heartbroken by Melanie's murder but were able to maintain a calm face to the outside world. It was clear from the moment Karen opened the door that her bereavement was ever-present and more than surface-deep.

'I'm sorry, just hearing you were coming set me off,' she said, her eyes red. 'I know you see Mum a bit. Thanks for that. The *Crimewatch* interview I did broke me.'

'I'm just here to say we're making good progress with the case. Not as fast as I'd like, not as fast as you'd like, but things seem to be moving.'

We sat in the sitting room of Karen's well-kept modern house in a village cul-de-sac.

She looked me straight in the eye: 'No one's ever told me what happened to Melanie. I mean, everything.'

I paused.

'Are you sure you want to know?'

'Yes. At the moment I have just blanks. In my mind she's died a thousand different ways. I just want to know. I think that'd be better, for me.'

'I'll tell you anything you want.'

'Please.'

I took a breath, trying not to show I was doing so. And I told her. The number of stab wounds, the sex attacks, the Green Blood Trail.

Everything.

At first she was silent. I felt she was trying to process the appalling details of what her little sister had endured years before. I didn't know whether no one had told her these details before or she had been informed and she had blanked the horror from her mind, but she wanted to know now, here.

Then she started to ask questions: 'Where were the wounds? What would Melanie have known?'

I answered. Openly, honestly, painfully.

She wanted to know more.

'When was Melanie alive?'

I told her as much as I knew.

Karen was beside herself, in tears, furious, but she managed a thank you.

'You know, you would think there would be nothing worse than knowing your sister had been raped and killed. But it is worse,' she said. 'It's worse because we haven't a clue who the bastard is.

'It's been, what, nearly thirty years. And I lie awake at night still, still thinking of Melanie's last moments. They're in my head, playing round and round. Every time it's different. Every time it's just as bad as the last. I'm on red alert, have been since 1984. My mind never stops. Look at me now, look at me. I have my daughters and they're amazing, but it's affected everything in my life: my relationships, my work, my home, my friendships. This is me …'

She patted her chest with one hand and wiped a tear with the other. 'This is me. This is my life. This has been me since I was twenty-six years old.

'Melanie was amazing. She was so amazing. As a child she had these glasses, you know, NHS ones. Our little duckling, we called her. And we knew, we just knew, one day she would grow into that beautiful swan. And she did. And she was …'

Karen couldn't carry on.

I took her hand.

'Melanie's life has been defined by murder. And so has mine.'

CHAPTER 19

OCTOBER 2013

'We need to do another familial run.'

'It's too expensive.'

'Well, we can't afford not to do it,' I said.

Duncan Goodwin looked back at me. With his neat beard, tweed jacket and brown boots, he looked like an academic. He always looked interested in what you were saying, even when he was refusing to budge.

'We can't spend another £20,000 on another familial DNA run. You did one just a couple of years ago and we simply don't have the budget for it. We have too many other cases. Live murders. This is not a priority.'

'But, Duncan, we could solve this case in a flash.'

The argument continued. He held the purse strings and was unpersuaded.

'Well, we need to review the exhibits. They haven't been looked at for years. There must be some science which can tell us something new.'

He agreed and my team in MCIT went back into the stores and started collecting the exhibits.

'Your geraniums are spectacular this year,' I said as I helped Jean Road into my car.

She chuckled and said it was all about knowing what to do with the first blooms of the year: regular dead-heading.

I had seen her less frequently over the last year, but had managed to pop in on her on the odd Saturday morning. It was great to see her looking so well. I'm only 5'4", but she isn't as tall as me. Like me, she refuses to leave the house without lipstick. Unlike me, her hair is always immaculate. She has never considered herself to be old and I'd noticed the frustration she felt when she couldn't physically do everything she felt she should be able to.

'Have you got your stick?' I asked.

'Yes, but I don't like using it.'

'See how you feel when we get there, we'll keep it in the boot in case.'

I got into the car and started driving.

Jean had been on a cruise to Iceland. She'd seen Adrian quite a bit recently, she said, but contact with her daughter Karen was more sporadic.

We reached the garden centre. I grabbed a trolley and we spent half an hour looking at rose trees. Then we made our way to the café. She had a cup of tea and a teacake as I drank black coffee and demolished a carrot cake.

Jean and I used to talk about her past. The challenges of growing up in post-war Britain. Then her marriage. She had lived around the country, then abroad with her husband Tony's job for the Ministry of Defence. As a child, I had moved around too with my parents.

What I loved about Jean was that she was completely accepting of me. I got the impression that she had always been like this and it had only been later, when she described streams of policemen coming through her front door, that I had realised she is just very polite. But if you took the time to ask – and listen – she would reveal her true feelings.

'We're doing a lot, Jean. I'm in this new team and we have all these resources, all these detectives. They usually work on live inquiries, but I can use them to work on Melanie's case.'

'That's good.'

'And we're doing a review. We're going to look at all the exhibits that've been kept in storage since '84 and will see what we can see with new science.'

'Can you really find new things?'

'Yes, and in the past we haven't done tests with some exhibits because we weren't sure if the science was good enough then. Sometimes you only get one go at it; the test will destroy things. So, it's often about timing.'

Jean didn't comment, she just took it in. Then she said: 'You know, I saw Sally last week. Melanie's friend, Sally.'

I nodded. Jean had told me about Melanie's friendship with Sally before.

'She was in the city centre, by the abbey. She's forty-seven now. Has two children, both teenagers. I've known Sally since she was fifteen. She and Melanie were in school together. She used to have a job, but gave it up for children. Now she's getting old. Not old like me. Ageing, that's what I mean. But she's had all of that *life*. And I'm happy for her, I really am. She's so nice. But I saw her hair and it was going a bit grey.'

CHAPTER 19

'And Melanie … Well, you've seen that photograph. You've seen what she looks like, what she *looked* like. She'll never grow old, she'll always be seventeen. That's her. No children, no job, no grey hairs.

'Always be seventeen.'

Jean paused.

'Who can do that to someone? Who could do that?'

I noticed the clatter of cups and the tinkle of cutlery around us. People ordering food, saying hello, chatting about gardens. And among this sat Jean and I, talking about her daughter's murder.

'I always thought if I got my hands on him, I'd like to stab him. I'd get a knife and stab him. But I wouldn't waste my effort on him now, he wouldn't be worth it.

'He's an insignificant little man.'

I looked at Jean. She hadn't raised her voice, her face hadn't reddened, she wasn't tearful: she was speaking with a passionate composure.

'I know you'll find him, Julie. I know you will.

'When you do, you make sure you lock him up and throw away the key. That's what they used to do, in the olden days. Leave him to rot. Leave him to think of what he did to my Melanie as he wastes away.

'He's not a man, he's a monster.'

'What are our options?'

We were sitting in a conference room in Kenneth Steele House, the three-storey modern grey office block named after Avon and Somerset's first chief constable.

173

Duncan Goodwin was there with Andy Mott, our forensic coordinator from the Review Team days. In an innovative
move, Motty had been promoted to become a senior investigating officer, unheard of for a civilian scientist. He really
was that good.

Meader, Hooky, Natalie Ace and Gary Mason were also
there.

'Well, there are 1,500 exhibits, Julie.' It was Duncan.

'I think we should look again at the clothing,' said Motty.
'We need to check that the stab wounds correspond with the
clothing. And if they do, that might tell us more about the
attack. Was she upright when she was attacked, was inter-
course the result of threats with the knife, was it consensual?
If we catch this guy, that will be his defence.

'And her knickers. They were found about fifty yards
away, in the opposite direction to the getaway. Why were
they there? What's the blood pattern on them? Was Melanie
wearing them when she was attacked? It might help us get a
better idea of the attack – and the attacker.'

'What about Melanie's shoes? Can we do anything with
them?' I asked.

'We've looked at them before. We could try for fingerprints,' said Motty.

Duncan Goodwin made a gentle gasp.

'You okay, Duncan?'

'Well, if you do that, that's the shoes gone for the future.'

'What do you mean?'

'Well, the lab will cover them in fingerprint powder.
You'll never be able to use them again. What if some new

science comes along in five years' time, something we don't know about now? You'll lose all the blood science.'

'That's true.'

'Yes, but we already have a full DNA profile of the killer. We know what the blood pattern is on the shoe, we have photographs, we can take more,' said Motty.

'Let's do it,' I said.

We organised the labs. A mannequin was set up. Gary went to a police cold case warehouse to get Melanie's clothing from storage. The last time there had been a review of these clothes had been twelve years earlier, the exhibits had been in paper bags since 2001.

The crime scene investigator (CSI) took the clothes and fitted them to the mannequin. She photographed Melanie's bloodstained top and trousers, working out exactly where the knife had penetrated. The CSI looked at the post-mortem report and worked out that the cuts from the murder weapon married with the stab wounds in the autopsy.

She would create a computer-generated image of the stab wounds to show a jury, if it ever got to that stage.

The CSI took off the clothes, repackaged them and fitted Melanie's knickers, photographing these on the mannequin.

It may have been three in the morning when I awoke in a panic.

What if the scientist hadn't cleaned the mannequin down between the clothes being fitted and the knickers? There could be cross-contamination. I had worked on enough cases where scientists had made mistakes which had undermined the whole prosecution. In one inquiry – the execution of a gang member – the scientist had missed a rip in the shoulder of a top. It had been caused by a knife and proved that one of my two suspects was a killer. But we only realised this at trial, it was too late to go back and review the evidence, and the suspect was found guilty of manslaughter, not murder.

First thing the next day, I phoned the CSI.

'Could you just tell me what you did between photographing the trousers and top and the knickers?'

'Don't worry, Julie. I did a proper job. I bagged the top and trousers away, cleaned the mannequin, waited for the correct amount of time then fitted the knickers. Relax.'

'Er, boss …'

It was Meader in the MCIT. He and Natalie Ace had been looking through the analysis of the exhibits. On their desk were photographs: clothing on the mannequins, images of her purse and the set of wooden keys which spelt 'Melanie'.

'I think we have something here.'

'What? From the exhibits?'

Meader nodded.

He had an A4 glossy picture of Melanie's shoe: it was covered in black powder.

'What is it?'

He smiled and his eyes widened a little.

'A fingerprint.'

I pointed to the photograph: 'On the shoe?'

He nodded.

'Fuck.'

'The report's just back from the lab. When they ran the fingerprint test, they found a print on the bottom of her shoe – on the lift.

'Melanie was dressed by her killer after her attack. The murderer put her shoes back on her.

'Our man was left-handed as well, wasn't he?'

I nodded.

'Then it's in the perfect position, just here.'

He showed me again and flicked the picture over to reveal a close-up photograph of the fingerprint.

'We've had this shoe in stores for twenty-nine years and we've never known this,' I said.

Meader nodded.

'The killer must have done something else,' I said. 'You don't do what he did to Melanie then go back to a law-abiding life. There's not a match on the National DNA Database. But if he was a thief or a rapist or a killer even years ago, his prints must be on that system.'

'He must be on record somewhere,' he agreed.

'Well, what are we doing? Let's run the fingerprint check.'

I remembered reading about a case from up north in the 1990s. A rapist who superglued his victims to their car steering wheels, or glued their eyes shut; one victim was thrown into the canal bound-up. Detectives had finally found him by carrying out fingerprint searches on vehicles which had been broken into near the sex attacks.

Genius.

I shouted for Duncan, but he wasn't in the MCIT. I phoned him, but he wasn't picking up. I emailed him and he called back half an hour later, muttering something about meetings.

'Duncan, you know about this fingerprint?'

He didn't and we showed him.

'Well, can we do a check?'

'It's not that straightforward, Julie. You can't just do a national fingerprint check, that's not how the system works. We have to do it methodically.'

'What?'

'It's the same with all cases. We look within force first, then we go regionally, then we look nationally.'

'You're kidding me. This is a category A murder. We have to go through a three-stage process?'

'Yes, we do, Julie.'

'Well, can we start?'

'Yes, Julie.'

Duncan asked Hooky to go to the force's fingerprint bureau, where they would start the work.

A fingerprint.

A fingerprint.

I thought of all the officers who had worked on the case over the years, all the people who had spent months, years even, of their lives working on this inquiry. Now we were tantalisingly close to finally finding Melanie Road's killer.

And I thought of Jean, sitting there in the garden centre coffee shop, talking of her daughter murdered a lifetime ago: 'She'll always be seventeen …

'Who can do that to someone? Who could do that?'

'He's not a man, he's a monster.'

CHAPTER 20

OCTOBER 2013

'Julie, we've got a problem.'

It was Gary.

The Inquiry Room was busy, and so was I. Most of MCIT was investigating a gangland shooting in Bristol. But I was a deputy senior investigating officer on a baby death. I was looking through photos which cut me to the core and I wasn't really paying attention to Gary Mason and his problems. But I did welcome the break from looking at those images.

'Sorry, Gary. What's up?'

'Have you heard of the Protection of Freedoms Act?'

'Er, vaguely.'

'It's creating a bit of an issue with our fingerprint inquiries on Rhodium.'

'What?'

I was more focused now. The fingerprint bureau had been looking at our print from the shoe for several days. I had been badgering them, but so far, we'd had no results.

'POFA, it came in last year. The government wants to protect people's freedoms – personal information, records kept on file. DNA files, that kind of thing.

179

'It includes fingerprints. Old ones.'

'What does that mean? What will happen to old finger-print records?'

'They're getting destroyed.'

'What?'

'Yes. If someone's been cautioned or convicted of a seri-ous offence, then the records stay. But if our killer was charged but not convicted, or was convicted of a minor offence, then the records will get destroyed.'

'When's that happening.'

'Now. They're shredding hundreds of thousands of fingerprint records.'

'When we're trying to match ours to find a killer? What can we do?'

'Er, do the search really quickly?'

I found Duncan Goodwin.

'Duncan, do you know about POFA?'

'Oh yes.'

'And you know that hundreds of thousands of finger-print records are being destroyed as we speak?'

'Yes.'

'And we're still fucking around with fingerprint records from our force, while other records are being destroyed around the country? Our killer could be anywhere. We have to speed this up.'

'We have a process to go through, wthin force, then region-ally, then nationally.'

'Duncan, this is a once-in-a-lifetime opportunity to catch Melanie's killer. We will never have this chance again. He could be Fred Bloggs, the Sheffield shoplifter, but we'll never know if his prints are going to be wiped out by the bloody government.'

He shrugged.

'Do you know how hard we've worked to get this chance? I'm trying to make things happen here.'

'Write me a report and tell me why we need to accelerate the process.'

'Thank you, Duncan.'

I breathed out and returned to my desk, muttering something unrepeatable. Then I opened my emails and started typing:

Dear Duncan.
We need to accelerate our checks of the
fingerprint records because they are not
going to be there in six months' time.
Thank you,
Julie Mac.

The fingerprint work went from days to weeks to months. Every so often, I would chase the bureau to check they hadn't secretly found a match and forgotten to tell me.

But no.

In my mind, there was a giant shredder, somewhere in the bowels of the Home Office in Whitehall. There was a mountain of papers beside it. Fingerprint records. And the Home Secretary was feeding them, one by one, into the mouth of the machine spewing out tiny, undecipherable shreds of paper.

Buried deep in the mountain was a golden sheet of paper, on it a fingerprint belonging to a man who had been a low-level criminal, who had always been cautioned for his minor offences. He had also murdered Melanie Road.

The mountain was getting smaller and smaller as Home Secretary Theresa May's hand closed in on the fingerprint record which was the key to us solving the case and delivering justice for Melanie's family.

Could I get to it before it was put in the shredding machine and wiped from the face of the earth?

'We're going to have to look at the fingerprints of everyone who touched the shoe over the years.'

Hooky groaned.

We were in the MCIT, gathered around the desk he shared with Natalie Ace.

'But everyone?' he said.

Three months had passed since the fingerprint bureau had started looking for matches. I had no idea how many old fingerprint records had been shredded in that time but I had to accept that this could be another occasion where we had made a brilliant lead for ourselves, only to fail.

Two steps forward, one step back.

'We have to. When we find the killer, his barrister might say, "That's not my client's fingerprint. My client had consensual sex with Melanie, someone else killed her." We have to close all our defences.'

'Okay, boss.'

Things must have been bad for Hooky to look so dejected at the prospect of all this overtime.

'In fact, we need to get this case match-ready. We need to start checking the continuity of all our exhibits. Any defence barrister will want to know, it's our weak point in a case this old.'

If we found Melanie's killer, we would be up against barristers who would want to know where all the hundreds of exhibits had been for over thirty years. Who had worked on them? Where they had been stored? Were they kept as purely as possible?

We went back through our fingerprint records, looking at detectives and scientists from 1984 and from the reviews of 1996 and 2001. We went back through our archives, comparing our newly found fingerprint on Melanie's shoe with those we had in storage of police officers who had worked on the inquiry in 1984. There were a few missing so Hooky and Natalie Ace tracked them down, finding them in person, taking their prints afresh.

No matches.

We went to the Forensic Science Service archives. The service had been privatised years earlier, but its store in Birmingham was still available to us.

Our fingerprint didn't compare with anyone on their records. They had a few names of scientists whose prints they didn't keep on record. Hooky and Natalie Ace went to see them. Soon afterwards, I was met by a grim-faced Hooky in the Inquiry Room.

'We've got a match. It was a scientist.'

'Oh no.'

'Yes, we went and took her print the other week. She was one of the first scientists at the scene.'

'Didn't scientists wear gloves in 1984?'

I looked around. Hooky, Natalie and Gary all looked deflated.

'This is disappointing, but it's good that we found it. We know there's no second attacker. We know whose fingerprint it is, we've closed that avenue off.

'You've told the fingerprint bureau to stop searching?'

Hooky nodded.

'We have other ways,' I found myself saying.

Unsure, really, what they would be.

'What's that sound?' I asked.

It was an MCIT briefing.

Three senior investigators had been talking about their jobs, the last was about a stabbing in East Bristol. As ever, I was the final SIO to give a talk and I felt a change in the room's mood as I went to the front of the briefing.

'This sound,' I continued, 'is the drip, drip, drip of me asking you guys to help me with Operation Rhodium.'

The detectives had been sitting forward in their chairs, but I noticed a few were starting to slouch back.

'We've got twenty more swabs to take in the Avon and Somerset Police area this week. I could really do with your help.

'Drip, drip, drip ... just like Chinese water torture. And I won't stop until I get my swabs.'

Their eyes were stony.

The room was silent.

'Come on, this is a category A murder. If this had happened yesterday, you'd be all over it.'

A few of the more polite detectives tried hard to look awake.

'Remember ... drip, drip, drip is me dripping on. I really won't stop, you know that. I'll hand the names out in a moment. Thank you.'

The briefing broke up. I heard a few snatches of words over the sound of scraping chairs: 'Fingerprint was a scientist', 'She's delusional', 'It's a fucking Review Team job'.

Melanie Road was 17 years old when she was murdered in the early
hours of Saturday 9 June 1984. She had been due to start her
A Level examinations the following Monday. She had moved
with her family to Bath two years earlier.

The garages where Melanie's body was found in a suburban cul-de-sac. Detectives always wondered why she was found here. Was she driven to this location by her murderer? Was she hiding from her attacker here when she died?

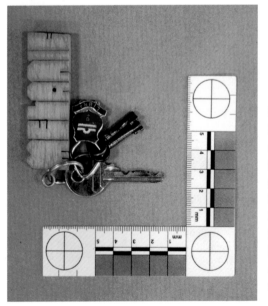

When police found Melanie's body, there were no identification cards at the scene, just a set of keys with a keyring that spelt 'Melanie'. Police used a loudhailer to broadcast her name in the neighbourhood to locate her family – a brutal way for Jean Road to discover her daughter's murder.

MURDER IN BATH

This girl was murdered in Bath in the early hours of SATURDAY 9th JUNE 1984

Melanie Anne Road
17 yrs, 5′ 7″, fair hair, wearing a black woollen cardigan, navy blue trousers that finish just below the knee and light-coloured slip-on shoes. She was carrying a black leather clasp purse.

1. **Did you know Melanie?**
2. **Could you have seen her Friday evening or early Saturday morning (8th/9th June 1984)?**
3. **Were you in or near the Broad Street or Lansdown Road area between 1 am — 6 am Saturday 9th June 1984?**

Bath Police need your help.
All information is useful.
Please call at
BATH POLICE STATION
or TELEPHONE BATH 60943

Police were desperate to find Melanie's killer. It became one of the country's biggest murder inquiries in 1984. Detectives arrested 94 men, then two more the following year.

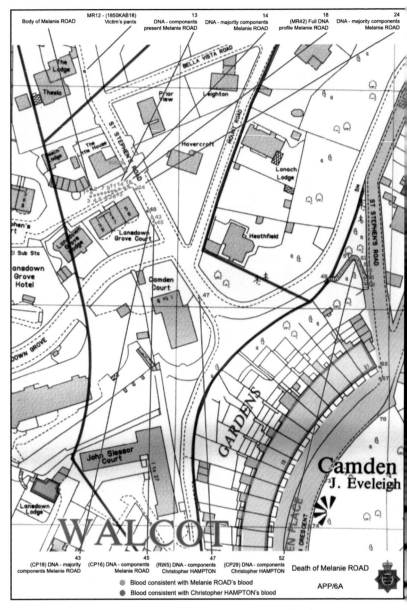

The Green Blood Trail. Forensic scientists were able to identify a rare protein makeup in the killer's blood. This was the map drawn to distinguish where the murderer's blood dropped – coloured green. It led from St Stephen's Road, down a set of stone steps to Camden Crescent.

The inquiry was codenamed Operation Rhodium. It was the last major homicide in Avon and Somerset Police before the introduction of computers. Here detectives and indexers sit side by side. There would be 30,000 documents in the final case file.

Face of a killer. This is the image Ben, our prime witness, drew of Melanie's murderer. Although the drawing is sketchy, Ben was able to tell us so much more than we knew: the killer was a white man, probably local to Bath, aged in his early thirties. This new information came to us 25 years after Melanie's murder, soon after I joined the inquiry.

The documents and exhibits were stored in a police warehouse in Weston-super-Mare. When I started working on Operation Rhodium disorganised evidence bags and crates were spread among those from homicides and rapes.

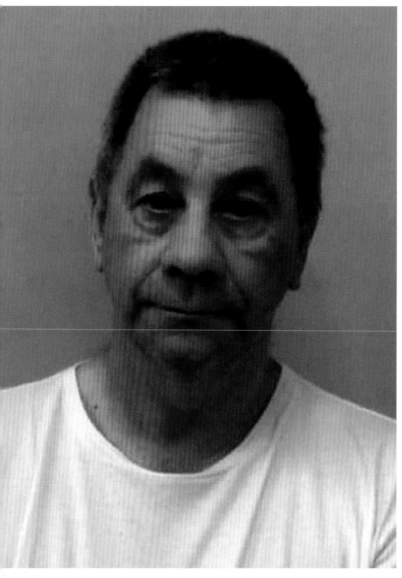

We were led to Christopher Hampton in July 2015. He had been born in Bath, had lived in the city in 1984 but was then living in Bristol with his second wife. He gave a 'no comment' interview on arrest.

Hampton was sentenced to life in prison with a minimum tariff of 22 years in 2016. 'You will very likely die in prison' said the judge, after hearing heart-breaking victim impact statements from Jean, Karen and Adrian Road.

Me, on the court steps following Hampton's sentencing. I told the media: 'The key to solving this case has been a combination of traditional police inquiries, advances in forensic science and the tenacity of a small group of officers and police staff.'

CHAPTER 20

I went back to my desk.

Ollie Day, a civilian investigator, came over.

'I can help with some of those swabs, boss.'

'Thanks, Ollie.'

'And this might help them a bit.'

He dropped a booklet on my desk.

'What's this?'

'Well, it's got all the fast food places in the force area. Thought that might help encourage a few of them to go out with the swabs. An army marches on its stomach, you know?'

'Ollie, you're a bloody legend.'

I picked up the phone and dialled Nathan Eason. A Londoner's voice answered.

'Hi, is that Nathan? Hi, it's Julie Mackay from Avon and Somerset Police. I was at the Review Conference in Cardiff a few years ago.

'Yes, I was really interested in your Offender in the System talk,' I continued. 'Wondered how I could apply it to an old case I'm working on. What help can I get from the powers that be?'

He said he'd used the College of Policing. They had analysts who came in and made up a matrix. They gave points to each suspect, depending on facts known about them. Five points if they had a criminal record, seven points for a sex offence, where they lived – that scored highly. Each case would be different and it took a little while to get the College of Policing involved, but they were helpful.

Just hearing him say the words again gave me hope: 'The offender was in the system.'

CHAPTER 21

OCTOBER 2013

It had been months since I had been at the scene of Melanie Road's murder. The last time, in the summer, had been one of those gentle, peaceful days when there was a lightness in the air and the sun had gently saturated the Bath stone. Today, it was as if someone had played with the colour settings. A dull October afternoon, short, grey and dank. The buildings, normally so vibrant, seemed to have lost their sparkle. And the wind whipped the leaves into a frenzied dance around Camden Crescent.

Gary Mason was with me, shivering in a long jacket. And so too was the Review Team from the College of Policing: Emma Spooner, a crime investigation support officer; Dr Terri Cole, a behavioural investigative advisor; Colin Johnson, a geographic profiler, and Liz Abraham from the Serious Crime Analysis Section (which we all called SCAS).

It had taken months, but at last I had expert assistance to help me understand what kind of a man Melanie's killer was. They had arrived earlier in the day in Bristol, and in a conference room, Gary and I had talked them through the case. Now they wanted to see the key locations.

We walked up the stone steps to the triangle of grass.

'This is where Ben saw Melanie and the killer arguing,' said Gary.

'And Melanie's body was found up there,' I pointed up St Stephen's Road, towards St Stephen's Court.

'That road on the left?' Colin Johnson asked.

'The one after.'

We walked up, Gary explaining this was also the route of the Green Blood Trail.

'I like this,' said Terri Cole. She was looking at the first left – the turning before St Stephen's Court, where Melanie was found.

'Lansdown Grove?'

'Yes, this looks good,' said Colin.

We went further up, making a left on St Stephen's Court.

I noticed them looking at the low blocks of flats which loomed over the road.

'Melanie was found here,' I said, pointing to the right-hand garage and the low wall.

I knew what they were thinking.

'This wasn't where the rape or stabbing happened,' said Terri. 'Those flats, they're too close. On a summer's night, people would have heard an attack like this.'

I nodded.

We talked about the scene and how Melanie was found: lying as if she were asleep.

'Can we look on that first road?' Colin said.

I shrugged.

We turned into Lansdown Grove.

The profilers were looking at each other.

'Looks good,' said Colin. 'All these bushes, far better for a rape attack. It's more secluded.'

'Did the original inquiry team look here?' asked Liz Abraham.

'They looked everywhere. Every square inch. And there's nothing in the files about bushes being flattened or even disturbed. There was nothing here forensically.'

They carried on looking at the road, approvingly.

'What I really want to know,' I said, 'is what kind of a man is he? Why rape Melanie twice? How does that happen?'

'We'll look at our research to see what's there to help you,' said Terri. 'We work with statistics. With data. What does the data show? We'll look at similar attacks to this and see what patterns of behaviour offenders have shown before or after.'

'Have you studied attackers like this before? Are there many men who do this kind of thing? Were there back in '84? What's their background? What contact do they tend to have with police and other authorities?'

'Hard to say, we'll have to look,' said Terri.

'This isn't the kind of place an out-of-towner would come, is it?' said Colin, the geographic profiler.

'We've always thought that. Tourists stay in the city centre, usually. We took the names of everyone staying in hotels in Bath that night, but we always thought it might be a local, or someone who knew these streets. Ben said he'd seen the guy around too, remember?'

'And Melanie, was she the kind of teenager who might have had consensual sex with a guy she met on the street?' That was Terri.

'No,' I replied.

'And nothing was stolen?'

'We've never found her purse or handbag, but there wasn't much in them. A couple of pounds and a library card.'

'Anything which might be a trophy?'

'We've always wondered about her knickers. But why drop them in one direction then run off in another?'

'And her clothes. The forensics show her knickers were covered in her blood, so they were on when she was stabbed. But there is no trace of semen on them, so they were removed for the rape. But when Melanie was found, she was dressed, her trousers were on, her shoes were on, but her pants were not. Strange.'

'Yes.'

That's why we've asked you here, I said to myself.

'If he removed at least one of the legs of Melanie's trousers and a shoe, that might show the offender is familiar with prostitutes,' said Terri. 'Were there any reports of sex workers coming across men with knives at that time? Any reports of aggression towards prostitutes, here in Bath or in Bristol or Swindon?'

'Nothing in our files.'

'How much do you think you can rely on the files?' asked Colin.

'It's the most extensive inquiry I've seen. Thirty thousand documents.'

'And was there anyone in Melanie's life who disliked her? Or she'd slighted, even without knowing it? And are you sure the boyfriend isn't the offender?'

'The original investigation spent months with Melanie's family and friends, building a picture of her. She was just a nice girl. She had no enemies, she wasn't abrasive or difficult. We swabbed the boyfriend back in 2001. And his brother. No DNA matches.

'And I've spent hours with her mum, she still lives just up there,' I nodded towards Jean Road's house.

'There's nothing she's told me about Melanie which makes me think anyone would want to harm her.

'She was just a nice girl.'

We returned to the grey warmth of a Kenneth Steele House conference room.

'Have you seen one of the matrices before?' asked Emma Spooner.

I nodded and she pushed a previous one across to me. On the left was a column with about twenty different boxes. Each box had a category: preconvictions, age, address at time of the offence.

'We'll go off and look at the statistics and research. We'll give you a list of scores you can give. You'll probably give five points if the man was aged between eighteen and thirty-five in 1984, three points if he was aged thirty-five to forty.

'The big one will be about offending.'

'With a sex crime, it doesn't always follow that they have a history of sex offending,' said Terri Cole. 'Often, we find we'll ask you to give a higher score for theft than a sexual assault.'

'Really? So, if a man in our system has nicked a TV, we should score him more points than if he raped a different seventeen-year-old girl?'

'We'll need to look at the research again,' said Terri calmly, 'but the statistics show that. It's about a person's dishonesty. Sometimes sex offenders aren't actual predators but they will nearly always have a dishonesty about them.'

'One thing we really need to ask,' said Emma. 'How much importance do you give Ben Schwarzkopf? How sure are you that what he says is true?'

'We've corroborated everything he's said,' I replied.

'What do you think?' Gary asked me when they had left.

'They are national experts. And it adds some credibility to our inquiry.'

In early December an email appeared in my inbox from the College of Policing. I clicked the attachment and saw a report which sprawled on for pages. I printed it off and saw work from both Colin Johnson, the geographic profiler, and Dr Terri Cole, the behavioural investigative advisor. On the final page was a matrix for Operation Rhodium.

I started with the behavioural report. It said the offender may have either known Melanie Road and had some form of vendetta against her or her family. Or, research showed it could have been because the offender felt inadequate, which could have led to the attack. Melanie may have belittled him in some way, even inadvertently.

Could anyone who knew where she lived have had these feelings? We should eliminate them.

Dr Cole said the offender was likely to have had a 'disorganised upbringing' and had contact with authorities: police, probation, schools or social services. And she was sceptical about three things: the sex was consensual, that the killer followed her home from the club or that Melanie accepted a lift. All unlikely.

Dr Cole said most probably Melanie was raped by the green triangle of grass; she managed to flee and dress herself. She dropped her bloodstained pants as she doubled back to the garages, thinking it safer to hide and was found and killed at that spot. Or, she said, both the rape and murder took place at the garages, even though they were just a few metres away from people's homes. If this had happened, Dr Cole said, then perhaps the killer redressed Melanie himself. Potentially as a way of 'making good' the crime. In his warped mind, he had been making it look as though she had been neither raped nor killed, and had posed the body in an attempt to cover up a sexual crime.

It seemed 'highly likely' that the killer had been 'engaged in additional criminality and was likely to have come to the attention of the police prior to or since the offence'.

The offender is in the system.

Dr Cole said sex offenders were no different from any other type of offender. They were more 'generalist than specialist'. Seventy-two per cent of sexual murderers had committed at least one crime against property, she said.

We should score thieves highly. But we should also score men who had a history of voyeurism or fetishism. Peeping Toms, indecent phone calls, exhibitionism, she said, were good traits to look for.

To me it was a relief to see people who had studied hundreds of crimes add their voices of authority to our investigation. The top brass at Avon and Somerset loved the academic stuff. And it made me feel that despite all our setbacks, we were on the right track.

Now I turned to the geographic profile written by Colin Johnson. I wondered if he would tell me if the killer lived on the north or south side of the river in Bath. He was not that specific, but his report was helpful.

A lot of it centred around a simple principle: 'Humans are basically lazy.' He said the same was true of killers, even in the moments before and after a murder.

Why had Melanie Road's killer chosen that location?

He said Melanie had been out on an unplanned and impromptu night out. If her movements were unplanned, it was unlikely that her killer had preplanned the attack as it happened. The area was suburban, residential, 'an unlikely place to specifically target lone females at that time of night'.

The killer was there for another reason.

What linked him to the St Stephen's Court area? Was it the thefts of car radios? Did he live there?

He used the steps. They are dark and not obvious. That showed local knowledge, Colin suggested.

He asked some questions:

Were inquiries made at properties after the blood stopped?

**What intelligence is there about people living
beyond the Trail?**

Did Melanie have any male associates in the area?

Have items ever been recovered in this area subsequently?

We had looked at all of that; we had been looking at all of these since 1984.

Colin suggested we score men who had some connection within five miles of the attack site seven points. If a man had been living between six and ten miles he should score ten points. And if a man on our system lived within five miles of where Melanie was found, we should score him twenty points.

Five miles? That was all of Bath.

We now had to apply this prioritisation matrix to the 8,500 men in our system.

The maximum score we could give was seventy-two. We needed to find a white male thief, preferably one with a history of voyeurism, who was aged between eighteen and thirty-five at the time, around six feet tall and who lived in Bath in 1984.

CHAPTER 22

JANUARY 2014

If anyone were to watch the petite cyclist on her daily route from her suburban home, through the congestion of the city's central streets and into the grey industrial estate, they might be forgiven for thinking they were watching a librarian or a bank clerk on her way to work.

When she reached the anonymous three-storey grey building and took off her helmet, you would see a smiley, bespectacled figure with long brown hair and a demeanour whispering 'understated'.

Compared with more outgoing people in the office – me, for example – Lesley Howse is like a mouse. But she is one of that special team who, quietly in the background, work on more murders than almost anyone in Avon and Somerset Police.

Lesley is an indexer. Like Barbara, who was so invaluable in the Review Team. If you were to talk to Lesley, you might think she lacks confidence, but behind those glasses and that quiet smile is a formidable steeliness. And in 2014, we were counting on Lesley's polite perseverance to help catch the killer of Melanie Road.

'Thanks for helping, Lesley,' I said as she came into the office and I showed her the prioritisation matrix.

'No problem, Julie.'

I explained how it worked: Lesley would take a man's name from the Operation Rhodium inquiry system and give him points in each box. Twenty for living in Bath in 1984, eight points for a theft conviction, adding an extra three for a crime with a female victim and another three for a knife offence.

The top scorers would be our top priority.

Lesley's job would be to apply this point-scoring matrix to all the names in our system.

'Of course, Julie. How many names do we have in this system?'

'Twelve thousand.'

'Oh.'

'But it's a male offender, so there's only eight and a half thousand men.'

'Okay.'

'And Gary will help you.'

Gary Mason waved from his desk.

Lesley smiled, pushed her glasses up her nose, logged on to the Holmes system where Barbara had uploaded all the names a few years earlier and she started scoring men.

Some names in the system had a lot of detail. If someone had been interviewed, we would have a Personal Descriptive Form or PDF to tell us their ethnic background, height and hair colour. For other names – for example, men whose names had been phoned in – we might know very little. Lesley would search for their details on the Police National

Computer, filling in the blanks about conviction histories, if they existed.

Gary would also unleash his investigative might, always ready to log on to a genealogy website, draw up a family tree or chase another police force for details. He lived for this.

'You can film Rhodium. I'm happy for you to show what we're doing.'

'Er, no, Julie.'

Superintendent Andy Bevan had called me into his office. MCIT was abuzz. At our last briefing, a few days earlier, there had been an announcement that a documentary team wanted to follow Avon and Somerset detectives on a murder case. Half of the team was horrified. I'd noticed others had got their hair cut and were dressing a little smarter.

'It's fine. It's probably easier for them to film a cold case than a live murder,' I continued. 'What are they going to do? Film a family liaison officer as he tells a mum her daughter's just been killed?'

'Well …' said Andy, his voice trailing off.

I liked Andy, had known him for years and could tell he was fighting for the most diplomatic words.

'It might be useful for the crews to practise being around police briefings, like you have. Try out the process with you. But the message from above is Operation Rhodium isn't …'

'What?'

'Appropriate.'

'Why not?'

'Well, I've heard from the Chief.'

'Nick Gargan?'

The Chief was new and had big ideas. My eyes bored into Andy.

'He's not keen on cold cases.'

'Sorry?'

'Doesn't see the point of them. He used the phrase "waste of money". It's not been solved in thirty years, it would be pointless for a crew to follow Operation Rhodium. You haven't caught him yet, the Chief thinks you're unlikely ever to catch him. I don't agree but that's from the top.'

What about the rights of the victims? What about Melanie? What about Jean? And Adrian? And Karen? What about proving to victims everywhere that the police will never give up? What about trust and confidence? I'm doing this around my day job. Live cases always take precedence. We have a tiny budget, just the cost of the swabbing.

If you were to see a victim or a witness decades after an attack and hear the impact that a rape or murder has had on them, has altered their lives forever, you wouldn't dismiss it as a cold case. The impact of Melanie's murder on Bath was indescribable, made worse twelve years later by Melanie Hall's killing. That's another cold case. Should we not investigate that?

What about proving that we never give up? Gary and I have already locked up cold case rapists. I will find Melanie's killer.

These were all the words which flashed through my mind in an instant. And for once my powers of diplomacy overrode my instinct to say exactly what I thought.

I smiled and left Andy with one word: 'Okay.'

I went to my desk underneath the large photograph of Melanie Road on the wall.

Nick Gargan has no idea what I'm doing – he's never even asked me about the case, how could he pass judgement? I thought.

I carried on working.

'Julie, you know this matrix?' asked Gary, 'What score are we using for top priority swabs?'

'I don't know. The maximum possible score is seventy-two, isn't it? Fifty? Make a list of anyone scoring over fifty. We'll do them first.'

'We've got twenty already,' said Lesley.

'Have you got the list there?'

She showed me a list of scores on her computer and I scanned through. I recognised a few names but most of them had lain buried in the system since 1984.

'David Wallis,' read one report. One of three musician brothers who were performing in Bath on 8 June 1984.

'Oh my God, these look amazing!'

Names in the system, but men we had never really looked at before. Things seemed to be bubbling up from the depths of our sea of names.

CHAPTER 23

FEBRUARY 2014

'Julie, there really was no need to do that. I'd have asked Adrian.'

'It's no trouble, it's brown bread, isn't it?'

Jean Road said yes as I carried the Morrisons bags into her kitchen, popping them on the worktop.

'I was there anyway for my shop. We've got five teenagers in the house – they're like locusts. Look what I got.' I grinned. 'Shortbread. I'll have a cup of tea, if you're offering.'

Jean filled the kettle and put it on.

Later, when the shopping was put away, a first cup of tea drunk and only half a packet of shortbread remaining on the coffee table between us, we finished catching up with each other's news and started talking about the inquiry.

'We've had scientists in, Jean. Profilers. They look at patterns in behaviour, at what other murderers have done.'

'What do you think that will do?'

'Well, we have thousands of names in our system. Eight thousand men. It'll help bring up some new names which were hidden away.

'We've already got three brilliant suspects, men we didn't really know about before. But they look great. We'll hunt them down.

'Gary, he's amazing. He can just find people even if they don't want to be found. Have you met him?'

Jean said she hadn't.

'He set up the Cold Case team. Before that, years ago, he was my boss just after I started. Now I'm his boss. You know what, we just get on with it. We've never had an issue.

'He's a bit scruffy. A dreadful driver. And he talks too much, but apart from that he's just a bloody dream to work with.

'Wish some of the others were like that.'

Jean smiled.

'They're just busy,' I continued. 'They've got live inquiries. Sometimes a couple of them are tricky, though. Not sure if it's because I'm a woman, not sure if it's me.

'But I'll whip them into shape.'

'Of course you will, Julie.'

'And I was thinking, Jean. Have you ever come into the Inquiry Room? The team's fab and they'd love to meet you.'

'No, I haven't. Tony went in. Back when it happened. They met him, showed him around. Talked him through what happened.

'I wasn't invited.'

'Do you want to come then? You'd be very welcome.'

'Okay, team, I have a new plan.'

No groan, just glazed eyes in the MCIT meeting. A murder had recently been detected, energy levels had dropped in the

Inquiry Room. That could be dangerous: when things got quiet, detectives got restless.

And a few were fidgeting as I stood at the front talking, again, about the murder of Melanie Road.

'I know you're sick of me dripping on about the swabs. And I know you've had doors slammed in your face and been called all kinds of names.

'Some of those names aren't even deserved.

'So, we're going to try something new. Something no cold case inquiry has ever done before. And you're going to be the pioneers.'

I noticed a few pairs of eyes which had been looking down or away were now focused on me.

'Yes, I really appreciate everything you've done, all the miles you've driven, all the swabs you've taken, all the time you've given. But we've got a new energy with our research and this is throwing up some brilliant suspects. Just brilliant.

'So, we're going to have a competition.'

I opened my blue book, fished out a laminated A4 sign and held it out to the team.

'Suspect of the Week,' I read it out. 'Yes, I'm starting a Suspect of the Week contest. Don't laugh, but I'm after a new man every Monday. One of you will be the lucky swabber who goes off to find him, or if he's dead, one of his relatives.

'A special prize for the winner.

'We have thousands of names. But ask yourself: could you be the one who wins the Suspect of the Week?'

I found myself grinning and even noticed a few smiles from the team.

The meeting broke up and I went to my desk. I stuck the sign on the wall, between Melanie's photograph and the map of the Green Blood Trail.

'Gary, do we have our first Suspect of the Week?'

'I think our first Suspect of the Week will have to be the musicians.

'The Wallis brothers. There's three of them, all dodgy. They were gigging in Bath on the night Melanie died. We looked at them at the time, but eliminated them. Wasn't any proof.

'All known to police. One was a suspect in the Beryl Culverwell murder.'

Beryl Culverwell was another Bath murder we had looked at in the Review Team. She had been killed in 1978. Her husband had returned home to find the house in darkness and his wife missing. Shopping was strewn over the kitchen table, dinner burning in the oven.

He went to the garage, where he found his wife had been beaten and stabbed numerous times.

Nothing had been stolen from the house, there was no sexual assault, no apparent motive.

And the case was still unsolved, more than thirty years later.

There was a stack of papers on the Wallis brothers.

The first was dated 17 June 1984:

Statement of David WALLIS, 10th June 1984.

They got to him quickly:

I am a musician and up until 8th June 1984 my brother John and I played music in 'Alex & Mark's Club', Walcot Street, Bath.

On Friday 8th June we got to the club at about 8.45pm and played in the club, which closed around 1130pm.

After the club had closed we packed our instruments and equipment in my Ford Capri JHJ 164P. I dropped my brother John off at his home at 3 Davison Place then I drove through Hedgemead Park, coming out at Lansdown Road by the Farmhouse Pub.

My spider sensors suddenly pricked up.

The killer ran through Hedgemead Park. The Farmhouse Pub was one of the points Melanie would have walked past.

I visited my brother Tom on Park Street, Bath and stayed about an hour and drove home. I cannot recall seeing anything untoward on my journey home and the city seemed quiet.

It smelled to me – it just smelled. They had a car. They were driving on the same roads where Melanie had walked that night. If her body had been moved in a vehicle, here was a clue. But there was a report written by a detective inspector in September 1984: 'There is no evidence to connect any of the above persons with our inquiry.'

I looked again through these papers: 'There is no evidence to connect any of the above persons with our inquiry …'

'Do we know if they're Green Blood?'

'Don't think they were ever tested.'

'And they're mentioned in the Culverwell murder from '78?'

'Tom is.'

'And they're in Gloucester now?'

'They hunt as a pack. Yes, they were all living in Bath, playing music in '84, and they're all about a mile from each other in Gloucester now.

'Although Tom's in the file index for the Culverwell killing, none of them actually has a criminal record. They're mentioned as witnesses and as being present in loads of inquiries, but they've never actually been charged with anything.

'They're always on the periphery.'

There was a statement from John Wallis's partner. Her name was Danielle Harvey and it was dated August 1984. Just three lines, saying that on 9 June, John had arrived home at about 01:00: 'He came straight to bed and was with me until 10:00 the same morning.'

Gary had found Dave Wallis on Facebook. He looked out from an image – he was on stage with a guitar strapped to a skinny body, a thick mop of grey, curly hair. According to his index card he'd be fifty-seven now.

He'd have been twenty-seven in 1984. Just about the right age, according to Ben Schwarzkopf.

Gary picked up his mobile and started dialling.

I carried on looking through the files.

Gary got off the phone: 'Gloucestershire Police know them. They've no record, but they know them well, all three of them.'

'How's that?'

'Well, there was a spate of robberies in Gloucester at venues where the brothers had been playing.'

Theft. That's eight points on the matrix, I thought.

'But Gloucester CID couldn't prove anything.'

'Well, our first Suspect of the Week is a group of three. Who wants to be our first contestant?'

DS Neil Meade had walked in moments earlier, clutching a bottle of champagne.

'Good idea, Meader,' I said. 'That'll do for a prize.'

'No, boss. I turned forty this weekend. We've got more bottles of fizz than I'll ever drink. Well, I'm a beer man. Thought I'd bring one in for when we solve Rhodium.'

He put the bottle of bubbly on top of a filing cabinet

'I'll take the brothers, boss,' said Meader. 'I can blag it.'

I went to the wall and stuck Tom Wallis's index cards from 1984 under the laminated sign which said Suspect of the Week.

MARCH 2014

'Meader, you said you were persuasive?'

'Yes, boss,' he sighed down the end of the phone.

'They've lodged a formal complaint about you.'

'What? The brothers?'

'Yes.' I looked at the email from Professional Standards. 'Inappropriate behaviour.'

'I only asked if I could swab him.'

'Were you inappropriate?'

'No.'

'What did you say?'

'Usual stuff, I was trying to solve the thirty-year-old murder of Melanie Road. Showed a photograph and spoke about what Bath was like in '84.'

'What were they like?'

'Well, I only met Dave. He was horrible. Wacky. Weird. Told me to fuck off.'

'Did you get a swab?'

'No.'

'When did you see him?'

'Two o'clock.'

I looked at the email from David Wallis to Avon and Somerset's Professional Standards department. It had taken less than twenty minutes for our Suspect of the Week to lodge the formal complaint.

'Boss, you might have to change the name of Suspect of the Week. These brothers are taking bloody ages. No way we'll get a swab by Monday,' said Meader.

The Wallis brothers were refusing to play ball.

When his attempt at Dave Wallis had failed, Meader tried his brother Tom but he'd slammed the door in his face.

'I read him the riot act,' Meader said. 'He just said he didn't speak to cops. Never had, never would.'

'Christ, does it have to be this hard? If we weren't suspicious beforehand, we are now,' I said.

I got Tom Wallis's phone number from Meader and dialled.

'Yeah?' the voice was deep, gruff and reeked with the superiority of a stupid man.

'My name is Detective Inspector Julie Mackay from Avon and Somerset P ...'

'Yeah, I had one of your boys up here yesterday. Accusing me of fucking murder.'

'We're not accusing you of anything. We're trying to find the killer of a schoolgirl in Bath in 1984 and we have a long list of ...'

'Yeah,' he said. 'Well, I told him we don't work with cops, never have. And if you keep on at us, we'll complain. We don't live in a fucking police state.'

'We're asking thousands of people to help us with this one inquiry. Just this inquiry, then your DNA gets destroyed.

Melanie's poor family have waited three decades for justice. How would you feel if it was your sister?'

'I ain't got a sister. This is coercion.'

'It's not. What have you got to hide?'

'Nothing. It's your job to find the murderer, it's not our job to cooperate with the cops.'

I could feel my throat go dry.

'If you don't cooperate, we'll launch an undercover operation on you. We'll follow you, or one of your brothers, we'll watch everything you do. Would you like that?

'I will hunt you down like a long dog unless you give us a sample of your DNA so do the right thing and help. This is a schoolgirl's murder, it's not about whether you cooperate with the police or not.'

'Fuck off.'

The line went dead.

I swore.

'Will you run a covert operation on them?' asked Gary.

'Too bloody right I will! I'll wait until we have a few more refusers and we'll do a big job on a load of them.'

'Hello, is that Danielle Harvey? Hello?'

I heard the distant reply from the end of Gary's phone.

'Yes, I'm sorry to call you out of the blue. I'm from Avon and Somerset Police …' he went on, bludgeoning the poor woman into submission. She said she would see him.

Yes, she had not been with John Wallis, for about twenty-five years.

Yes, he had left her for another woman.

No, she no longer had contact with Wallis.

Yes, he could rot in hell and yes, she would speak with Gary, for whatever it was about.

'Hello John, this is Detective Sergeant Neil Meade. Yes, I'm the same one who came to your house a couple of weeks ago.'

I watched as Meader recoiled from the phone, almost certainly at the end of a barrage of abuse.

'Yes, well, we've been continuing our research. We've been speaking with your partner – sorry, your former partner,' Meader looked at a piece of paper. 'Danielle Harvey is it, I think you were together back in 1984.

'Well, she made a statement at the time, but she's worried she may have made it under duress.

'I really do think the best way we can eliminate you for sure and to keep us off your backs is to give us a swab. It'll take ten minutes and you won't even have to tell your brothers. If you're eliminated as you say you will be, we'll just magically disappear.'

Meader slipped up to Gloucester to swab John Wallis at the third time of asking.

We had other leads …

We'd tracked a man to Hong Kong. He said he couldn't come to Bristol but he'd be passing through Heathrow Airport on the way to Berlin. Gary went to the airport transfer lounge, where he took the swab. This was international territory and we wondered what the legals would be if he was the killer: would it be accepted by a British court?

There was a man in Tokyo who said he wasn't leaving Japan. He sent us a paternity test he'd recently taken. We said thanks but that wouldn't be the same as an official swab. How would we know that he had taken the test and not asked a friend?

I sent the swabs off to the laboratory for another eight-week wait.

CHAPTER 25

MARCH 2014

'I don't want my stick.'

'Take it just in case,' I said.

'They'll think I'm a little old lady.'

I'd pulled up outside Kenneth Steele House and helped Jean Road from my passenger seat. Jean's mobility had improved and I was confident of her on two feet, but it was always safer just to have her stick handy.

We made our way in, through security and up the lift to level two. We got out of the lift and I could hear the chatter of idle detectives through the double doors.

'Here we are,' I said as we went through. And it was as if a magician had conjured a silence spell. I looked at the room. There were fifty, maybe sixty detectives, indexers and civilian investigators who seemed to have lost their power of speech.

'So this is the Inquiry Room, we work on all major crimes here,' I said, my voice booming.

Even the loudest, laziest detectives were gently shuffling bits of paper or quickly finding something to input on a computer.

'Hello,' said Jean to a couple of detectives who passed by. They smiled and said hi.

'This is Dave. He has been doing some swabbing and so has Ollie here, and Rich and Russ there.'

I ushered Jean to the Rhodium area and showed her the wall.

'See, we have Melanie's picture up on the wall. That's so important, helps inspire us.

'This here, Jean, is the DNA profile of the offender.' I pointed to the chart next to Melanie's picture – the chart with parallel lines and spikes with numbers.

'You see these points here,' I said, touching one of the spikes, 'these are what makes this man's DNA unique. Gary and I know every point of this profile, we've been looking at it for so long. We've become kind of experts in DNA forensics.

'I did sciences at A level, Jean. I wasn't like your Melanie, I preferred partying to studying and failed everything. I've learnt more here in an Inquiry Room than I ever did in a classroom.'

The Suspect of the Week sign had the names of the Wallis brothers written underneath.

'I've started a competition just to gee things along, Jean. This job's as much about persuasion as policing,' I explained.

I showed her the image Ben Schwarzkopf had drawn of the offender in 2010. I remembered seeing that picture for the first time, wondering how long it would be before I saw the killer in the flesh. Four years later, I was still waiting.

'Look, we're just setting up for our team meeting.'

There were no yawns among the team, no scraping of chairs, no low chatter of gossip and banter as the detectives assembled and I made my way to the front.

'Hi there, you'll see we have a visitor with us today. This is Jean Road, Melanie's mum.'

'Hello.' Jean waved with a smile.

'Jean's just come along to see what we do. And you know, it just struck me how all of you have put so much effort into Operation Rhodium.

'Jean, is there anything you would like to say?'

'I'd just like to thank you, thanks for what you are doing. I really appreciate it.'

'Er, Jean,' I said, 'You've not come here to thank us, we're here to show you that Melanie's case is with all of us, we take it so seriously. We're here to show you how important it is.'

I looked out at the dozens of alert, quiet, attentive detectives. In fact, they seemed more like pupils in assembly than police in a briefing. Jean smiled.

'I think every single one of you has been involved in this case in some way. Whether it's research for a Suspect of the Week, or swabbing, or on exhibits.

'It means so much. So, thank you.

'Anyway, I'm going to carry on dripping. We've got a new suspect – we're having to call it Suspect of the Month now. Anyone interested?'

Jean sat, poised and dignified, watching the silent show of hands. And not for the first time she reminded me of the Queen.

'Ian Botham?'

'What do you mean? Beefy?'

'Yes, he's in the system.'

I looked at Gary: 'You are bloody kidding me.'

'He was Somerset's club captain at the time. There was a report that he injured his hand the weekend Melanie was killed.

'Somerset were playing Middlesex in Bath. I don't really like cricket but it says here he bowled someone out. Edmonds? But when it comes to batting, he's absent. Hurt.

'I put him through the Operation Rhodium prioritisation matrix. He scored forty-four out of seventy-two.

'He scored 850 runs that season,' said Meader.

'We need to eliminate him,' I said. 'What if it's him?'

I had images in my mind of tabloid newspapers with Ian Botham's picture next to Melanie's. But that was too extraordinary, surely?

'England cricketer, charity fundraiser, national figure, swabbed for cold case murder. Bit embarrassing for him if he's found to be the killer,' I said. 'How'd he hurt his hand?'

'There was a charity cricket match on the Saturday, the day before the game against Middlesex, and there were what's described as "celebrations" afterwards. He injured himself somehow then.'

'Well, we're swabbing him.'

It took Gary two days to find Ian Botham's phone number.

'Hello, is that Mr Botham?' Gary had suddenly become incredibly polite. 'Okay, yes, this is an unusual phone call for you. But my name's Gary Mason, I work for Avon and Somerset Police …'

As Gary did his usual spiel, I noticed a touch more deference than usual.

'Well, we're in that part of the country next week. No? Okay? You're where? The week after?'

He put the phone down.

'Botham's happy to be swabbed, but he's having his wisdom teeth out.'

'Could we pop along to the dentist and do it while his mouth's open?'

Gary smiled.

Ian bloody Botham.

It couldn't be, could it?

There was no shortage of volunteers keen to make the 600-mile round trip to swab the former England cricketer. Some of these detectives had complained about driving thirty minutes to Swindon but four hours up north to eliminate Ian Botham was apparently no problem.

'What about the Fake Doctor?'

Among the thousands of names and characters which had passed before me and the inquiry, there was something which stood out about the flashy, secretive Essex doctor Brent Bowen. We hadn't tried him for a year or so. I was looking at his website and found the perma-tanned, sparkly teeth look deeply off-putting.

What if he really were Melanie's killer? And while Jean and her family were living through thirty years of grief, here he was, living it up, laughing at us through his brightly polished smile.

'He just smells,' I told Meader.

'He lives in this big, gated house, you just can't get anywhere near him,' he said.

Gary volunteered to go. If anyone could wear down a fake doctor through an intercom, it would be Gary Mason.

And I said a silent prayer for all the other motorists who would be on the M25 that day.

Weeks were passing and the Suspect of the Month was changing. The Gloucester brothers had been taken down, replaced
by a man who'd raped and stabbed a woman in London days
after Melanie's death. He in turn had been succeeded by a
deviant choirmaster from Gwent.

The inquiry was feeling a bit like a conveyor belt: we
would find a suspect, research him, visit then swab him, send
that off, start on another suspect and halfway through that
process, the result would come in from the first. And we
were halfway through our third Suspect of the Month when
an email arrived from the forensic services company with the
results from the earlier swabs:

> Operation Rhodium.
> The DNA profiles of the following individual were
> obtained from their reference mouth swabs.
> John WALLIS
> This DNA profile has been compared to the
> unknown DNA profile (MR8) obtained in Operation
> Rhodium.
> John Wallis can be excluded as a potential contributor
> of the semen. Using Y-STR, his brothers David
> WALLIS and Tom WALLIS can be excluded as
> potential contributors of the semen.

The scientists said we could cross Ian Botham and the
Hong Kong man off the list. The paternity test from Tokyo
would go into 'pending'.

Could something work in our favour for once?

I was searching in the shadows. Looking in one corner of
the inquiry, pulling up stones, shining a light on parts of the
investigation which had been in the dark for decades. But
everywhere I looked, it seemed the murderer had just
melted away. Vanished elsewhere.

Somewhere in these files, on a card, on an index was the name of Melanie's killer. I was convinced I would find him. I was sure his days of twisting and turning, wrestling away from me were numbered.

I felt I was closing in on him. I had no idea when I would catch him, or how, but I was closing in.

CHAPTER 26

MAY 2014

'What are we doing for the thirtieth anniversary, boss?' Hooky asked.

I had spent years looking at the date, 9 June 1984, but I had been so involved in the case that I had failed to realise this important milestone was just a few weeks away.

What should we do? How could we exploit this?

I knew from other inquiries that allegiances really do change. People who were partners in crime do fall out. Consciences can be appealed to. People grow up: become parents, lose children, face death themselves and want to offload their darkest secret rather than take it to the grave.

Some find God, others lose their minds. People change. But all it would take was for someone to come forward.

Jon Hook suggested Jean write a letter to the people of Bath. I called her and she said, 'Why not?' Jean had never spoken publicly about her daughter's death. I knew what she had gone through but people in Bath didn't understand. If a mother could write a letter summing up what it was like to be on the dark side of a cold case, that might just persuade someone to do the right thing.

I called at her home and she led me through to the kitchen table. It was a mass of papers and bills, letters from the doctors and notes from Tony's care home.

'I've done it, there you go,' she said, ripping out a page from a reporter's notebook, as if it were a shopping list. 'Let me know if that's okay.'

In blue ink, Jean's handwriting was small and precise. A lot like the woman herself.

I sat at her table and read:

I beg the people of Bath to search their memories of 30 years ago on 9th June.

I know it's a long time ago, to me it's only yesterday. Some people say 'Why churn the memories all over again? Let it rest.' But I can't. This whole episode in our family has torn us apart – not sure if it will ever heal.

While the perpetrator walks the streets – that's if he is still alive – free getting on with his life, he has left the Road family in limbo.

Yes, we go about our business/life, we put on a face for the world to see that we are coping, but we mourn for our daughter, sister, Melanie every minute, hour of the day and night.

So once again, people of Bath, search your memories. If you were anywhere near the area in which Melanie was found or walked that fateful night, and you know of anything suspicious happening, then please, I beg you, come forward and tell us.

Don't protect him because he also is in need of help.

'Jean,' I said. 'That's heartbreaking.'
She fixed me one of her little looks and said nothing.

220

I admired her eloquence. She had obviously given this so much thought. There, on a little, single sheet of lined paper from an everyday notebook were words which gave a window into the heart-wrenching loss and desperate questions Jean Road and her family had faced every day for three decades.

I just wanted to wrap Jean in my arms and tell her I was so sorry for her.

Yet again, I swore to myself that I would find Melanie's killer.

Hooky continued organising the thirtieth anniversary. He printed Jean's letter and arranged for billboards and posters. Together, our team tidied up MCIT to keep restricted and operational evidence away from journalists and TV cameras.

Karen Road had also written a note. She had spoken before, but not publicly since the *Crimewatch UK* campaign. Had that really been five years ago?

Melanie Road, my little sister, died a horrific death in 1984 and her murderer has never been caught. As much as this was 30 years ago, it's every day and it never gets easier, and I can't move on. The pain remains as strong today as it did when Melanie died.

When this nightmare started, three decades ago, I never believed I would still be appealing for information to find her murderer.

Melanie's last night was an unbelievable, horrific experience and this monster should not be able to get away with it. This man has to be found and tried and should not be walking around free. I believe someone out there knows something. If you have any information, no matter how small, please come forward, even if you think it's irrelevant.

I ask you to imagine it was your little sister and feel the way I feel, knowing there is someone who knows, but for whatever reason has decided not to help.

Finding the man who killed my sister won't bring Melanie back, but she deserves justice and I want to begin recalling happy memories of Melanie, rather than continuing this torment.

I want closure, for the pain to go and to be able to move on and for this nightmare to end.

Could Melanie have had a more eloquent family? I wondered as I read her note in MCIT.

Adrian Road was still keeping his distance. He'd told me that he didn't want to see me until I'd found Melanie's killer. Finding the killer was a vow I had promised to keep.

We hoped to persuade any accomplice by releasing to the press more details about the inquiry. We decided to give a few basic details about Ben Schwarzkopf – we would say we had a witness, he had seen the moments before and after the attack. And we described in greater detail the DNA progress we were making.

If we suggested that solving the case was inevitable, perhaps a confidant would want to help, rather than be charged with assisting an offender.

By the time the press arrived, MCIT was tidy in a way I had rarely seen. There was Ali Vowles from the BBC, who I knew; a bloke from ITV called Rob Murphy I'd never met; Siobhan Stayt from the *Bath Chronicle* and a few radio journalists, including Nigel Dando, brother of the television presenter Jill.

The questions were fine. The ITV bloke asked the obvious one – how would I find Melanie's killer when generations of other detectives had failed?

'Methodology is really important to us, we've got a terrific team here who are dedicated to that. And we've identified people who are living all around the UK and we've visited them. We've identified some people living abroad and we've identified some people who have died. And even if they're dead it doesn't mean that we can't eliminate them. There are some ways we can still do that,' I explained.

We printed Jean and Karen's letters in press releases and they appeared in both regional and national newspapers a few days before 9 June. And on the day itself I'd arranged for a small team of us to go to Bath city centre with our newly printed posters.

It was a bright Saturday. I woke early, sorted the horses and took Toby to his rugby club. Things had become uneasy at home between Matt and me. My children were still firmly *my* children. Connie had qualified recently for the Pony Club National Championships, a brilliant achievement. She had beaten thousands of competitors to get there. But on the day of the finals, I travelled up to Cheshire alone to watch her ride – Matt had refused to come. I was feeling like a single parent again.

But today was about Melanie. The city was busy. It's always tourist season in Bath and we had a spot right outside the Roman Baths: ground zero for visitors. The air was buzzing with accents from Japan, the US, Australia, China and Europe.

I had a little van with some big posters of Melanie. I had leaflets and started shoving them into the hands of people passing by. It didn't matter to me if they were a tourist, if this was their first morning in Bath, if they clearly didn't speak English – it was about getting people talking.

Bath may look like a city, but it acts like a village. And people who live there know each other well. After a little while a few locals started chatting to the detective who was dishing out leaflets.

'Oh, Melanie Road, I remember that one' or 'Melanie Road? Is that the one who went missing from Cadillacs?' or 'I thought you'd found him'.

The BBC turned up and I was interviewed. That was brilliant, because a camera crew made even more people stop, watch and start talking to me'.

'One name, that's all we want,' I said. 'It doesn't matter if it's the wrong name because we can eliminate them, we have the science. So, if you have even a second thought about someone, just let us know and we can say for sure.

'You might be thinking now, after all this time, this man said something to me and I wasn't happy about him. Just let us know.

'It's not fair, is it, that Melanie's family have lived for thirty years without justice, but her killer is roaming around. He could still be out killing now.

'Talk to your friends and family about it. Remind them, chat to your parents. Just one name …'

A lot of people just seemed bemused by what was happening. Who was this woman? What was she on about? But I had long ago abandoned any self-consciousness as I thrust leaflets out and talked to Italians and was interviewed on the radio.

Just one name …

We got four.

Each name was phoned into the Inquiry Room. Two we found quickly – there was little intelligence of any criminal history, they looked neither shady nor left us with a feeling we were on to something. Research on them was straightforward. They were swabbed within forty-eight hours. We fast-tracked the results, which returned negative.

The third name was that of a man who had died two years earlier: John Stewart. He'd been convicted for drugging his girlfriend. Rape couldn't be proven, but we assumed it had happened.

It took a week, but we got a sample from a brother in Liverpool. A fast-track test using Y-STR proved Stewart wasn't our man.

But a fourth name was called into the Inquiry Room after my day of leafleting in Bath. Again, he was dead. And his list of offences would prove to be long and complicated. But it was the intelligence, the information police had never been able to prove about him, which made us focus our attention on this one criminal.

He became June's Suspect of the Month.

His name was Alan Martin.

I looked up, seeing Gary's eyes twinkling away behind his glasses. I have only ever seen him excited like this when he's got the whiff of a lead – he's like a sniffer dog.

I looked down at the papers, then back up at him.

'It's not just the score which is interesting, it's everything about him,' he said.

'And he was in the system?'

'We've had a card for him all the time.'

'Perhaps it was worth me embarrassing myself in Bath,' I said.

I looked at the prioritisation matrix:

Name: Alan MARTIN
Criminality: deceased
Sixty-six points out of seventy-two.

Findmypast.com records showed he had died in 2002.

Gary had photocopied Martin's index card. He had been six feet tall, unemployed, had lived with his mother just a few streets away from Melanie in 1984.

Martin had been picked up by a stop check the week after Melanie's murder:

Attended Beau Nash club until 0200 9th June 1984. Could subject be the man seen talking to the deceased?

I looked through.

'Alibied by his mother,' I muttered to myself.

I turned the page: Restricted Intelligence Report. It was dated 2004, two years after his death.

Report title: Rape

It has been suggested that a male called Alan MARTIN from Bath could be a suspect for the Bath Raper. He would be in his late 30s now and is a builder-type.

Apparently, he raped a girl called Jade about 14 years ago following an all-day drinking session. He was particularly brutal with her, tearing her clothes and her underwear.

The source of this intelligence was not a registered inform-ant. Reliable, but untested.

A suspect for the Operation Eagle rape inquiry had been in the Beau Nash nightclub at the same time as Melanie Road in the hours before she was murdered.

The next page was a photocopy of a document written in old typeface:

8th September 1984
Alan MARTIN, Unemployed.

Why did it take them three months to get to him?

I am a single man living at the above address with my mother.

On Friday 8th June 1984, I went alone to the Beau Nash nightclub, arriving there at about 11.30pm. Prior to that I had been drinking in various pubs in Bath but I can't remember which ones.

I remained in the club and spoke to numerous people that I know only casually. I can't recall any names.

I have seen photographs of the deceased Melanie ROAD but I do not recall seeing anyone in the club answering her description. I left the club at about 2am when it was closing and walked straight on to the taxi rank at the Abbey.

I certainly didn't go anywhere else. I can't recall having to wait for a taxi. I know I arrived home at about 2.15am.

My mother was asleep on the settee when I arrived home and we had a brief conversation and I think I would have gone to bed at about 2.45am where I remained until about 10am the next day, Saturday 9th June.

And after that was another single page typed in the same font, with the same date. An alibi, a statement from his mother. She'd watched the late film, fallen asleep on the settee.

Alan seemed quite normal and relaxed when he arrived home but it was apparent that he had been drinking.

Mums lie for their sons, I said to myself.

Gary was back.

'What more do we know about the rape? Or his other offences?' I asked.

'They're all on the old PNC.'

'How tedious! Can you get them, Gary?'

Old Police National Computer records were archived on microfiche with the Metropolitan Police. We would have to apply to Scotland Yard.

'He's dead – does he have any male relatives?'

'I think there's a dad, who'll be ancient.'

'Well, we'd better get that microfiche before he croaks.'

Gary went to call Scotland Yard.

It had taken Gary a week, but finally he had the microfiche from Scotland Yard: Alan Martin's criminal record.

He had driven up the M4 to London personally to get it and held it up in a small cardboard box: 'This should tell us what we need to know before we swab his father.'

'Brilliant, Gary. Wonderful work. Do we have a microfiche reader anywhere?'

His face fell.

'At last, Julie, here you go.'

Gary threw Alan Martin's criminal record on my desk. A small but weighty pile of A4, printed from microfiche records:

13/5/1979: Attempted theft from a cash box in GPO telephone kiosk

5/6/1979: Attempting to steal monies from the Post Office
22/4/1984: Assaulting Nick TOLHURST
25/8/1984: Assaulting two police officers
30/11/1984: Common assault
20/08/1992: Failing to leave licensed premises
20/08/1992: Offensive conduct likely to cause distress
(Public Order Act).

Gary found Alan Martin's father Cyril in a housing association flat on the south side of Bath. He was not with Alan's mother, hadn't been in 1984. There were no photos of Alan anywhere. Gary said he just sat on a settee, watching a daytime quiz show.

Cyril had little time for his son, Gary said. A shame when he died, he said. But he always knew that son wouldn't amount to much.

I pictured the scene in my mind: Gary there, chatting, trying to find out as much as possible about this old man's son.

A son whose death had brought to an end a depressing existence of low-level crime, potentially a secret life as the Bath rapist and a high-scoring chance of being the murderer of Melanie Road.

We fast-tracked the swab and waited.

CHAPTER 27

SEPTEMBER 2014

Normally, I would have been checking my emails for the results of Martin's DNA swab, but I got sideswiped by a homicide in Somerset. A twenty-seven-year-old had spent a night drinking four bottles of wine and snorting cocaine. He claimed he couldn't remember anything, including killing his mum with a knitting needle, a knife and electric cables.

This live inquiry took precedence. All of the processes had been improved since 1984 – the scenes of crime work, the house-to-house interviews, the forensic investigations – but often the principles were the same. And in this case there was one big difference: we had a prime suspect. Detectives investigating Melanie Road's murder never had one in their sights. Now, thirty years later, Alan Martin was as good a lead as we'd ever had. I hadn't allowed myself to get too hopeful but in my quieter moments, I thought what an incredible achievement it would be if we had caught the killer of Melanie Road and the Bath rapist at the same time.

And then came the email:

This sample has been compared to the unknown DNA profile obtained in Operation Rhodium (MR8). This profile does not match therefore Alan MARTIN can be excluded as a potential contributor of the semen.

Could we not just have a bit of luck in this case? Something. Anything?

Alan Martin was also cleared of being the Bath rapist.

MCIT had a new boss, Liz Tunks. Liz was an inspiration. Years earlier, she'd been the first female senior investigating officer I had come across. Having her as a boss was going to be superb.

Soon after starting, she came to me: 'Julie, you're resilient, aren't you?'

'Yes, Liz?'

'We'd like to try something new. You see, we're good at holding informal reviews of our big cases but we don't really do proper peer reviews. We'd like you to test that.'

'Great.'

'On Operation Rhodium. Would you like that?'

Of course I'd like my work pulled to bits and picked over by a bunch of DCIs.

'Yes, Liz.'

I looked through the window of the big conference room at Kenneth Steele House as the detectives arrived. I'd been peer-reviewed in the past and it had been vile. I had reviewed other cases and knew that most of the time the lead detectives had done a good job, but something somewhere had just been missing: an inquiry had a blind spot.

Liz Tunks came in, bringing with her the senior investigating officers from the three forces: Avon and Somerset, Gloucestershire and Wiltshire.

Fifteen senior detectives looking at my work.

I read through my notes and looked up, smiling at the detectives as they sat down.

I started with a little presentation.

'Oh, hi Duncan.'

'Sorry.' Duncan Goodwin, the forensic coordinator, squeezed into the room late and found a place to sit.

I told them everything we had done: the Review Team work, Ben Schwarzkopf's arrival, getting everything on the system, the familial work in 2011, the Suspect of the Month, the thirtieth anniversary, all the swabs, all the false leads. It felt as much a tale of woe as a presentation about a crime.

Some of the detectives were smiling gently at me as I spoke. Was that pity? I finished and noticed a sharp intake of breath from the room.

There was a silence. I knew from experience that the tone of the first few questions would set the pattern for the ones to follow.

'What about mental health hospitals in 1984? What about patients from there?'

'Yes, we've checked as far as we can. There've been about three NHS reforms since then and all the trusts and organisations have changed. We've spent many months looking at this; we kept hitting brick walls.'

'Who died in 1984? Have you looked at sudden deaths? Suicides? It sounds as if this person just suddenly stopped living. Just disappeared.'

'Yes we have, we have been through all the coronial files for 1984 which still exist. There aren't many. The storage facilities have changed many times over the decades and every time they move things seem to get lost. And lots of the paperwork is destroyed after seven years. We've looked at newspaper cuttings, police records, the Police National Computer, but these records simply don't exist in an accessible place.'

'What about the boyfriend? How sure are you that he wasn't the killer?'

'He was eliminated by DNA in a previous review. All his friends were too.'

'Are you sure about that?'

It carried on: what evidence was there really that the prioritisation matrix was accurate? Contact the DNA Strategy Board. Have you looked at a voters' list from 1984? You could create a paper-based house-to-house inquiry with wider parameters than the 1984 investigation. How many people were refusing to be swabbed?

'We have ten refusals at the moment. One's really good, I call him the Fake Doctor …'

'Can you get swabs from their relatives instead? Or you could mount a covert operation on them, try to get a sample of their DNA …'

More questions and suggestions: What about abroad? These Saudis? Have you looked at a list of students from Bath University and Bath College who were in the city in '84? How many nominals are listed as 'Unable to locate'? You could have an intelligence officer just dedicated to these.

'I think there are just sixty of our nominals who we've tried to find and can't.'

'I really think you should go back to the Bath coronial files and look again at suicides from 1984.'

'What about other murders? Shelley Morgan. Two women sexually assaulted, stabbed and murdered in two days, ten miles apart, have you looked at similarities?'

'Yes, in a painstaking way.'

'What about your forensic strategy?'

'Yes,' I replied.

'There are other DNA sources apart from the National DNA Database, can you compare your scene-mark with those? Green Blood? It's rare in this country, but in other societies, is it three per cent of the population or more? If it's more common in other communities, Romany, Irish, for example, should you focus your attention there? The Republic of Ireland has only just set up its National DNA Database.'

I was writing down these ideas in my blue detective's book.

'What about another familial DNA run?'

'Yes, I'd love to do that, but it's expensive.'

Sean Memory was asking the question. He was a Wiltshire DCI, a cold case officer who would later investigate sexual abuse claims against the former Prime Minister Sir Edward Heath and would, the following year, secure a murder conviction against the killer cabbie Christopher Halliwell.

'I had a cold case rape,' he said. 'I did a familial run four years ago and there was nothing on the National DNA Database. But I did one again last year and we got a hit. When was your last run?'

'Two thousand and eleven.'

'There'll be a million more names on the database since then.'

'But there's the cost,' I said, looking at Duncan Goodwin.

'Duncan,' said Liz Tunks, 'how much will it be?'

'Well, the last run was £20,000; we simply don't have that budget. We need to balance with ...'

'Live cases, yes, I know,' said Liz. 'Could you just find today's cost?'

'Of course, Liz.'

'What has been your budget?'

'Very little in terms of personnel,' I said. 'Just Gary Mason; most of the work is done by MCIT detectives around live cases. The biggest cost is the swabbing.'

I looked at my files.

'We've spent, I think, about £100,000 on swabbing in the last few years. We've eliminated hundreds of people.'

'I really think you should look at the coroner's archive from Bath in 1984 ...' the DCI was still banging on about that.

I was reminded of all the hours Gary and I had spent in a coroner's archive in Bristol, looking for every file we could find. We had exhausted this line of inquiry and this detective just seemed to like the sound of his own voice.

I wrote up a set of actions. We would look again at Melanie's then boyfriend; he was now living in the USA. We would try again to find Bath coronial files from 1984. Any sudden deaths or suicides. Keep that bloody DCI happy. I would check our sample against other DNA databases. I'd used the Missing Person's Bureau Database on Operation Santos – the human tissue inquiry in 2011.

This was separate from the National DNA Database. If a family member goes missing, families can have their DNA loaded on their system. And if the worst happens and a body is recovered, DNA from that can be compared with the database record.

I wrote asking if we could try to match our Melanie Road scene-mark. They answered politely, but firmly: no. They were set up to solve missing persons inquiries, not to detect crimes.

It was late summer 2014 and I was holding an informal team meeting. We were talking through our live cases and then we turned to Operation Rhodium.

'Oh, I got that costing for the familial run, Julie,' said Duncan.

'Okay?'

'Yes. It's about £3,000.'

'Three grand?! We've just spent a hundred grand on swabbing because it's the cheaper option and now you're saying it's £3,000?'

'Well, you know the costing now,' Duncan said back at me.

'Okay, great. What do we need to do?'

The forms were as excruciating as last time. Reams of papers, writing down the circumstances of the case as I had done thousands of times before. I sent them to Liz Tunks for a superintendent's consent.

The next step was a Chief Officer Review. Louisa Rolfe and I had been on that fast-track accelerated development course twenty-six years before. She had risen brilliantly through the ranks and was now assistant chief constable.

My career had stalled before the sudden, late spurt over the past few years.

'Julie, you've done this once before, why do you think it's going to work this time? What's it going to cost? Is it a good investment for the force?'

But Louisa signed the form and it was sent to the College of Policing for a panel discussion and another level of approval.

I tried the National Missing Person's Bureau again. I said I understood that they were not a crime fighting organisation, 'but what about the human rights of our victim? What about the safety of the public and duty of care? What's the process for appealing your decision?' It was a bit of a rant. The bureau wrote back: there was no process for appealing its decision and it would not assist us with our inquiries.

The MCIT was busy. The swabbing continued, but became more sporadic as a series of homicides came in.

On Christmas Day 2014, I was the duty senior investigating officer. Connie, Toby and I went out riding with the horses, a family tradition.

And then came the call: a murder. A body had been found in Bath.

Matt was looking at me when the phone rang and my stomach turned.

'Okay, yes, I'll be there shortly,' I said before hanging up on the DS.

'It's Christmas Day,' said Matt.

'I know, and I'm the on-call grown-up.'

'But it's Christmas Day,' he protested.

'Look, I'll go in, I'll do everything that's possible today then I'll be back, hopefully. I've bought all the presents, I've got all the food. Everything's sorted. Just relax and enjoy the day.'

He shrugged.

There was only so much I could do on Christmas Day. We secured the scene, started the actions. A senseless case of a homeless man found with fatal head injuries near the railway station.

I had been in touch with the victim's home police force up north. I thought of his family, sitting down to Christmas dinner, remembering loved ones from afar. I thought of the officer who would have to knock at their door.

When I returned home, the house was dark and cold. No smell of Christmas dinner and as little sense of festive cheer.

My children were on their screens. Matt was on the settee. The oven wasn't even on and the children were complaining they were hungry.

I set about cooking dinner and we were just sitting down to eat when my dad arrived with my stepmum. He had a pile of presents and a bottle of something. But even their cheery appearance couldn't lighten the mood.

'You only eating now?'

'Dad, I've been called out.'

'On Christmas Day?'

'Murder doesn't take public holidays, Dad.'

My phone rang, its cheery tone in stark contrast to the mood. It was a forensics officer wanting to talk about strategies. We spoke briefly and efficiently and I went back to join the others.

'Can you believe she's been called out on Christmas Day?' Dad asked Matt, politely.

He didn't reply.

My phone went again: it was the superintendent. I briefed her, saying everything was under control. That was true of the murder inquiry, but not accurate when it came to the mood in my house.

My dad left. Then it exploded. Matt made accusations about work being more important than home. This made me feel terrible as my family was my priority, but like him I had a challenging job. Where was the empathy? I felt embarrassed and torn, but also that it had now crossed the line. It was Christmas and this argument should not have ruined it.

I rounded up the children, we took our selection boxes and the Monopoly board game, went into a bedroom and shut the door.

CHAPTER 28

'You've been living like this for how long?'

'Five years,' I replied.

My village GP looked at me. I couldn't quite read his expression. Disbelief? Sympathy?

'And you're in pain how often?'

'Most of the time. Sometimes it's okay, sometimes I want to kill someone. Sometimes I don't want to get out of bed.'

'And when it's like that, do you get out of bed?'

'I have a demanding, full-time job, horses which need caring for and three teenage children,' was what I didn't say.

'I'm up at five thirty most days,' I said.

'Do you ever take a break?'

I didn't answer.

The agony in my abdomen had become excruciating. Five years earlier, I had been diagnosed with fibroids. And I hadn't been back to the doctor since.

'Any other symptoms?'

'Like heavy periods? Yes, can happen at any time. I spend a lot of time out and about and that's a constant worry. If anything happens it's embarrassing, hideous really. I never wear light colours, always dark skirts.

'I work in a job dominated by men. The culture's not really to think about comfort breaks.

'Severe pain, awful cramps. I never sleep.'

My GP looked back at me.

'Okay, Mrs Mackay, I think you do need to see a specialist about this. Five years?'

'Five years.'

Matt and I were living in a strange existence now. Together in name, but our bonds seemed to be breaking. We were arguing less, a tranquillity had descended on the house. Not an easy one, but at least there was a sense of calm. And that was just as well, because the first few weeks of 2015 did little for my health or the inquiry into the murder of Melanie Road.

It was relentless.

On 19 February, a teenage girl called Becky Watts had vanished from her house in Bristol. She had last been seen by her stepmother Anjie and was reported missing the following day. Most of MCIT was focused on finding Becky. The investigation was made trickier because of the fractious family set-up. Becky had been living with her father and Anjie. There was a stepbrother, Nathan. Becky's birth mother was difficult to deal with, there was no sign of this poor schoolgirl anywhere and the whole of Bristol wanted to be involved in the search.

A few days later, in Somerset, a man murdered his estranged wife in front of their children.

Lisa Winn had contacted Avon and Somerset Police many times over the years, complaining about her husband,

Neil. He stabbed Lisa multiple times, leaving her body in the garden. The few resources left were sent to Somerset to deal with that inquiry.

I was finishing a course at HQ when I had a call: 'Julie, another murder. Can you look after the surveillance?'

I had been made the officer in charge of the force's covert operations.

A man had been found dead in the town of Yate, near Bristol. Intelligence suggested he was part of a County Lines drugs gang from London. Gangs from the capital had thought selling drugs in the provinces an easy touch. And they brought violence with them. Teams were monitoring a phone which we assumed was being carried by the Yate man's murderer.

'Julie, we need you in the Green Room.'

'Okay, just coming …'

My phone rang with its cheerful tone: Mrs Miller, Toby's teacher.

I groaned.

'Hello, Mrs Miller, is everything okay?'

'Hello, Mrs Mackay, we just have a little issue with Toby.'

'Really? What's that?'

'Well, it's actually a big enough issue that he needs to be away from school again. Can you pick him up?'

'Does he have his phone with him?'

'I think so.'

'Leave it with me.'

I dialled Toby's number. It went straight to voicemail.

'Toby …'

I called Callum.

'Callum?'

CHAPTER 28

'Mum?'

'Do you have your motorbike?'

'Yeah.'

'Toby's going to be suspended again. Can you go to school and get him? Have you got a spare helmet?'

'Yeah.'

'*Now*. Can you go now?'

'Mum, you told me not to use the bike.'

'Use the bike today.'

I tried Toby. This time the call connected.

'Mum, the teachers just don't understand …'

'I know they don't get it but it's best that you just come home, Callum will pick you up.'

'But, Mum …'

'Say sorry. Callum's coming to get you. I've got this murder to deal with and I'll be back home.'

I hung up and dialled his teacher.

'Mrs Miller?'

'Mrs Mackay.'

'Callum's on his way. Toby's very sorry. I've just got a little thing at work and I'll come into school as soon as I can to talk about his behaviour.'

That night, I got home after 1 a.m. I was up at 5 to tend the horses and make packed lunches, then drove to Bristol and the Green Room before sunrise. This pattern continued for the next four days.

I didn't blame Toby one bit for his outburst. His home life was a mess, living in another man's home with a teenage boy who was very nice, but someone he didn't get on with. He was right: his teachers didn't get him, they didn't understand.

He was – and is – a clever, caring boy who needed extra support, not to be told he was awful all the time. His dad was barely around and his one parent had a full-time demanding job which could mean that she was away for four days at a time. And he was fifteen years old.

Also, in the back of my mind, something was whirring. What had happened to that familial DNA run for Operation Rhodium? I'd applied late last year, months before. It had gone to the College of Policing and I'd heard nothing.

The four days ended in an exhausted chase, our surveillance teams catching two men and charging them with murder.

I felt like a failure at work. I felt like a failure at home. A failure as a mother, as a partner.

I had ended my first marriage and I didn't want my next relationship to disintegrate. And I had no way out. I was financially committed. We had a big mortgage. I had nowhere to go.

Every day I would drive into work, thinking of the mess my personal life was in. I would get out of my car, fix a smile and be the quick-talking, fun, joking, demanding, professional 'Julie Mac' for the day. Then I would get into my car and wonder what I would come home to. What was it now? A child on drugs? A furious argument with Matt? It seemed that the only bit of stability in my life was the inquiry into Melanie Road's death. That conveyor belt of progress and setback. The calm permanence of Jean Road.

But was I failing her too?

'Emma, you know I submitted that application for a familial DNA run? Any idea where we are with that?'

There was a worrying silence.

'I don't know, Julie. I'll look.'

DS Emma Spooner from the College of Policing rang off and called back later: 'Terribly sorry, Julie. We don't seem to have the papers anywhere.'

'Don't worry, I have a copy,' I said, looking at my laptop, finding the application and resending it as we were on the phone.

'Thanks, Julie. I'll let you know if you get it.'

I put my phone down.

Nearly thwarted, but not quite.

'I know there's no chance in June. Half the force is knee-deep in mud. Could we do something after the Glastonbury Festival? In July? If I get the permissions?'

I was on the phone to the head of Avon and Somerset's Surveillance Unit. The Fake Doctor was just one of the names in our system who refused to be swabbed – there were nine others. I had told one of the Wallis brothers we would 'hunt him down like a long dog' and that was a speech I'd repeated to many reluctant suspects, with varying levels of success.

If you watch police shows on TV and films, you might think you can just leap out of police HQ and start following suspects undercover.

If only.

There's the Regulation of Investigatory Powers Act 2000. RIPA. It's a nightmare – the gatekeepers rarely let anything through. There are forms, more forms, returned forms, revised forms and, if you're lucky, approved forms. Even if it's an urgent job. An 'i' undotted or a 't' uncrossed would see the form sent back with a request to fill it in again. And properly, this time.

Why did we want RIPA authority? It's all about 'reasonable necessity': is our request to follow someone to covertly get their DNA reasonable? Is it really necessary? Which of their human rights would we be breaching? Article eight, the suspect's right to a private life under the Human Rights Act, for sure. But what about Melanie Road's right to life? That was covered by article two. Far more important, in my opinion.

I had to list what we had done to engage with the Fake Doctor and others: why was there no other means possible? What did I propose to do? When would I start the surveillance and when would I stop it? If we're following him to a coffee shop, what if he's with someone else? How would our operation impact them? How would I ensure that we would only take his DNA?

I'd been an undercover officer and understood the demands and challenges of the job: long hours and short notice. Now I was the Undercover SIO for MCIT. I knew all about the rules, regulations and RIPA headaches.

I'm a believer that if something's not working, you should try something new. Shake the tree. It might not be the right thing to do, but sometimes doing the wrong thing can make the right thing happen later, and this can be better than continuing with a failing status quo.

'We've never really done covert on a cold case before. I guess it's no different to a live inquiry?' asked the Head of Surveillance.

'Just the same,' I said. 'Except the suspects are thirty years older than when the crime happened. They can't run as fast as they used to, easier for you to follow.'

Thirty surveillance officers were dedicated just to Operation Rhodium. I was excited – this was the first time since 1984 there had been any covert ops on the Melanie Road case.

'I'll give you fourteen days,' said the Head of Surveillance.

I made sure Dr Brent Bowen, the Fake Doctor, was at the top of the hit list.

I had a few qualms about the operation: it was expensive, it meant the surveillance team being out-of-force for days. What if they were needed to deal with Bristol's never-ending gun problems?

I had to jump through loads of hoops and disclose to each force whose area we would be operating in. We would be using intrusive methods which had to be signed off by each chief constable.

'Julie, this is the biggest undercover swabbing job we've ever done. Who's going to pay for it? Where's your funding?'

I didn't need to look at a spreadsheet to know I'd blown my minuscule £10,000 investigation budget months ago: the inquiry was in the red.

This was at least £30,000 worth of work.

This led to another protracted series of conversations: Liz Tunks, back to the surveillance teams, the Head of CID, the Assistant Chief Constable chairing covert tasking.

'Julie, is this really the only way of getting these swabs?'

'Yes. The Fake Doctor's been refusing for years.'

'Julie, will you be on call 24/7 for the 2 weeks to answer our questions?'

'Yes.'

So, we were set. A groundbreaking surveillance operation was planned by Avon and Somerset Police. We'd have to wait for the Glastonbury Festival to finish, give the undercover ops a week to shower themselves down and deal with anything in-force, then they were mine.

Dr Brent Bowen, the wide-boy Fake Doctor from Essex, was in my sights.

CHAPTER 29

MAY 2015

MCIT was buzzing. Although nearly three months had passed since the week of the three murders, detectives were faced with the aftermath.

The Becky Watts inquiry was in full swing. The poor teenager had been found dismembered in a shed, her stepbrother, Nathan Matthews, had been charged with her murder and his girlfriend, Shauna Hoare, had been charged with perverting the course of justice. But we were looking at what evidence there was to upgrade that to murder.

Just to the left of the buzz of the Becky Watts investigation was the quiet solitude of the Operation Rhodium inquiry. Four desks. On the wall was the poster of Melanie, Ben's drawing, the Suspect of the Month and the DNA chart.

'Hang on, Gary,' I said, looking at my inbox. 'The familial list's back.'

I forwarded it to him along with the passwords.

'It's only taken six months,' he grumbled under his breath.

He logged on and downloaded the list.

'We have a new Screamer,' he said gently.

'What?'

Gary didn't smile, he just gave me a quiet, knowing look. 'We have a new Screamer,' he repeated.

He pointed at the chart on his screen.

Trish Blackmore, the woman whose DNA was 44,000 times more likely to be related to the offender than anyone else, was at number two.

'Are there likelihood ratios? I can't see any.'

'Not on this list.'

I looked above and saw again the new name at the top. 'Clare Hampton,' it read.

'Well, she's got to be more than 44,000 times more likely than Joe Public,' said Gary.

'Julie, can you come and check this?' It was a detective inspector from the Becky Watts inquiry.

I was running the surveillance in the prison where Nathan Matthews was in custody. We wanted to see if he said anything to anyone about a taser we'd found and believed he'd used to incapacitate Becky, or about his clean-up job in the bathroom after he killed her.

'Gary, did you know you can use cat litter to get rid of the smell of a body?'

He shook his head, adding, 'Who the hell thinks of these things? Matthews must have been watching too many crime documentaries.'

I left to deal with my RIPA forms and surveillance crews as Gary stayed to research the new Screamer.

It was a few hours later when I passed Gary in MCIT. His eyes were sparkling.

'Julie, I've just been looking at the files for Clare Hampton. She lives in Bath; she was arrested in Bath in November.'

'What for?'

'Low-level. A row with her boyfriend. She broke his necklace. Neighbours heard shouting and called the police and it was listed as a domestic violence case. That's why she was swabbed, even though she was only cautioned.'

'Have you got a phone number for her?'

'Just found one, I'll call her in a minute.'

'Julie …' a shout from the other end of the room.

'Let me know how you get on.'

Another two hours passed, writing up RIPA forms and setting surveillance strategy before I saw Gary again.

'You spoken to her?'

'Yes, she's got a dad. Christopher Hampton, lives in Bristol. He's sixty-three. Would have been thirty-two in June '84. Painter and decorator. Have done a check on him.'

'Is he in the system?'

'No, I don't think so. No criminal record. No cautions. Nothing.'

'Julie, can you please get back here?' It was another DI shouting about a prison visit to Nathan Matthews.

'Let me know how it goes.'

I slipped away from the Becky Watts inquiry towards the end of the day to catch up with Gary.

'I've arranged to see him,' said Gary.

'He's consenting? Well done.'

'He can do Friday, but I've got the grandkids so I'm swabbing him on Monday.'

'Gary, he's our new fucking Screamer.'

'It's my grandchildren, Julie.'

'Where are you meeting him?'

'He's decorating a primary school in South Bristol. I'll see him before work.'

'Well done.'

'But Julie, there's another.'

'What?'

'Number four on the list. He's called Gareth Jenkins-West, he's from Cardiff. I called him too.'

'Okay?'

'I told him what it was all about and he said he had a brother, Tommy. Said he hadn't seen Tommy in thirty years.

'Tommy left Wales in a hurry around 1984. Went to Scotland. But before that he'd worked around here. Gareth said the rumour was Tommy had murdered someone then vanished.'

'No fucking way.'

'So I'm swabbing Gareth in the afternoon.'

'Can't we get his brother?'

'He's up in Scotland. It's all so complicated up there, isn't it? Procurator fiscals and the long drive. I can get to the brother in an hour and swab him. Use Y-STR to eliminate or see if we need to go to Scotland for a follow-up.'

'Cardiff? In an hour? With your driving?'

Tommy Jenkins-West had a criminal record. Mostly theft, no violence. But that rumour of murder from his brother and that familial DNA link was exhilarating.

Monday came. Gary was in the office early, but I was in even earlier.

He shuffled over to his desk, grabbed a couple of swabbing kits and carried on looking up everything he could about Christopher Hampton.

'What do you think, Gary? It really could be one of these.'

'How many times have we been here before? We don't even know the likelihood ratios of Hampton or Tommy Jenkins-West.'

'Let me know how they go. As soon as you've swabbed them, call me and tell me what they were like.'

Gary nodded and headed out. He returned about two hours later, carrying a completed swab and a grin I couldn't quite decipher.

'Gary, you said you would call.'

'Well, it's only round the corner from the school. I thought I'd come back in before going to Cardiff.'

'What was he like?'

'Hampton? Nothing. He was like nothing.'

'Was he nervous? Tell me everything.'

'No more than anyone else. I did the usual thing – pulled up, called him on his phone. He came over and sat in the passenger seat of my car. I explained the case, said he was one of many thousands of swabs we were doing. I said he would be eliminated, unless he was the murderer, and if he was the murderer, would he like to tell me? Save me from swabbing him.'

'Funny.'

'Yes, it's a new line I'm trying out.'

'He signed the consent forms, I took two swabs, we shook hands. I asked him if he wanted to be told the result, he said he did, and off he went.'

'And you have the Cardiff bloke this afternoon, Jenkins-West? Have you found out anything more about his brother in Scotland?'

'No more than we knew.'

'This time, call me when you've swabbed him.'

Gary headed out.

The familial list had lots of new names in the top thirty.

I had my two weeks of covert operations booked for ten men refusing to comply. We had nearly exhausted all the men in the system who scored above fifty on the prioritisation matrix. I had also considered reviewing the house-to-house files, adding thousands more names to our system. That was a huge piece of work. We were convinced that Melanie's killer had lived in Bath at the time. Perhaps he was lurking somewhere on a house-to-house form ready to be found, but that would take months to do.

It was late in the day when Gary called to say that Gareth Jenkins-West was a very nice man, but that, of course, didn't mean his brother wasn't a murderer.

'What did he say about Tommy?'

'Just repeated the story. Tommy moved away from Wales years ago. Rumour always was he'd killed someone. He hasn't seen Tommy in thirty years, he doesn't even have a photo of him.'

My heart skipped a beat. There was something about this new, strange name in Scotland which I liked.

I liked it a lot.

Gary had told Christopher Hampton and Gareth Jenkins-West that they would know the results in about eight weeks. We had twenty swabs ready to be processed by the lab and we added these two to the batch and sent them off.

Eight weeks to wait.

And the other inquiries continued. Surveillance operations in prisons, building a prosecution against the County Lines murderers who had left a man dead in Yate.

Work was busy.

The man who had stabbed his mother with a knitting needle as she slept was appearing at Exeter Crown Court. He was given a life prison sentence in June 2015. After the hearing, I was interviewed on television and spoke about the horror and pointlessness of the attack.

I'd booked a week's leave and a few days away with Matt in Marrakesh. Morocco was beautiful. Just the hit of the dry heat and the dusty smell, the chatter and chants in a different language were a joy to experience and a welcome distraction from the uneasy mood between Matt and me.

I had a lot on my mind. The pain in my abdomen – the gaps between long days of cramps and agony were becoming shorter, the feeling of agony more persistent. I had somehow managed to get an appointment on the NHS at the private Bath Clinic to look again at my fibroids.

Connie was finishing her GCSEs and had mentioned something about moving abroad to train with a dressage champion. And there was Matt. We were connected financially in a way we were no longer emotionally. What was I doing?

Work was exciting, but I wanted to start moving up the ranks further. I had been in the police for twenty-seven years now. I had three years left of my career. Could I make detective chief inspector? That would involve more work, more boards, more responsibilities. And, of course, there was Operation Rhodium. There was Jean. And there was Melanie.

Would I ever find her killer?

CHAPTER 30

2 JULY 2015

'I fucking hate this house!'

The scream came from Callum's room, as did the waft of weed smoke under the door.

When Matt and I had got back from Marrakesh the day before, the children were on edge. But now it was just Callum and me in the house and he was fuming.

'Why the fuck do we have to live here? It's your fault, Mum. It's all your fault.'

There was a silence – a silence that often preceded an explosion.

Then it happened.

A crash, glass smashing, a crunch, splitting wood. Something heavy thrown on the floor.

'I fucking HATE this house!'

Callum's door burst open. He looked like he'd been taking something and he wasn't in any mood for negotiation.

'And I hate you,' he pointed at me.

Callum slammed the front door and I went into his room.

A wardrobe door was in pieces, hanging off its hinges, his clothes inside were falling out and over the splintered wood. What had been a full-length mirror was now shards of glass scattered on the carpet. Bedclothes were ripped and thrown over the bed and a poster was hanging from the wall.

Marrakesh already seemed a million miles away.

What are we doing? I thought to myself.

What more could I do? Where could I turn? I felt that everyone had backed me into a corner and no one, not a single person in my life, was helping themselves or helping me. I felt so sad. I – we – had been going around in circles for years and could find no way out of this.

My phone rang: it was a withheld number. It might be work, but I just couldn't face another question about surveillance operations. I was on annual leave and my family was breaking apart in front of my eyes.

I went to the kitchen, got a bag and a dustpan and brush and started sweeping up.

I cut myself on one of the splinters as I picked the mirror up. I swore; I felt like crying. The glass made a rattling sound as I brushed it from the carpet into the dustpan.

I started collecting the broken parts of the louvred wardrobe door.

The phone rang again: it was Gary.

I caught sight of myself in part of the mirror which was hanging off the wall.

'Hi Gary, you've not got another fixed penalty notice, have you?' I had no idea how I managed to make my voice sound normal.

'Julie, we've been trying to get hold of you.'

'I saw a withheld number, I thought it was the bank. Why didn't you use your phone?'

'I didn't want to use my minutes.'

'Christ, Gary! Look, I'm on annual leave. Is it a bus lane ticket?'

'Julie, we've got a hit.'

'On what?' I was looking at the smashed glass and broken wood and wondered how he knew about Callum's outburst.

'On Rhodium.'

Then it clicked.

'Jesus fuck! On Rhodium?'

My voice was suddenly not sounding normal.

'Who is it?'

Gary would have said it instantly. He's not one for dramatic pauses and the silence between my question and his response would have been momentary. But it felt like time slowed, it seemed like forever.

'Hampton.'

'Hampton? The Screamer?'

'Yes.'

'Oh my fucking God! After all that familial work, they were right in the end.'

I breathed out.

'Christopher Hampton,' Gary repeated. 'Born in Bath, lived in Bath. We've done it, Julie.'

It was him. The person we had been hunting for thirty-one years. This insignificant man Gary had swabbed weeks before, a man at the top of a list sent by scientists, was Melanie's murderer.

I couldn't believe what Gary was saying. His words made sense, but somehow they didn't: we had done it.

'How did you hear?'

'Got an email from the lab this morning.'

'What's happening?

'Liz Tunks has organised the teams. We're arresting him tonight. He's still at work, painting that school, but we'll pick him up at home. We've got a wraparound team heading there now.'

'You got live ANPR (automatic number plate recognition) on him?'

'Yes, Liz is doing all of that, but I thought you'd want to know.'

'I'm coming in, tell Liz I'll be in within the hour. Fuck, Gary, we've done it!'

He hung up.

I realised I was sitting on my son's floor, shattered glass around my feet, broken wood to my side. An image came into my mind: the picture of Melanie Road which had been on the inside of my detectives' book, the same photo hanging on the wall of the Inquiry Room. A seventeen-year-old schoolgirl who had left her parents' home thirty-one years ago, gone out one night and never returned.

It had taken thirty-one years. Thirty-one years for us to find out who had taken the life of this vibrant, clever, funny, talented teenager.

I spoke to that image in my mind: *We've done it for you, Melanie, we've done it for you.*

This time, we've done it for you.

I knew I'd find him. I don't know why I was so sure, but I knew I'd find him.

Christopher Hampton.

My brain was whirring. Did I dare believe that we had found Melanie's killer? Gary was saying we had. We had done it. It was real. For years I had believed that this moment would happen, but I hadn't quite prepared myself for when it did.

I had been convinced I would find Melanie's killer. Convinced. But now I was hearing his name, now I had confirmation, it was taking a little while to work through my disbelief. But the hard-wiring of the detective in me was starting to crank into action.

What do we know about this man?

The drive from home to the Bristol Inquiry Room took forty minutes. I may not have been paying much attention to the speed limit. I don't know why it felt appropriate, but I put on the Fleetwood Mac album *Rumours* and was singing along as I played it at top volume.

I'd called Matt to say we'd got a hit. He'd congratulated me, but I felt that behind the 'well done' was a question about why I was going in to work while on annual leave.

'This is just something I've been working on for a little while,' I'd said as politely as I could.

I'd tried to call my children, leaving them voicemails that I'd left supper in the fridge.

And as I drove, I was thinking about what we needed to do: arrest teams, intelligence, putting Hampton in Bath in 1984, his family, evidence, linking him to other killings, Jean,

Karen and Adrian Road. We needed to make sure nothing leaked to the media. Nothing before an arrest, before family liaison officers had spoken to the Road family.

I got to the office and saw a line of unmarked police cars pulling out from Kenneth Steele House. Jon Hook was in one. We got out at the same time and hugged each other.

'We did it, boss! You coming to arrest him?'

I looked at the line of police cars filled with officers ready to go to Hampton's home, then I looked up at the windows of the Inquiry Room.

'No, I'll have too much to do in there. Let me know when you've got him.'

Hooky smiled, got in the car and I watched the convoy disappear.

I opened the door of the Briefing Room and caught a glimpse of the team before I started shouting. About sixty officers were assembling, getting ready for Liz Tunks to speak. I noticed heads turn towards me and then I heard the cheer.

'You've done it!' I found myself shouting. 'You've bloody done it!'

The commotion stopped and Liz started the briefing.

Cell-site analysis showed that Hampton's phone was near the school he was decorating. And the ANPR analyst had plotted his car's movements that morning. His car, like his phone, was near the school. A further analysis of ANPR records showed his route and timings in recent days. We knew which way he was likely to drive home and when.

And if he followed the pattern of the last few days, he would start moving in the next few minutes.

But who was at home? Until this morning, he had been just a name on a list. We had stopped making detailed biographies of suspects. Now we had the hit, we were playing catch-up.

Liz said there were a few details that Gary had already discovered. Hampton was sixty-three, lived in East Bristol with his second wife, Julie, and their daughter and his stepson.

We had no idea who was in the house. Would it be just Hampton when we arrested him? Would we have an audience of his family members?

In between wife number one and Julie had been a girlfriend. That had been in 1984, when he was living in Bath. We had two addresses for him, first in Broad Street then in Great Bedford Street. Both were near the end of the Green Blood Trail.

Christopher Hampton had no criminal record. He had lived an apparently law-abiding life since he'd raped and murdered Melanie Road.

'Are you sure about arresting now?' This was a question from a detective in the briefing. 'If we wait till tomorrow morning, we'll have time on our side, we'll be working daylight hours, easier for interviews, easier for getting results back from the lab. At the moment, we'll be arresting him at five in the evening, that means we'll waste the first fifteen hours of custody time. You know, with his eight-hour sleep break and waiting around.'

It was something which had flashed through my mind but I'd discounted it.

'No,' said Liz. And I gave an inward sigh of relief. 'He knows he's given us a positive match. He's expecting us to come back in eight weeks' time, but the lab's been more efficient than we thought. We got the hit in five weeks. We don't want him hurting himself so we lose a confession, we don't want him harming anyone else. And there's a chance he might try to leave the country. No, we go now and deal with it.'

Well done, Liz.

'Come on, let's bring him in.'

I started mentally drawing up a list of things we would need to do after the arrest: seize his phone and computer, search his house, interview his current wife, ex-wife and girlfriend from 1984. What had been his motive? What actually happened that night? Were there any friends? What about other crimes? Could this quiet, grey man be not just the killer of Melanie Road, but other victims too? Shelley Morgan? Melanie Hall? Could he be the Bath rapist?

Other actions: take samples for an evidential DNA swab. At the moment, the swab we had taken from Hampton was only what's known as an intelligence swab. This meant it was good enough to be used for investigative purposes to try to find a match, but wouldn't cut it in a court of law. We would need to get a second mouth-swab and make sure this DNA confirmed the match found in semen from the murder scene.

In a few hours, Jean Road would at last know who had murdered her daughter. I wanted to ring her, I wanted to see her. I wanted to tell her myself, but there was too much to do.

'Is there a visual live feed?' I asked.

'No, just the radio,' said Liz.

Meader had a radio on and was monitoring the team as they deployed.

'Can you turn that up?' I shouted.

'It's as loud as it will go …'

'Ssshhhhhh, everyone,' I ordered.

The room fell silent.

'What's happening?'

'It's quiet at the moment. They're just waiting,' said Meader.

A metallic voice in the earpiece: 'Front of the house covered.'

My heart skipped a beat.

The metallic voice through the radio of the arrest commander: 'Rear of the house covered. We're just in place until subject returns home, keeping our distance.'

'Subject moving,' it was an ANPR analyst. Hampton's car was triggering the automatic number plate recognition cameras as he took what looked like his normal route home.

'Should be home in seven minutes.'

'Team on the outer cordon should pick him up shortly.'

'Stand by, stand by, stand by … Car one has a visual, single occupant, wait for ID …'

Silence on the radio.

'I can confirm the sole occupant is Hampton and is heading towards home address, all units await an update.'

I wondered what the scene looked like. He lived on a main road, a street I knew well. A busy road, but still difficult to secrete a team of twelve arresting officers.

I hope Hampton doesn't see them and run, I thought.

Were the windows of his house open? Were the lights on? Was his wife there? Would we have to arrest him in front of her or their daughter? Or his stepson?

I looked at Gary, who remained impassive, looking at his computer screen, finding whatever intelligence he could to help the interview teams. Where had Hampton been on 9 June 1984? If he could prove he was elsewhere, our whole case would be blown.

'Subject with you in a few seconds, he's just travelling into Staplehill Road now.'

'We've got a visual on him,' the radio voice.

'Subject's parking his car. He's just getting out. He's walking to the front door of his house … and he's in … confirming he is inside the address.'

I breathed in.

Seconds to go. Just seconds … and this is it.

'We're going to knock on the door now, we're going in.'

Then silence.

CHAPTER 31

2 JULY 2015

The silence on the radio continued.

I looked across at Gary. He was tapping away at his computer keyboard, looking at the monitor, making notes on a pad.

I glanced at Liz, also on the radio, pacing the floor.

I had started working away on my policy book, setting the direction for the inquiry: search teams, forensic recovery from Hampton at the police station, management of him, organising the interview teams, making a list of witnesses we needed to speak with that night, organising the family liaison teams for Jean, Adrian and Karen Road, as well as Julie Hampton and her son and daughter.

Most of the team were not on radios and a hush remained in the large open-plan office. There was a gentle tapping of keyboards, a low murmur of quiet conversation, even people's ringtones seemed to have quietened somehow.

I looked again at the wall: pinned up were the image of Melanie, Ben Schwarzkopf's drawing of the killer, the murderer's DNA chart, the Suspect of the Month. I couldn't even remember the name of the latest one.

Irrelevant now.

I looked at the radio, checking it was still turned on.

How long did it take to make an arrest these days?

There was a brief ping of static, then came the metallic words: 'Confirm: one in custody.'

I hadn't realised I'd been holding my breath, but I exhaled and felt a shiver.

I looked at Gary and nodded. He nodded back.

My skin had goose bumps, I realised. I wished I was there, I wished I was looking this man in the eye. We had no pictures of him, we'd performed no surveillance work, he had no social media profiles. All I had was Gary's description of a quiet, grey man.

Unable to take it any longer, I picked up the phone and called Hooky.

'Hooky, what was he like?'

'Calm, really calm.'

'What did he say?'

'You'll love this, boss. You'll bloody love it. We went in, he was there, sat down, reading the paper. His wife was there, wondering what was happening. Then we cautioned him, you know, we're arresting you on suspicion of the rape and murder of Melanie Road in June 1984.

'And his wife says, "What's going on?" He says nothing.

'Then as we're leading him out of the house, she says, "I'll see you later," and he turns to her and says, "No, you won't." She says, "Well, I'll see you tomorrow," and he says again, "No, you won't." Last words he said to her.'

'Fuck, yes,' I said.

Poor woman, I also thought to myself.

He knows: he knows that after thirty-one years, we have finally caught up with him.

'First things first,' I said to Liz. 'We need to get a download from his phone. And his car and computer, check his sat nav. Who knows, he may have been back to St Stephen's Court or Melanie's grave or somewhere relevant since we swabbed him.'

'Good idea. Oh, the tech guys go home in ten minutes.'

'Christ, can we get them in first thing in the morning? Tell them to look not just for Melanie Road, but any possible offence. Shelley Morgan. Melanie Hall, the Bath rapist. We have no idea who we're dealing with here.

'Are the search teams in yet?'

'We're just waiting for his wife to collect some things. She's off to a relative's tonight.'

'They need to look for anything involving any crime in Bath or Bristol. Did he keep trophies? Newspaper cuttings? Knives?

'And Julie Hampton, we need to give her a dedicated family liaison officer. She may not want one, but we've got to protect her. And we need to find out what Hampton's been like in the last few weeks. Has he mentioned the swab? Has he been different? Edgy? Anxious?'

I asked for John Lord and Gwen Bevan – both experienced officers – to conduct Hampton's interviews.

'Do an early interview,' I said. 'See what he says. He might confess, lighten his conscience. Just tell him why he's been arrested and ask him what he can tell you.'

'With a solicitor sitting next to him?' asked John.

'Let's at least give him the chance.'

Gwen and John went off to the Patchway custody suite. It would be hours before they would be able to speak with Hampton. He would need to be booked in, processed and permitted to speak with the duty solicitor, but in the next few hours we would get an idea which way this inquiry would go.

Would he confess or contest?

And what about Jean, Karen and Adrian Road?

I found the family liaison officers, Tim Coppick and Karen Thomas. We agreed to ask Adrian to go to Jean's, where we would tell her. Then we would move quickly over to Karen's to inform her.

I would have loved to have been with Jean, I would have loved to have been the one to break the news, but I needed to stay in the Inquiry Room to oversee the investigation and set the focus and direction for the case. As I wrote out my actions and formulated our policies for the next few hours and days, I heard Karen Thomas dial Jean's number. I couldn't help but hear Jean's distinctive voice from the end of the phone.

Karen: 'Hello Jean, how are you?'

Jean: 'Oh, hello Karen. Yes, I'm very well.'

Karen: 'Jean, we'd like to come and see you this evening.'

Jean: 'This evening? But it's six o'clock already. I have choir practice.'

Karen: 'Oh, I'm sorry about that, Jean, this is really quite important. Is there any chance you might miss tonight's choir?'

Jean: 'Really? Why? Is it important?'

Karen: 'We've got some news for you. We're going to ask Adrian to come over.'

Jean: 'Adrian? Why's that?'

Karen: 'We'll see you at seven thirty.'

Karen dialled Adrian. The last time I had spoken with him had been five years earlier, in 2009. He had severed contact with us.

Karen: 'Hello, is that Adrian?'

Adrian: 'Yes, who is this, please?'

Karen: 'Karen Thomas, from Avon and Somerset Police. It's been a few years …'

Adrian: 'Karen, I told Julie. I don't want to have anything to do with the police investigation.'

Karen: 'Yes, I understand, I'm with Julie now. We were wondering if you might go to see your mother tonight. We'd like to meet with you.'

Adrian: 'I told you, I just can't handle this. I don't want anything to do with the police until you've …'

A pause.

Karen: 'Why do you think we're ringing?'

Silence.

'Could you go to your mum's please, Adrian? It's important.'

Adrian had no words. I could hear him crying down the line.

Karen, speaking gently: 'We'll see you at seven thirty, Adrian. Drive carefully.'

'We've got a new swab from Hampton,' said Hooky.

'Great. I need a traffic officer to take it to the lab.'

I dialled a traffic inspector, who made one of those sharp intakes of breath which are usually the preserve of car mechanics and boiler maintenance engineers before they hit you with a bill.

'Where's the lab, Julie?'

'Abingdon. It's a murder case, absolute top priority. And we have just a day to get it turned around.'

'So, Julie, what's going to happen if there's a problem? A collision? Can you justify it?'

'Of course I can justify it. Do you want an email saying that?'

'Yes. It's late, we don't really have anybody.'

'You must have one traffic guy somewhere who can drive a really, really important DNA swab to Oxfordshire for an hour.'

I typed it as we spoke.

I hope your traffic officer isn't so incompetent that he causes a crash and makes me do a load of paperwork. Why does everything have to be a battle? I thought to myself.

They got a motorcyclist to whip the swab to the Abingdon laboratory.

The reports were coming back. An initial search from Hampton's house had shown little of interest. Now they were making a deep-dive of the property.

Julie Hampton had been interviewed. She had said she didn't believe a word of it. Her husband was no killer. He hadn't acted strangely or differently over the last few weeks. He had mentioned that the police had spoken to him, but there was no talk of a DNA swab.

The intelligence guys were in full swing. I was amazed at what they had discovered in just a few hours. Already they had spoken to some of Hampton's work colleagues. What was he like? A quiet man, something a little seedy about him. Was caught looking at porn on the job, once. Talked about sex a bit too much. But wasn't forward or suggestive with women. Wasn't violent.

Meader got off the phone.

'The interview teams have just finished with Hampton's first wife, Pauline. She and Hampton were divorced in '84. They'd split a couple of years earlier. They'd been married ten years, had three kids, including Clare.

'They had hardly any contact at the time of Melanie's murder. Pauline said we should speak with Terry Salmon. Terry was his best mate, they did everything together. He'd have a better idea.

'And he had a girlfriend at the time – a Tracy Delaney.'

'Great. Where is she?'

'We've found two. One in Bristol, one in West Sussex.'

Meader went off to find which Tracy Delaney was Christopher Hampton's former partner.

The intelligence guys found Terry Salmon, Hampton's old workmate, quickly, and within half an hour an interview team cold called at his home in an affluent village outside Bath.

'Chris Hampton? Christ, haven't seen him in years,' he'd said. 'We used to decorate together when we worked for Steve Hanrahan. Then my brother set up in the fascia business and I started with him. I've only seen him a few times in the last, what must it be, thirty years?'

'What was he like with women?'

'Very appealing. He wasn't a looker, really. But he always had an eye out, you know. Never knew how he did it.'

'Was there anything unusual about him and women? Did he treat them badly?'

'You'd better ask my wife.'

Diane Salmon was there and the team interviewed her later.

'Yes, Chris called at our house. It must have been 1973. Terry and me had been married, what was it, a year? It was strange. He said he was there to see Terry, but he would've known Terry was at work.

'We go inside and he starts chatting. I said I was just taking the Teasmade upstairs. I started going up with it, took it into the bedroom, looked round and he was there. Then before I knew it, he was all over me. Arms, hands, kissing. I started hitting him, hitting him away, but he was saying he loved me. Said we could start a new future together. Then he started, you know, groping ...'

'Had he ever done this before?'

'No. And he didn't do it again. I told Terry and that was that.'

So, he went too far once. An awful, creepy sex assault on his friend's wife. But that didn't make him a killer. I was mulling this over, alone in the office, writing up my policy book.

How could we prove he was in Bath in 1984? Did we have phone books from back then? Where exactly was he living then? Who might have seen him on the night out?

I looked at the clock: 10.15 p.m. I'd been desperate to call Jean Road for hours. At last I was alone in the office.

I picked up my phone and dialled.

'Hello?'

I heard the warmth in Jean's voice and wanted to cry.

'Hi Jean, it's Julie.'

'Oh Julie!'

'I just wanted to call to see how you're doing?'

'You know, I saw you on the TV, down in Exeter a few weeks ago. You were on the court steps. I thought, one day you'll be there for my Melanie. You know, I thought that.'

'You okay?'

'I didn't believe them. When they told me, I didn't believe them. I still don't believe it now. But I had faith in you, I knew you'd find him.'

'It's true. We've done it. I'll come to see you as soon as I can, it's just very busy here. Hopefully in a day or so.'

'Good night, Julie.'

'Night, Jean.'

'He's still not talking,' Gwen Bevan said on the phone from Patchway custody unit. 'He's just sitting there next to his lawyer. He gave a prepared statement: "I am not responsible for the rape and murder of Melanie Road in 1984." Apart from that, nothing.'

'Did you ask all the questions?'

'Of course.'

We had agreed a set of questions between us which were designed as much to appeal to his conscience as to elicit information. Gwen was as good an interviewer as it gets. A former air hostess, always immaculately presented, her looks were disarming – especially to a sex fiend like Hampton.

But the questions, so far, were not working.

I had them written down in front of me and could imagine the scene in the small interview room. Gwen and John Lord, Hampton and his lawyer. Outside, our Tier Five officer would be listening in case any actions emerged from the interview to follow-up quick-time.

Gwen: 'What was your involvement in the rape and murder of Melanie Road?'

Hampton: 'No comment.'

'Where were you living in June 1984?'

'No comment.'

'Where were you working?'

'No comment.'

'What vehicles did you use?'

'No comment.'

'Did you know Melanie Road?'

'No comment.'

'How did you meet her?'

'No comment.'

'Where did you meet?'

'No comment.'

'Did you rape Melanie?'

'No comment.'

'How was Melanie when you left her?'

'No comment.'

'Did you murder Melanie Road?'

'No comment.'

'Why?'

'No comment.'

'Describe what happened.'

'No comment.'

'What weapon did you use?'

'No comment.'

'Melanie was stabbed twenty-six times. Can you help with an explanation?'

'No comment.'

'Thanks, Gwen,' I said. 'Put him to bed, give him his eight hours. We'll try again in the morning.'

It would be the hard way. Of course it would be. Everything about this case had been hard. It was Christopher Hampton and his lawyer against me and my team.

CHAPTER 32

3 JULY 2015

'There is just nothing about him that says murderer,' I said.

Although it was first thing on Friday morning, the Inquiry Room was busy and I was briefing the team.

'No history of domestic violence, no criminal record. We have a sexual assault and he's a bit seedy. But he has no history of carrying a knife. You can see how he's slipped under the radar.'

'We've found his ex-girlfriend – Tracy Delaney,' said Hooky.

'Brilliant,' I replied. 'Is she the Bristol one?'

'Brighton.'

'Why can't anything in this case be straightforward?'

'I know. I've got her number, chatted to her. She doesn't really want to be interviewed, says she wants to just speak on the phone.'

'We can't do that. We have to see her, we've got a duty of care. Send a DS. Pete Walker's good.'

'Okay, ma'am.'

'And can you get the interview videoed too, protect her if we need to use it in court. See what kit Sussex Police have got.'

'At last minute on a Friday?'

'Yes, last minute on a Friday.'

'We've found what car he had, boss.' It was Meader.

'What was it?'

'A white Ford Cortina. It's not registered to him at Broad Street, but at a different address, in Great Bedford Street.'

'In June '84?'

'Yes.'

'Have you got a number plate? How did you find that out?'

'Magic, boss, magic.'

'Or the DVLA. Well, take your wand and see what Pete Walker's found out about the ex-girlfriend.'

The news about the car was a breakthrough in our investigation. Although we would have testimony from his ex-wife and friends that he was living in Bath in 1984, here was hard, documented proof which put him in the city – the kind of thing prosecuting lawyers love.

What was it about a white Ford Cortina? Why did that mean something to me? I could look through the files. But there was a quicker way to find out.

Down the phone line I heard the sound of young children playing in the background.

'Gary?'

'Everything okay, Julie?'

'Was there a white Ford Cortina seen on the night of Melanie's murder?'

A pause. More childish chatter and a click of plastic toys.

'Yes. It was parked badly. It's in a witness statement. Can't remember whose. But someone saw a woman who they thought was Melanie walking home and she walked past a badly parked white Ford Cortina. I'll have a think.'

'Thanks, Gary.'

I asked Gwen Bevan to reinterview Hampton to tell him we could prove he lived in Bath and had a car registered to a flat in Great Bedford Street. We had to disclose our evidence to him. It also might persuade him to admit what he'd done.

DS Pete Walker called. He and Liz Cousins had sped to Brighton to interview Tracy Delaney.

'Not great news,' he said.

'What did she say?'

'She doesn't like Hampton, doesn't like him one bit. Obviously, she's moved away and she's moved on with her life. She says that she and Hampton did live together in June 1984. They'd been together for a couple of years, they split up in '87.

'She says they were living in Great Bedford Street in '84. In fact, she was pregnant. There was an illness and the pregnancy didn't reach full term. That's why she remembers the time.

'But she has no recollection of him coming in either injured or covered in blood. She doesn't remember him being quiet or subdued or manic. She doesn't remember him even talking about Melanie Road at all.

'He wasn't violent, he didn't abuse her. She said there's no way he could have murdered someone. Get this, she said she left him because he was boring.

'She says he did have decorating tools, but she didn't recall any knives, only large scissors.'

'Thanks, Pete.'

CHAPTER 32

It was mid-afternoon and I was starting to worry about the ticking custody limits. We'd arrested Hampton at 5 p.m. the previous day. We had twenty-four hours on our clock and I'd obtained a twelve-hour extension. That would mean Hampton's time would expire at 5 a.m. on Saturday. We would need to apply to a magistrate for a warrant of further detention but we would have a period of grace to continue holding him until the court opened. That would be at 10 a.m. and we would ask for another thirty-six hours, and we would subtract from that the time he had spent in custody from 5 a.m., when his time had expired. But none of this would happen unless we got the results of the swab back from the laboratory.

I phoned the lab.

'Hi Mike, any news on that fast-track swab?'

'Er, Julie, it's 4.30 on a Friday afternoon. We can't do that now.'

'What?'

'We're going home for the weekend.'

'What the fuck?!'

'Don't swear, Julie.'

'What do you mean, you're going home? No! It has taken us thirty years to find this killer. All we need is a report from you saying this is a match to the scene DNA. If we don't get that, we're going to have to release him and we're not doing that.'

'But those reports take hours.'

'Mike, we have spent hundreds of thousands of taxpayers' pounds on you. This is when we need you to step up. We've had meetings with you, we've had conferences with you, we've worked with you for years.

'We have a contract with you to provide a service. What do you want me to do? Let him walk free? Somebody needs to write that statement. I don't need a long essay, just three lines saying this man's DNA matches the scene-mark.

'We'll never have this chance again. If we release him, we won't be able to arrest him again. Not unless there's new evidence. And we're not going to get new evidence. *This* is the evidence.'

I slammed the phone down and shouted a few more words which Mike would not have approved of.

The email confirming that Hampton's new, evidential swab matched the murder scene appeared in my inbox later that night. But it was too late to put to Christopher Hampton. He was now on his eight-hour rest period. And his time expired at 5 a.m.

All we needed to do was to put formally to Hampton that this second swab he had given on Thursday was a DNA match to the semen found at the murder scene. He could respond, then we would charge him with Melanie Road's murder. This late email ensured that the only way we could proceed was through a warrant of further detention hearing at Bristol Magistrates' Court on the Saturday.

I called the Crown Prosecution Service to let them know the state of play. My CPS contact told me that their lawyer, Huw Rogers, would be taking care of Saturday court and would help with any charging decision.

We had a swab, we had a plan, we had a tried-and-tested method of extending the warrant.

What could go wrong?

CHAPTER 33

I slept little that night. As I lay in bed, watching the ceiling grow lighter by degrees as the sun started to rise, I wondered if I was following the right lines of inquiry, doing the right things, following the right processes.

At 5.30 a.m. I got up to muck out the horses. I returned to the house, got ready for work, looked in on Callum, Connie and Toby as they slept, left a note on the table with details about lunch and dinner and drove to the Inquiry Room.

Hampton's time was up. He was being transported to Bristol Magistrates' Court for the warrant of further detention hearing. While these hearings could be tricky, they were so commonplace that the police usually represented themselves. Meader said he would take care of it while I stayed and ran the investigation. For the first time in days, I was starting to relax a little. We just needed to present the lab email to the judge, get our time extended and then interview Hampton to explain this.

My phone rang, Meader's name flashing on the screen.

'Julie, we've got a problem …'

'Funny, Meader.'

'No. Julie, we've really got a problem.'

'What?'

'It's a district judge. She's refusing to approve the warrant.'

'You're fucking kidding me! Why not?'

'She's agreeing with Hampton's lawyer, claiming abuse of process.'

'Abuse of what? If we don't get this, he's going to walk free.'

'Yes, Julie. That's why I'm calling you.'

'Is the CPS there? Huw's doing Saturday court.'

'I'm trying to find him. The judge has broken until 11.20, then we'll have an argument in court.'

'Do not let that man out of the dock. I'll charge him myself if I have to. I'm coming down.'

Charging was processed on computers, but I knew there wouldn't be any decent tech in court. I found an old paper form, wrote out the charge and got in the car. I had never heard of a detective ever doing anything like this before, but I was determined this man would not walk free.

I don't remember much about the journey down, except I drove quickly, swore a lot and tried to think clearly. If we had found Melanie's killer after thirty years, got proof of a DNA match, then had to let the murderer go because we had run out of custody time to conduct an interview it would be a disaster for the force, the end of my career and more importantly, a tragedy for Melanie's family, compounding the one they had been living through for three decades.

I parked on yellow lines outside the court and tried to get in. The doors were locked, the weekend entry was tighter than from Monday to Friday. I banged on the window and a guard came over slowly.

'I've got a hearing now. I need to be in.'

He nodded slowly and opened the door, put me and my bag through the security screening and I dashed upstairs.

I saw Meader's face lift with relief when I appeared.

'What are they arguing about?' I asked.

'Abuse of process.'

'Abuse of what? How?'

Huw Rogers, the CPS lawyer, appeared. Smart as ever, with a round, cheery face. I'd worked with Huw many times before, he was a great prosecutor.

'Hi Julie,' he said, relaxed, not quite registering the look of shredded terror on my face.

'The defence is banging on about abuse of process, Huw.'

'I'm sure it's something over nothing. Leave it to me, I'll represent you.'

'Thanks, Huw, but I'm warning you. If she doesn't give us a warrant, I'm going to charge him there in the dock. He's not walking out of this courtroom.'

For a moment, he thought I was joking. Then the penny dropped and he stopped smiling.

'You can't do that, Julie, that'll be a whole new can of worms ...'

'Watch me, Huw, just watch me. If there's even a sniff Hampton's going to walk, I'll do that.'

We were called in. Bristol Magistrates is a modern courthouse, the rooms all greys and creams, light wooden furniture.

Huw went to the front, in the prosecutor's position. I sat behind him. Hampton's lawyer sat next to Huw.

There was a knock at the door.

'All rise,' said the clerk.

We stood and the District Judge swept in and sat down. She offered us a serious smile.

There was a clinking of keys and the door opened behind the dock.

A small grey man in a tracksuit shuffled in. He nodded to the dock officer and sat down. I was about to study him more closely but his lawyer started talking: 'This is a case of poor police procedure. They've had this DNA swab for over a month. A month …'

He allowed the silence to hang.

'And now, only now, are they using it. Why have they sat on this for a month? It's without precedent.'

Now I understood.

I started whispering to Huw.

'We have not been sitting on this for a month. We took the first swab in May, but we only got the results on Thursday. We arrested him within eight hours of the results. Since then, we've taken a second, evidential swab.

'Within twenty-four hours of that swab we've sent it to the lab, had it tested, had the results confirmed. We couldn't have acted any quicker.

'Both swabs are a perfect match for the scene-mark DNA.'

He looked down and nodded.

Hampton's lawyer had stopped talking. Huw got to his feet and outlined my argument.

The District Judge looked unimpressed.

'Well, bearing in mind police took the swab a month ago, it is unacceptable that it has taken so long for the results to be processed and the arrest to be made.'

My heart sank. Huw stuck to his guns. Hampton's lawyer carried on with his line of attack. Like a spectator at Wimbledon watching balls knocked from one end to another, the judge started nodding from left to right as the two lawyers traded arguments. Then she looked at a legal reference book.

The exchange lasted over an hour. There were points of law and case law, but in truth, the lawyers were stuck on the original point. Eventually, the judge sighed and said: 'With those developments you have outlined about the last forty-eight hours I will grant you the warrant of further detention. You'll have another six hours.'

Six hours? I thought to myself. *Only six hours?*

It didn't matter, though. What we needed to do would take just ten minutes.

Huw, Meader and I left the court.

'We're going to charge him this afternoon, Huw.'

'Okay, okay,' he replied. 'I'll finish with the hearings here and I'll see you back in the Inquiry Room.'

'Meader, that was too close,' I said as we reached my car on the double yellow lines.

I took the parking ticket from under the windscreen wiper, got in and drove back to the office.

CHAPTER 34

4 JULY 2015

I tapped my fingers and looked again at the pinboard on the Inquiry Room wall. The custody photo of Christopher Hampton was askew, I noticed. How many times had I looked at this wall? And how long had I waited to be able to put up an image of Melanie Read's killer?

On the desk next to me was the file with all the documents and evidence Huw Rogers needed to read before authorising the charge. I looked at Hooky, who was sitting next to me.

'No, ma'am, I still don't know where Huw is,' he said, deadpan, having read my mind.

I walked to the wall and straightened the image of Hampton.

'Have you tried his phone?'

I looked again at the image of Hampton. Everything about him looked grey – his hair, his skin, his eyes, even the white T-shirt he was wearing had a dull complexion.

Somehow the photo didn't look right straight, so I turned it back to wonky.

I went to my bag, got my phone and dialled Huw Rogers. There was a recording in his chirpy Welsh accent: 'This is Huw Rogers from the Crown Prosecution Service. Sorry I can't take your call. There's a good chance I'm in court so probably better to text.'

'Huw, it's Julie. We have three hours left until our custody clock's up. Where are you?'

This was the third voicemail I had left.

I sat down again and tapped out a text:

Huw. Call me ASAP. Julie.

I can't remember exactly what I did for the next forty-five minutes but it was nearly 4 p.m. when Huw Rogers breezed into the Inquiry Room.

'Huw …'

'Not now, Julie. You have no idea how difficult today's been. Right, what have you got?'

'Our time runs out at six. Can you authorise the charge for Hampton?'

He blinked at me.

'Well, let's look at what you have, Julie. You have the lab report proving the DNA match?'

He held his hand out. I found the report and passed it over.

'What about the familial evidence? Have you got the statement from the officer who took the intelligence swab?'

I flicked through my papers and found Gary's statement. He carried on looking at it while asking questions: 'How do you know he was in Bath at the time?'

I told him about the registered car and the statements from his then-girlfriend and ex-wife.

'Have you got the confirmation from the DVLA?'

'Yes.' I passed the written confirmation of Hampton's car over. I looked at Huw, so pleased that intel officer had been determined to get this one document.

'What address do you have him in?'

'The electoral roll says Broad Street, but the car is registered to Great Bedford Street. So, we're saying Bedford. His ex-girlfriend says that too.'

I looked through my papers and started handing more over: 'We've done an incredible job in just over a day, Huw. I think you'll agree. Here's a statement from his former friend, putting him in Bath in '84. And here's a statement from his friend's wife describing how Hampton sexually assaulted her.'

I passed the papers over.

'What about the exhibits? How can you prove they haven't been compromised over thirty years?'

I knew this would be coming.

'The key piece of evidence is MR8, that's the semen sample found at the scene. Gary's been working on that. And we can account for it for every day since 9 June 1984. Every single day.'

I gave Huw those papers.

'Okay,' he sighed. 'I don't know, Julie. This is thirty-one years old, what's the rush to get him before the courts now? I think we should bail him and improve the evidence, give you time to work on your inquiries. I'm not sure this quite reaches the threshold to charge.'

'Bail?' I could feel my cheeks redden. 'Can you imagine the anger in the press and in Bath if we let a man with a full DNA hit for the murder of a schoolgirl out on the streets?

'The public wouldn't expect that. That's not what Melanie's family would expect. What if he does a runner? What if he kills himself? No, Huw, there are too many things at play here. It's too risky.'

The photo of Christopher Hampton looked down at us from the wall. A grey man with a blank expression, impassively watching us argue over his fate. Above his image was the photo of Melanie Road: laughing, colourful.

Huw breathed out and looked at Hampton's DNA profile and the profile from MR8.

'These don't match,' he said.

Three words which hit me in the stomach.

'What?'

'These don't match. This isn't a full match.'

'What are you saying?'

'Look … look here,' he said.

Huw placed our new, evidential DNA chart next to the one showing our old sample from the scene of Melanie's murder. Side by side, two DNA charts. One from thirty-one years ago, one from thirty-one hours ago. He pointed to nineteen hit-points on the charts which followed an identical pattern. Then he pointed to the final point: 'The twentieth point, it's a fail.'

He looked me in the eye.

No! No way! No …

I pulled the papers together and looked through the points on the chart (scientists call them alleles, the points in a person's DNA scientists look at to distinguish one person from another). The chart which had returned from the lab late last night had a full profile: the twenty alleles were filled out. The chart I had been looking at for six years had hits at markers one to nineteen. And in the twentieth spot was the letter 'F'.

F for Fail.

He was right.

No! No way! No … How did I miss that? I'd been looking at the murderer's chart since 2009. For bloody years.

Huw leaned back in his chair and frowned at me.

'I'm not charging without a full DNA profile.'

'No, Huw. No. We've been using this chart as the scene-mark for ages, it's the killer's DNA.'

'It's not a full profile, Julie. It's not good enough.'

I felt drained.

The door opened. Andy Mott came in.

'Hey guys, well done on Rhodium.' His sing-song northern accent seemed to puncture the mood.

'I'm not sure we're there, Andy.'

'What? Why not?'

'Actually, could you help us here? Look at the charts.'

Motty sauntered over and looked at the pieces of paper.

'What's wrong?' he frowned.

'The twentieth allele, it's a fail.'

He looked at them. Motty has never said a word he hasn't thought about at least three times before opening his mouth. He's a scientist originally, never a risk-taker. A man for whom evidence is king.

'That's a match, that's fine. You don't need to worry about that.'

'It's only a partial profile,' said Huw.

'That's so close, it's got to be a match. It could be explained by anything. Sometimes you get a speck of something somewhere, a minuscule fleck of dust, a little anomaly. That's a full DNA profile. You'll run the tests from the exhibits again and you'll get a twenty-out-of-twenty match – you can charge with that.'

'Well, I'm not authorising the charge,' said Huw. 'I need the statistical probability. You don't have that. Is this a one-in-a-million match? Is this one-in-ten-million? Or could it be one-in-a-hundred? That wouldn't be good enough. I think we should bail him and decide when we know for sure. This is too risky.'

I grabbed the file and found the large photo of Melanie.

'Huw, this isn't a poxy burglary, this is the murder of this girl, Melanie. Look at that picture. This is who we're talking about. We've been looking for her killer for thirty-one years. Thirty-one years! Now we have him. And you have everything you need to charge him. It's the right thing to do.'

I found myself pointing at Melanie's image.

'You can't make a decision of "you've not got enough" when clearly we have. We have Hampton in Bath in '84. He's as good as admitted the murder to his wife and we have a full DNA profile.'

'It's not a full match,' Huw insisted.

'It's a full match, Huw,' said Motty.

Huw sat for a moment and stared at something vague in the room, he was looking at neither Motty nor me.

I realised no one else had said a word: Hooky and the others were sitting, silently watching the show. I stared at Huw, I could see the cogs whirring in his brain. He was either going to say 'charge' or he wasn't. One word. Just one word would make the difference between us and justice.

'Come on, Huw.'

I felt like I was hanging by a thread. A thread that could be snapped if he chose.

I was terrified.

I thought of the hours of work we'd put in, the generations of detectives who had tried and failed. I thought of Jean, Karen and Adrian Road in their homes, waiting for news. Waiting for us to tell them we'd charged Melanie's killer.

I thought of Melanie.

'Come on, Huw!'

'Okay, but it's against my better judgement.'

'Thank you, Huw.'

He nodded.

The room seemed to breathe out.

'Okay, let's talk about next steps,' said Huw.

'We don't have time for that,' I told him. 'We've got to tell Hampton's solicitor that we're charging, we've got to build the charge on the computer and his time's going to run out in an hour and a half. I'd love to stop and chat, but it'll have to be another time.'

CHAPTER 35

4 JULY 2015

'Do all policemen have to drive so slowly?' I said to Hooky as he pulled out from Kenneth Steele House on to the main road.

The speedometer was nowhere near the 30 mph mark.

'I know you're on overtime, but you don't have to eke it out. We've got thirty-five minutes to get to Patchway.'

I tapped my blue detective's book which was on my lap, looking down at the sentences I'd written in blue ink. Trying to take in the words: 'I am charging you …'

'… murder of Melanie Road …'

'… remanded in custody …'

'You're not going to make me look like a bloody idiot, are you? I don't have a clue what I'm doing.'

'When was the last time you charged someone, ma'am?' Hooky asked.

I couldn't remember.

For years, it hadn't been my job to charge suspects: as a detective inspector now, as a DS beforehand, or further back in my deeper past during my time in the Cold Case or Professional Standards teams – 2007?

'Eight years ago, I think. Can you speed up? Look, we're on a dual carriageway.'

'How are you feeling?' he smiled.

'Okay. Bit nervous,' I said, rapping my fingernails on my blue book. 'They've changed the wording, haven't they? Since I last charged someone?'

I opened the book again and read the words.

'You'll be all right, ma'am. Not sure I've ever known a senior investigating officer charge a murderer. Could be a first time?'

'Do they know I'm doing it?'

'Yes, they're all ready. They know it's a special one.'

There was a pause.

'What do you think he'll be like?' I asked. 'I mean, he's been living free for thirty years. He knows he's going away, he knows I'm taking his freedom.'

'Remember, everything's recorded,' said Hooky after a while. 'Everything in that suite is filmed and recorded. Don't say anything to prejudice the case. Don't chat to the custody sergeant beforehand, don't say you've got good evidence, don't mention the DNA hit. Just go in, charge him and get out.'

We crawled through the Saturday afternoon traffic northwards towards the Patchway custody suite.

'Please, Hooky, please can you put your foot down. You are officially slower than Gary.'

We rumbled into a car parking space, I leapt from the car and headed inside. Hooky meandered in after me.

The custody suite is set out like the bridge of a spaceship, a raised central section where the custody sergeant sits above lower areas, little pods with computer terminals.

'Hello, Detective Inspector Julie Mackay, I've got the authorisation to charge Christopher Hampton with murder.'

The custody sergeant looked at his screen and nodded.

'You're cutting it a bit fine, just a few minutes left on the clock. Do you have authorisation from the CPS?'

'Yes, of course.'

He carried on tapping away at his keyboard.

'Are you okay, Julie?' Gwen Bevan and John Lord, the interviewing officers, appeared. 'You look a bit flustered.'

'I'm fine. How is he?'

'Silent.'

'Does his solicitor know we're charging him?'

Gwen nodded.

A prisoner was brought in; not Hampton. A tall man with long, dank hair and a thin face. A second sergeant started talking to him about his custody time period.

'Do you have him?' I asked the custody sergeant.

'He's on his way.'

I heard the distant turn of a key and a murmur of voices, then the metallic creak of heavy-duty hinges.

Then a slam.

Then footsteps.

In the distance I noticed a small figure in a grey tracksuit walking towards me along the corridor. Behind him towered a detention officer. He was indistinct from afar, a blurred figure, walking in slow motion. But with every creeping step he emerged into focus. Now he'd left the corridor and was in the suite, just metres away. If there were the usual bangs and chatter of the custody unit, I didn't notice. The only thing on my mind was this grey man who was now four metres away from me.

Now three.

Now two.

Now he was there in front of me, face to face.

'Christopher Hampton, ma'am,' said the custody sergeant.

Hampton looked at the custody sergeant behind me, then turned his head and fixed his gaze on me. His eyes were impassive, lacking spark, giving no clue as to what was happening behind them. A grey stubble was sprouting through his deadpan face. He smelt of sweat.

You're the man I've been looking for, I thought.

I pulled the computer monitor round so I could read the charge.

'Christopher Hampton,' I started.

I looked again at the screen, then looked back at him. His eyes were still on me.

What are you thinking? I wondered.

He said nothing.

I looked again at the screen.

'I am charging you with the murder of Melanie Anne Road on the 8th to 9th June 1984. You do not have to say anything …'

I can't mess this up now, I thought to myself. *What's the next bit of the new caution?*

I fought to find the words.

'… but it may harm your defence if you do not mention now something you later rely on in court …'

Keep your voice calm, I told myself.

'You will be remanded in custody until a hearing at Bath Magistrates' Court on Monday 6 July.'

His breathing was still, his face pale. He gazed at me; he was somehow looking at me yet not at me. Not a flicker from his eyes. No recognition, nor fear, nor resentment, nor acquiescence nor remorse.

You're the man I've been looking for all this time. You are that man. It's you. You killed Melanie.

You raped Melanie twice and stabbed her twenty-six times all those years ago. How did you do that? How could you live with yourself? How could you have had a family? How could you live your life after depriving Melanie of hers? Do you have any idea what you've done to Adrian? And Karen? And Jean?

I noticed that the room was silent. The phones seemed to have stopped ringing. There was no murmur of chatter. Through the corner of my eye I could see Hooky, Gwen and John staring open-mouthed at the murder detective and the man she had been hunting for six years. A man who had evaded police for thirty-one years.

The other prisoner had turned round and was watching, as if realising something important was happening and he should understand its gravity. Above me, on the bridge, the silhouettes of the custody sergeant and detention officers were frozen, looking down at us.

I noticed my heartbeat, slow but strong. What was happening behind the glazed eyes of the killer before me? I nodded to the custody officer, who motioned for Hampton to return to his cell.

As he walked away, I stared into the back of this small, shabby man in a grey tracksuit. A man I wouldn't have noticed if I'd passed him on the street.

You are him.

The drive back to Kenneth Steele House was the polar opposite from the one to the custody suite. My nerves had been replaced by a feeling of elation I couldn't remember ever experiencing before, certainly not as a detective.

I kept thinking of Jean Road in her home. A few hours ago, there had been a good chance that Melanie's killer could have been released either on bail or on a technicality. How would Jean have felt? But not now. Now Hampton was behind bars and would face trial.

We went back into the Inquiry Room and I drafted a media release detailing Hampton's charge and the date of his first court hearing. This would be the first time his name would be released to the wider public; the first time people in Bath would know who the killer was.

We called the court clerk to say there would be big interest in Monday's listings. Among the drink-drive and theft hearings would be a cold case murder. The press would be there; we would need extra security.

Karen Thomas, the family liaison officer, told Jean, Adrian and Karen that Hampton had been charged. They would have their first chance to see Melanie's killer in court on Monday 6 July. There would be a trial, perhaps in six months' time. But this would be his first appearance in court, in public, named as the man we suspected of being Melanie's killer.

CHAPTER 35

A procedural hearing.

'Do you think we can get our shit together for a trial?' asked Hooky. 'I mean, the case is massive and there are new rules for old inquiries. Will we have to serve the documents which are relevant to Hampton? That'll be just a few hundred. Or everything? Because last time I looked, we were at 30,000 documents. The old bean-counters won't like that. And what about our exhibits? Can we really prove they've not been contaminated? A good defence barrister loves a cold case to get his teeth into.'

'Let's see what the judge thinks. Hang on …'

I went to the kitchen and grabbed a tube of plastic cups. It was late now and everyone had gone home except the inter-viewers, my two brilliant sergeants and Hooky. Then I went to the filing cabinet and pulled down the dusty bottle of champagne Meader had left there two years earlier, the one he had said we would open when we caught Melanie's killer.

'What about Gary?' someone asked.

'He should work weekends.'

I popped the cork and poured the fizz into the cups, pass-ing them round: Meader, Gwen, John, Hooky and my sergeant John Dowding.

'We've done it,' I said.

The champagne was warm and acidic and the plastic cups would have terrified any sommelier, but this may have been the best drink I had ever tasted. I looked at the team around me. They had bags under their eyes, but smiles on their faces. We sat down, sipping our warm fizz surrounded by piles of papers, files, index cards and policy books.

This was just the start of it.

CHAPTER 36

6 JULY 2015

'Julie, you were a bit out of order on Friday, talking to the lab like that.'

I was driving to Bath Magistrates' Court when Liz Tunks called me.

'What? Telling them they should do their job? Telling them we should get the service we pay for? Ensuring a killer didn't end up being let out with no chance of us arresting him again? Not sure about that, Liz.'

'Well, I'm having to soothe a few egos today, Julie. Build some bridges. Don't forget, we need them for the prosecution case too …'

'Tell them I say sorry.'

'Are you?'

'Not for saying it, but yes for upsetting them.'

'Good luck today. It's just an up-and-downer, isn't it?'

'I hope so,' I said, hanging up.

And I really did hope so. I was in excruciating pain. The excitement of Hampton's arrest and charge had acted as a balm to the constant agony in my abdomen. Now the drama had subsided and the pain was back. I was booked for an appointment in the Bath Clinic at 1 p.m. If I didn't make it, I would have to wait six months for another spot.

I parked in Bath Cricket Club's ground, opposite the courtroom. It was the same car park where Ben Schwarzkopf had seen Melanie's killer before her murder more than thirty years earlier.

A gentle rain was falling and a small huddle of press camera crews and reporters were sheltering under umbrellas, chatting. They snapped me as I walked across the road and headed into court.

Poor Jean will have to go through this, I thought. *As if today wasn't going to be hard enough*.

I had spoken with Jean Road over the weekend and tried to explain what would happen: 'Just a formality, not usually dramatic, but this will be tough for you, Jean.'

I made my way through security and up the stairs to the lobby outside the courts. My phone kept ringing, so I took calls while looking for the listings to find which court Hampton was appearing in.

Jean arrived a little before 10 a.m., walking slowly on her cane. She offered a little smile, but I could tell from one glance that behind her eyes was a bottled fury. Adrian and Karen were with her. He was pale, looking as if he were trying to calm himself. And Karen's red eyes betrayed the surface-level pain in which she existed.

This was the first time I had seen all three of them together.

'I've got a room for you here,' I said, opening a door to reveal something little larger than a cubicle.

As Adrian walked in, he tapped me on the shoulder: 'Thanks for finding him, you don't know what this means to us.'

'I'll be back in a minute,' I smiled.

I heard a tap-tap-tap on the tiled floor and saw a small blonde woman with a walking stick. She was younger than Jean, much younger. Late fifties, I guessed, but the expression on her face seemed to have aged her. She was with a small woman who must have been in her late teens and a tall twenty-something man dressed smartly. They stood silently, looking confused.

That must be Hampton's family: Julie and her children. Poor woman.

A few news reporters were making their way to the top of the stairs, chattering loudly.

I had asked a detective constable to see when our hearing might take place. Ours was clearly the most important job of the day here: 'They're going through the list, they're not prioritising custody hearings. They're keeping Hampton in his place in the queue.'

What about the families?

What about my bloody appointment?

I snuck away and called my friend who worked at the Bath Clinic.

'Liz, this hearing's taking forever. Is there any way I can reschedule my appointment? The only reason I can't make it is because of this case.'

'Let me see, I know his secretary. When will you know?'

'No idea.'

I hung up and walked back through the lobby, past Julie Hampton, her family and their family liaison officer. Julie

Hampton looked as if she were suffering some kind of trauma, as if she were still taking everything in: her husband the murderer. Reporters flitted about.

I went back to Jean, Karen and Adrian in their cubicle.

'Why's it taking so long?' Adrian asked.

I explained and filled the time describing what would happen in court: where they should sit, what they should do.

I looked again at my watch.

'*Liz, I'm sorry, I really don't think I'll make it,*' I text-messaged.

'*I told them you've just solved a thirty-year-old murder in Bath. Can you make Thursday?*'

Liz, you're a bloody genius.

'*Yes,*' I replied.

There was a shout from a distance. A court usher: 'Hampton. Everyone in the case of Hampton?'

'Okay?'

Jean, Adrian and Karen got up, I held the door open and they paraded out. They reached the courtroom and made their way in. Inside, there were two rows of fold-down seats. I ushered the Road family to the far corner and sat next to Jean.

Julie Hampton and her children sat behind.

The rest of the seats were filled with news reporters. Every spot was taken.

The three magistrates sat ahead: a grey-haired woman in the middle flanked by two men in their sixties.

There was an empty, large, pale-wooden dock with toughened glass extending all the way around and up to the ceiling. Behind this were six seats, behind these a locked door.

The clerk was working out the running order for the following hearings. There was everyday courtroom chatter as beside me Jean, Adrian and Karen prepared for the moment they had waited more than three decades for.

A key turned. A metallic scraping, then the clink of a turning lock.

The door opened and the small figure of a grey man in a grey tracksuit appeared, bent over, handcuffed. I could feel every pair of eyes in the room following my gaze, boring into him. The security officer removed the cuffs and Christopher Hampton made his way to stand in front of the seats in the dock.

Jean, sitting next to me, seemed rigid, her knuckles white, clasping the handle of her stick. I could hear her breathing.

'You are Christopher Hampton?' asked the court clerk in a clear voice.

Hampton's face was fixed with its deadpan expression, granite, unmoving, looking at the magistrates. Ignoring the people in the public benches.

I heard a sob from behind me.

The clerk read out his date of birth and address. Hampton nodded that they were both correct.

'You have been charged with the murder of Melanie Anne Road on the 8th/9th June 1984. Do you understand?'

Hampton mumbled a confirmation.

There was another burst from behind me. Another woman's sobbing.

I looked across at Jean, her gaze focused on Hampton. Her eyes were wide, staring at this man who had destroyed her family, who had destroyed her life.

Adrian was pale; he was also looking directly at Hampton, a hand on his mother's. And beyond him sat Karen. Her face was red, tears flowing from angry eyes. She looked as if she were about to leap from the chair and start pounding the security glass.

'You will be remanded in custody until Wednesday, July 8th when you will appear before Bristol Crown Court,' continued the clerk.

Hampton nodded.

The security officer cuffed his wrists and led him through the door, which slammed shut.

We got up, I looked to the line of chairs behind me and saw Julie Hampton doubled up over her walking cane, a tissue to her eyes. Her son was persuading her to get up, trying to lead her away, out of the courtroom.

'I just want to go now,' said Jean.

CHAPTER 37

9 JULY 2015

'Look, I'm a detective. I'm straight-talking, down-to-earth, you don't have to dress things up,' I said to the doctor in the Bath Clinic.

'How is the pain?' He was a serious man and did nothing to try to lighten the mood.

'Awful.'

'You've been living with the cramps and that agony for five years?'

'Yes.'

'Right, well, let's have a look then.'

I got on the bed and we went through it. No matter how lovely or professional the doctor, or how matter-of-fact my job, the internal examination was still humiliating.

Rape victims go through something far worse after their attack, I thought to myself.

It was little comfort.

Afterwards, the doctor said: 'And the medication is no longer working?'

It never really had.

'Fibroids can develop over time. There is nothing to say yours are cancerous, but sometimes things reach a point where it is better to be safe than sorry.

'We have a few options. You could continue to manage the pain. The fact you're here suggests that's no longer something you want to do. Or another possibility is a hysterectomy. It's a big procedure, but we do it through keyhole surgery. We can get you in and out of hospital in two days, but it will take a long time to recover.'

'How long?'

'Six weeks? Maybe longer. I know why you rescheduled this week. Are you working on any important cases which require you to be in work? Are you able to take time off?'

I've got the case of my life which will dominate the next year, I thought to myself.

'I have a lot to do in the coming weeks, but there may be a bit of a lull. I'll need to be back in work for early next year.'

He looked at his diary on the computer: 'We can do 10 September.'

'Book me in.'

'Do you like lilies?'

Jean had opened her front door and of all the greetings I had expected, that was not one of them.

'I love them.'

'Good. Bloody people, they keep sending me flowers. And all the bunches have lilies, I can't stand the smell.'

She let me through and I walked into what had been a kitchen, but now seemed more like a botanical collection.

Vases bursting with flowers were scattered on all the work-tops. In her conservatory were the lilies, away from the main house so she didn't have to smell them.

'It's like Melanie's died again,' she explained. 'All the attention. People I haven't seen for years. Suddenly, there's a knock at the door and they're there with their head tilting, saying they're sorry, but here's a bunch of flowers.'

'There are some nice ones here.'

'Oh, they mean well. They're doing their best. I sound ungracious. I don't mean to, but ever since last week, it's as if we're going through the whole …'

She searched for the word.

' … *thing* again. It's brought it all back. It's like June 1984, a second time around.

'And now my house is invaded by *lilies*.'

'I'll help you with the lilies, Jean.'

She made me a cup of tea and we started work on a packet of biscuits.

'Jean, I just wanted to let you know, there's going to be a trial. Probably early next year. It'll be a few weeks long, maybe a month. And there's a chance you'll be a witness. You probably won't have to give evidence in court, but we'll need a statement from you about what Melanie was like and to describe the last time you saw her.'

'Will there really be a trial? He won't plead guilty?'

I shook my head.

'He's going to fight. He's got a solicitor, soon he'll have a barrister. There will be a trial.'

'Are they going to start digging things up about Melanie? Saying she shouldn't have been walking home alone?'

'I don't know. Maybe. With you being a witness, I can't tell you too much about Hampton ...'

'It's okay, I don't want to know anything about him.'

I left the house with two bunches of lilies and, if it were possible, more love for Jean Road than ever before.

The wheels of justice were already starting to grind.

It took the judge three hearings to decide about documents. There had been a change in the law in 1997. The judge had to determine if the case would use the old or new rules. Under the new legislation, we would have to disclose just the documents which related to the accused, to Christopher Hampton. Under the old rules, from the time of Melanie's murder, we would have to disclose everything. The whole case over thirty years; all 30,000 documents.

The judge looked torn as he made his announcement: 'Old rules. Disclose everything.'

Okay, that's just made my job ten times harder. But if it's old rules, that's how we'll play it.

Many of the documents had not been entered on to the computer. The team would have to read everything, add a summary on the Holmes system; if the document was actually relevant to the case we would add a code to it as well as writing a more detailed description of what was in it. We would then share all of this with the defence barrister, when one was appointed.

I built a unit of six disclosure officers just to work on this. And I didn't envy their job. The rest of the team was already in place. Meader would be my deputy, the immaculately turned out John Dowding the receiver, Hooky the officer in charge, Karen Thomas would continue the family liaison work. Gary Mason would work on the exhibits alongside Andy Mott. And Kate Brunner QC would be our prosecuting barrister. I had worked with Kate before and had been delighted when she was appointed. She was clever, organised and meticulous, so we knew we were in safe hands.

My biggest worries were around the integrity of our exhibits. What would a good defence counsel do with thirty-year-old evidence? What if they could prove that, at some point in the past, a vital piece of evidence had been contaminated or handled in a way which compromised it? The whole case would be blown, Christopher Hampton would walk from court a free man.

The key piece of evidence was the semen sample from the murder scene: MR8. I was confident it had been kept in the correct way but we needed to check. We needed to ensure that our timeline of where it had been for every day of its thirty-one-year life was bulletproof. From the moment it was taken from the scene, travelling from one laboratory to another, into storage, back to a new lab.

The Metropolitan Police had secured convictions against two men who had murdered Stephen Lawrence. Stephen's racially motivated murder in London in 1993 had been one of the most controversial inquiries in recent history. It had taken eighteen years to bring his killers to justice. Proving the integrity of the exhibits had been a big issue in that case, so Andy Mott headed to London to see how they managed the sprawling inquiry. And back in Bristol we had a new blood sample from Hampton. We needed to check it was Green Blood but the PGM (phosphoglucomutase) science which had been so important back in 1984 was now out of date, superseded by DNA. We could only find one scientist in the country who could make those checks on the blood. And there was further bad news.

'Boss, you know that scientist at King's College London? The blood expert?'

'Yes.'

'Well, the defence has just got to her. She's working for them.'

'Shit! And she's the only one in the country?'

'Yes.'

'We'll have to find a way around this.'

We faced other challenges too. I had ordered a search of the flat Hampton had been living in at the time of Melanie's murder. Initially a judge had refused the warrant, saying he needed to know more about the person who was living there now. 'Weren't we being a bit presumptive that the resident would deny a search anyway?' the judge had asked.

We obtained consent from the residents, our teams descended on Great Bedford Street and started pulling it gently apart. There was nothing in the fireplaces or behind cupboards or obvious spots under the floorboards. We decided against taking the whole apartment to pieces, feeling that the cost of the operation would be too high and the likelihood of actually finding the murder weapon too low to be worth it.

'Boss, what do you think the chances are of Hampton being the Bath rapist?' It was Hooky.

'Not sure if we can prove anything forensically, but why do you ask?'

'We've had a call from one of the victims.'

'What?'

'Sarah Molloy. She was attacked by the rapist by the Holburne Museum in '94. He grabbed her, she managed to get away. But the following week, in one of the side streets near there, he attacked another woman so we always linked those two offences.'

'What's that got to do with Hampton?'

'Well, Sarah was watching the coverage on telly the other day and saw the court artist's drawing of Hampton. Stopped her dead, she said. It's him, the man who went for her.'

'Christ! Can you get a statement from her?'

And more links were emerging. We spoke with three former workmates of Hampton's. In June 1984 he was working for a decorating company based in Bath but the building he was painting was in Clevedon.

Meader was telling me this when the penny dropped.

'Bath to Clevedon?'

I checked the map. The most direct route passed Backwell, the North Somerset village where the remains of Shelley Morgan were found. Shelley had not been seen after dropping her children at school two days after Melanie's murder. Her body had been found in a copse just a mile or so from the road between Bath and Clevedon.

A forensic review of Shelley Morgan's exhibits had been conducted a year earlier. Could we link the two cases? Was Hampton responsible for both? Or were two knife-wielding rapist-killers operating in the same area days apart?

'What about Ben?' I asked. 'He's our key witness. Can we show him a photo of Hampton from around the time? Could he pick him out? Check with the CPS, make sure they're happy to arrange an old-fashioned ID line-up but with photos.'

'We can try, boss,' said Hooky.

'He's autistic, he's on the spectrum, he has that kind of mind. Puts things in boxes. Have we got an image of Hampton at the time? From the 1980s?'

'The nearest we've got is one from a few years later, Clare Hampton gave us a picture.'

Hooky arranged to see Ben Schwarzkopf. He would go armed with a collection of photos, including one of a younger Christopher Hampton, along with others who matched his appearance.

And, as ever, Gary Mason was working his magic.

'I think you might be interested in this,' he said in his quiet way, pushing a statement on the table. It was in an old typeface, the kind I had been used to reading in the Review Team.

**Statement of Ryan MICHAELS. DoB: 3/10/1965.
Date of statement 13.6.1984.**

At 1.35am on Saturday 9th June 1984 I left a friend's house at Keynsham. I drove my Blue Vauxhall Viva to Saltford where I dropped another friend at his house ...

He gave the details of his friend and said he drove back to Bath:

I reached the traffic lights at George Street with its junction with Lansdown Road at 0150am. The lights just changed to red as I came to them and I stopped at the white line.

Whilst I stopped at the lights a girl crossed the road from the top of Broad Street in front of me onto the nearside pavement going up Lansdown Road.

As I drove over the junction I saw the girl walking up beside the Lansdown Arms. I also noticed a white MkIII Cortina parked in a slip beside the Lansdown Arms with its bonnet protruding slightly.

I took quite a bit of notice because I thought it was rather quiet and the girl was young and alone. I would describe her as aged about 18, 5'5", slim build, fair hair which was just over the shoulders …

Under the same conditions I would recognise the girl again. I have seen the photograph of Melanie ROAD and can say that she is similar to the girl I saw.

'Brilliant, Gary! If we can find that car in the system, it might match Hampton's?'

'Ryan Michaels is still around,' said Gary. 'He could be a live witness.'

We were an index card away from putting Melanie Road near Hampton's car minutes before he killed her.

CHAPTER 38

JULY 2015

'We need to know more about Hampton,' I said.

I looked at the team.

'What we have isn't enough. What was he like in '84? What's he been doing in the in-between time? Was he a sexual deviant? Did he carry a knife? Did he have lots of girlfriends? Did he go to work on that Monday morning? Did anyone notice anything different about him? Who were his mates? Was he on drugs? Did he comment about the murder to anyone?'

'What else have we got?'

'We have spoken with a couple of his old workmates, ma'am. We got them through Terry Salmon,' said Hooky. 'The first, a guy called Harry Summers, he didn't know him at the time but met him on sites in the 1990s. Said Hampton was an absolute sex maniac. Caught him looking at porn one lunchtime. Had a temper too.

'But we've found his employer from 1984, Steve Hanrahan. Said Hampton was one of the best workers he ever had. Reliable, quiet, did a good job.'

'It's hardly building a picture, is it?'

'Well, it's showing two sides of the man,' said Hooky.

Quiet sex fiend, responsible face to the rest of the world.

'Terry Salmon said Hampton had flings. He worked in Plymouth, decorating a shoe shop, cheated on his first wife there. He didn't tell Terry much about it, he was discreet. But he did the dirty on Pauline for a long while with this shoe shop worker and there were other women as well.'

Gary had gone back to the Forensic Science Service's archive in Birmingham. We had been in constant contact with the archive throughout our inquiry but now, when we asked for everything to do with the case, they suddenly found more.

A blood sample from Melanie. Until now, we had been working on a composite profile for her. We had combined samples from Jean and Tony Road to create what was likely to be Melanie's DNA profile. We had used this to determine which spots of the blood at the scene were likely to be Melanie's and which were her killer's. And all that time, on a shelf in Birmingham, sat a sample which could have given us a guaranteed reading.

'For Christ's sake, why didn't they tell us about this?' I asked Gary.

'They changed their reference numbers a few years ago, they didn't realise they had it.'

Gary found a lock of Melanie's hair which we didn't know existed. We divided the sample into three locket boxes and gave one each to Jean, Karen and Adrian.

Andy Mott came back from London after seeing the Stephen Lawrence inquiry officers.

'It's really simple what they did with the exhibits,' he said. 'It was just a spreadsheet. In one column they had the name of each exhibit and then a list of where each exhibit was for its life. And if there's a gap in the continuity, if we're not sure, we'll just have to say so.'

'It's like saying to the defence, "Here's the chink in our armour, attack here,"' I said. 'The important thing is the key exhibit, MR8. The killer's DNA sample. And we can prove where that has been for every single day for thirty-one years. It's watertight.'

I trusted Motty implicitly but I had been guaranteed so many things for so many years only to be let down that I lost sleep over it.

Now we knew who the killer was, we were able to build a picture of Melanie's last minutes. We already knew she was upright when she was attacked but now we had to work out a storyboard to present to a jury. Could we show what happened?

We went back to Melanie's clothing, fitted it again to a mannequin, then showed how the small patches, which were cut by scientists for forensic sampling, fitted perfectly. They still did, thirty-one years later. We had every single scrap.

We sent Melanie's pants away for testing. The results confirmed what we already knew: they were heavily stained with her blood but there was no evidence of the killer's semen on them. This meant she had been stabbed while wearing them. But her killer had removed them to carry out his sexual assault.

Stabbed first, sexually assaulted afterwards.

We still had no idea why they were found fifty yards in the opposite direction to the Green Blood Trail, to Hampton's getaway.

'It says here,' said Gary, 'that the original inquiry brought in an expert to see if a fox could have picked the pants up and run away with them. The fox expert said no, it wouldn't have gone near the pants.'

Motty was also upgrading all the main exhibits to a new, more precise testing system called DNA 17.

I was getting paranoid about the science. I had discovered at the moment I needed it the most that the DNA profile had been incomplete, a nineteen out of twenty match. That had nearly caused the charge against Hampton to collapse – I couldn't let a lapse cause the trial to fold.

We tested blood spot 47 again. That was a key sample for us as it was a small spot on its own, halfway between where Melanie was found and the top of the old stone steps, where the killer bled more profusely. It linked the attack to the getaway. We had never tested the spot for DNA before, knowing that when we did, it would destroy the sample for future scientific use. Now was the time to do it, but we would have only one go at it.

The results of the new DNA 17 testing came back: blood spot 47 was an exact match with Christopher Hampton and able to offer a statistical probability with a much greater accuracy than the old science. It read: a one in a billion chance it was not him. I read that figure with a mixture of shock and satisfaction.

'We have a bit of a problem with Ben, boss.' It was Hooky.

'What?'

'You know he has this brilliant mind, puts things in boxes, remembers everything?'

'Yes.'

'Well, I showed him the photos. He picked someone else, not Hampton.'

'Shit! He's our key witness.'

And there was more unwelcome news. This time it was Gary: 'The stab wounds are all to the right side of Melanie's body. We've always thought the killer would be left-handed.'

'Yes?'

'Hampton's right-handed.'

'Well, it's not a deal-breaker. He could have been using his left hand to carry the knife, he could have used his right hand in an unusual way.'

'Might be something the defence looks at.'

'Thanks, Gary.'

Now, knowing who the killer was, we found that when we went back through the documents, it was like finding missing parts of a puzzle. Pieces we had never been sure were important or not.

We found the man who had been sitting on the church wall. And he was the same man who had been pushing the bike up Lansdown Hill. He had been a key part of the original inquiry back in 1984; hundreds of police hours had been spent trying to find him.

He was in the system, buried under thousands of documents.

He was completely irrelevant to the inquiry apart from one freakish coincidence. Two of his friends in the 1970s had been a couple: Pauline and Christopher Hampton.

We never discovered who the jogger was.

Other parts of this puzzle didn't fit. We had become really excited about the witness who had seen the badly parked Ford Cortina as the young woman had crossed the street soon before Melanie's murder. That car was tracked down in our index card system. It didn't match the registration we had for Hampton's car in 1984.

Two vehicles. No link. A potentially brilliant piece of corroboration down the pan.

And the weeks were passing. If we didn't disclose all these documents to the defence, Hampton's barrister would have a good case for an abuse of process argument. This was a race against time. Yes, we had six months, but we also had 30,000 documents.

Glen Boxer was my disclosure officer. Glen was a dark-haired detective sergeant in his forties. He usually had a few days' growth on his face and he wore his shirt in the same way Gary Mason did: hanging out.

'Glen, how are we doing?' I would ask gently each week.

'One per cent, boss.'

'Christ!'

'A lot of documents, boss, we're going as fast as we can.'

The following week: 'Glen, how's it looking?'

'One point four per cent. We are working really hard.'

'Well done,' I said, silently screaming.

With all the names, addresses and details which were in this mountain of paperwork, one person, it was now becoming clear, was not mentioned: Christopher Hampton.

The offender was not in the system.

And he never had been.

At home, the uneasy truce was wearing thin: Matt and I rarely talked. There were two camps, mine and his. And there was trouble in my camp. Toby was still refusing to try in class. His dyslexia was a huge drawback and his teachers simply didn't connect with him. I was still being called into school every week.

Callum had finished school, but he preferred a life of drugs and parties rather than work and earning. Every time he left the house I wondered when I would see him again. Sometimes he would be away for days. And when he returned we'd fight and I'd tell him to find somewhere else to smoke his dope, which he did.

Connie, in the meantime, had sailed through her education without a blip and had just completed her GCSE exams.

'What are you going to do?' I asked, expecting her answer would include A levels and university.

'I've got a placement with an Olympic eventer. I can take my horse and I think it'd be good for me, good experience.'

Okay, not A levels, but at least she was following her passion.

'It's a good idea,' I said. 'Where is this trainer?'

'Belgium.'

'Connie, you're sixteen. That's the other side of Europe.'

'I'd like to do it, Mum. You've always wanted me to ride, I'll be doing what I love.'

I said we would see. We'd research the trainer and find out if people we knew had had dealings with her.

At work, I had the biggest case of my career, a multi-stranded, precarious, high-profile murder inquiry which needed complete attention otherwise a defence barrister would start screaming 'abuse of process'.

At home, I was living in a house which had never felt like mine, in a relationship with a man I barely talked to, and I was effectively a single mother with three children at what was arguably the toughest time of their lives.

And I was unwell. Hardly anyone knew – and fewer people seemed to care.

CHAPTER 39

AUGUST 2015

It started with a plane ticket to San Francisco.

Matt and I had been talking about going to see his brother in America in a few months' time. He had bought a ticket. Just one. For him. And that was the spark.

'I can't do this any more,' I said.

It was a conversation I'd been putting off for ages. Something else, like my medical check, which was five years overdue.

I had been trying to keep things going. Appeasing his ego, mollifying him after my promotions, feeling guilty about the demands and hours of my job.

'We'll sell the house, split things in two,' I said.

'No, you won't.'

'We haven't got much choice, neither of us can afford to buy the other out. This is not negotiable.'

Where was I going to move? What impact would this have on the children? Yes, soon Connie would be in Belgium, Callum was talking about going to Australia, but this was their home and I worried that what little stability they had would be taken away. Apart from their home, I was the only permanent thing in their lives and that was pressure.

Matt had also been planning to help me move Connie and her horse to Belgium. Instead, I arranged for a transporter to come. I loaded her things into the car and drove her myself across the Channel. I had never driven so far in my life; I had never been in the Channel Tunnel before, I had never taken a horse abroad, and I had never been so worried about my daughter.

What am I letting her do? I thought to myself as we found ourselves on the flat Belgian motorways.

And any worries I had were compounded when we arrived late at night to find Connie's new accommodation. I've busted human trafficking rings with fewer people sharing a room. But the trainer was an Olympian, Connie was excited and what choice did I really have?

Leaving Connie, I set off, already tired and anxious, heading back to a house which would soon no longer be home.

'What's happened to your lawn, Jean?'

I was looking out of Jean Road's kitchen window and saw little mounds of earth across her immaculate garden. I'd been doing my weekly shop and had got a couple of bags of groceries for her. I hadn't seen her for a little while. I didn't really need to talk to her about the case, Jean didn't really need any shopping, but I just wanted to see her.

'It's those bloody badgers,' she said. 'They keep coming in from next door. You can't stop them once they're on that run.'

We went outside and peered at the hole.

'It's not a sett, they're just tunnelling through,' she explained. 'But I don't know what to do. I've asked Dave to come and look at it, but he's always so busy.'

'I'll get Toby to have a look at it, he's strong.'

Jean glanced at me: 'How's everything?'

'It's all a bit tricky, really. At home.'

We went inside and sat in her front room. Jean in her chair, me on her settee.

'I drove Connie to Belgium the other week. Callum's off to Australia soon. God knows what he'll get up to. And Toby's lovely but struggling at school. And things are tough.'

'Try not to worry,' she said.

'I don't know what I'm going to do. Things are just horrible. Matt and I, things are coming to an end. It's so hard.'

'I understand that. That's not very nice.'

I breathed out, sat back on the settee and listened to silence. I realised Jean's home was the one place I could go to get any peace. Then I saw the picture of Melanie, her niece on her knee, taken just hours before her murder was on the cabinet.

Jean understood pain better than me. Better than anyone I knew.

'Okay, team, how are we getting on with disclosure?' I asked.

'Thirty-six per cent.'

'We have three more months, please go as fast as you can.'

The case was taking shape. The results had come back from the scientist who analysed Christopher Hampton's

CHAPTER 39

blood to see if it was Green. The expert was also working for Hampton's defence team, but we had agreed this could be achieved with no conflict. And the results were clear: Hampton had Green Blood.

The tech analysts had been through Hampton's phone and tablet. This showed nothing relevant, apart from an internet search about Melanie around the thirtieth anniversary of her murder.

Our search teams had seized a knife from Hampton's garage. It looked old and incongruous. We had wondered if it had been a trophy but forensic scientists said its shape was different to the weapon used to murder Melanie.

I also asked that my work be reviewed by a retired DCI, Gareth Bevan. I thought it worth someone looking at the state of the inquiry and adding ideas while I was away for my operation.

Andy Mott, the former forensic supervisor turned senior investigating officer, would lead the inquiry while I was away.

'Is it a big operation?' Hooky asked.

'No, but they say the recovery will take a little while. I've just had the odd pain here and there, nothing serious. The doctor says it's better to be safe than sorry.

'Gary says he'll come to see me, so if anything's going to get me moving, it'll be the sight of him approaching with a bunch of grapes.'

The car jiggled under the uneven weight of loose paving slabs in the boot as Toby and I passed along the country lane into Bath.

'Mum, do you have cancer?'

'No.'

'But you're having an operation to take out the growths.'

'Yes, but they're not cancerous.'

'But they might become cancerous?'

'I don't think so. And Toby, I know you're worried, but I'm not. And please don't go around telling people that. It's not true and it might never be true.'

'Are we going to leave our house?'

'I think so – we need to sell it first.'

'Thank God,' he said.

We got to Jean Road's home and Toby carried the paving slabs up the steps to her lawn.

'Lovely to meet you, Toby,' said Jean. 'Your mum's told me so much about you.'

Toby flushed a little and asked where the badger's tunnel was.

'You'll need to dig deep, Tobs.'

He smiled, got a spade from the car and started shovelling.

'I'm going to be off from the inquiry from next week. I've got this op and they say to have six weeks off. I've got a replacement, Andy, who is brilliant. But if you have any questions or worries, just call me,' I told Jean.

She gave me one of her looks. Knowing but subtle.

'How do you feel about this operation?'

'I'm okay about the operation, I've been in agony for years. But I don't like the idea of general anaesthetic.'

'I understand it's scary. The doctors know what they're doing.'

CHAPTER 39

I was dropped at the hospital by my dad. He lived nearby and had been a rock of stability in the turbulence of my home life. Matt and I were living under the same roof but leading separate lives. I hadn't wanted him to take me. Callum was out somewhere, Connie was in Belgium, Toby was with friends.

I went to the reception and was checked in.

A nurse greeted me and said she'd show me to my room. We walked through corridors with rooms either side. I glanced in as we walked past. People in bed with cards, 'Get Well' messages and cuddly toys. A few had visitors.

I was shown to my bed and unpacked my book and a magazine. I tried to make myself as comfortable as possible on a nil-by-mouth regime and in a panic about anaesthetic. I lay there, looking at the ceiling. What if there was a problem with the operation? What if I had left things too late? Who would look after my children? They weren't old enough to care for themselves, no matter what they thought. They had no one else who could do it.

What would happen with the trial? Andy was brilliant but he didn't know the case like I did. I knew what levers to push to get the team firing on all cylinders.

What would a defence barrister do if we came unstuck?

'Are you okay, Mrs Mackay?' said the nurse.

I nodded, my mouth was dry.

'You'll be pleased to know the operation was a success. Do you have any visitors?'

I shook my head.

'Just take it easy. You should do absolutely nothing for the next week. Don't lift a kettle, don't make a cup of tea, be careful with stairs, even. You won't be able to walk far without feeling faint. Baby steps. This was major surgery.'

Matt brought me home from hospital. He had said he would help. But we didn't talk. I looked out of the window, watching the countryside pass as we drove along the lanes to our village. I just wanted to get home without an argument. I shuffled through the door and inside, doubled up in pain, light-headed and faint.

'Why don't you go to bed?' asked Matt. They were just about the first words we had said to each other.

'I don't want to go to bed. I've just been on my own for a whole day having major fucking surgery.'

Wiped out, I couldn't summon the energy to argue so I went to bed. The next morning, I woke late and found myself alone in the house.

Don't lift a kettle, don't make a cup of tea, be careful with stairs, even, the words of the doctor were replaying in my ear.

I rang Matt: 'Where are you?'

'I'm playing golf, I told you.'

'I've just had major surgery. I can't do anything for myself, I'm fucking trapped!

'I don't need you to be here, I just need to know what you're doing. I can make my own arrangements. I just need to know. I just can't do anything for myself.'

I called my friend Sian and told her what had happened.

'You can come here, of course, you're welcome to spend as long as you need to.'

'Thank you.'

'You know I can't cook?'

'Can you do omelette and chips?'

'Just about.'

The next day, Sian's son Boz picked me up and drove me to her home in the countryside. I spent a week on her sofa, being fed omelette and chips, wondering how on earth I could get out of this mess.

A week later, I had returned home.

My friend Liz, who had helped me with the appointment a few months earlier, lived around the corner. She would come round and after a few days we'd walk a little way. Some days for ten minutes, other days it was twenty. Then we'd be back down to a quarter of an hour.

It didn't matter, I was getting out. Slowly, I started rebuilding my fitness.

Gary arrived. He knew Matt through work and it was very cordial. Handshakes and hellos. Matt left us to it.

Something about seeing Gary was so normal to me that I was able to summon some banter: 'How long did it take you to get here, Gary? Three days?'

He grinned and started updating me on the case.

'Disclosure's at 56 per cent,' he said.

I knew that would be the case. Other officers may have added 10 per cent for luck to make me feel better, but Gary's a straight talker.

He didn't bring grapes.

I started to feel better by increments and soon I could start driving again. And I was so desperate to see Connie, and determined to get away from the house, that I found myself driving to Belgium.

I had become paranoid about how she was living after saying goodbye to her in a room filled with fifteen wannabe jockeys. But when I got there, Connie was brilliant – level-headed, streetwise and safe.

She knew how to handle herself.

Physically I was slowly starting to get better. Walking further, feeling stronger. But mentally I knew I had to dig deep, to start preparing for the split I knew was on the horizon.

I was walking each day in the fields near the house. I would pass the cows grazing on the flat heights and descend the hills which fell away to steep banks to the stream at the bottom of the valley. Just me in the soothing air with my dog, who would scamper from one scent to another. This was the only place I could get any peace. I rarely cry but I found myself in tears.

And I thought I was alone.

'Julie?'

Fuck off, someone who knows me.

'Julie?'

It was my neighbour, Tess. Clerk to the parish council. I think she may even have been a bell-ringer at the church, she was so much a part of the village establishment.

'I heard you had an operation.'

I wiped away a tear and looked at her.

She gave me one of those looks Jean Road gives me. You can say what you want, but she knows if you're telling the truth.

'It's not the operation, is it?'

And it spilled out. Matt and I were splitting up. The pressure at home was too much.

There were many things at play and I could no longer cope. She suggested a support group that helped people in the situation I was in. I'm not one for group therapy, but I was so desperate I thought it worth a go.

'You won't believe how many people are living through the same thing,' she said. 'I'll get you the number. I'll take you if you need me to.'

Three days later, Matt drove me into Chippenham. It was now late autumn 2015 and the evenings had a chill, an early sign that winter was around the corner.

'I'm glad you're doing this. It's good you're getting help for your issues,' he said as I got out of the car outside the community hall. I shuffled across the pavement and went inside.

There was a sister group meeting upstairs. Down here was a large room and five chairs with a mixture of men and women.

One of the guys started talking. He was a different age to me, from a different place. But what he said resonated exactly with what I'd been going through.

Dawn, the group leader, asked, 'What about you, Julie?'

I talked about the conflict in my home, the competing pressures and demands and the behaviours of everyone. How despite me trying to help, it didn't work and quite frankly I didn't understand it.

I looked around. Everyone else just knew. The behaviours were not deliberate or aimed at us, they were just a consequence. As I started to understand it and feel the help and support around me, I felt I could actually deal with it, if only on a personal level.

Later, I sat down with Callum and Toby at home.

'I've got these leaflets and I want you all to read them. I think we all need to realise that how we act impacts others around us.

'Callum, your weed smoking's out of control, it's having a huge effect on your life. You're not yourself, you're angry, you're doing things you wouldn't normally do. And those things are affecting me. And Toby.

'I'm trying to get us all help. Things have to change.'

Cal looked back at me blankly. I gave the leaflets to Matt and his son George.

'Matt, please read this …'

Months later things hadn't changed. Despite all my efforts, no one else wanted to make a difference.

And I hit a new low.

I had walked further than usual. The dog and I strode beyond the fields, down the valley, into a copse of trees by the stream. My head was swirling with the same thoughts: how did things get to this? This was my life. What was the point of anything?

The sun was high now in a cloudless, late-morning sky. I noticed the light dancing through the reds and browns of the turning leaves from the giant trees above. The only sound was the occasional yap from my dog above the gentle gush of the little brook.

Why was nature so much calmer than humankind?

I looked around and took the place in: it was just so tranquil.

Who would care if I wasn't around?

Everything about this place was soothing: the water, the air, the trees, even the muddy simplicity of ground underneath. My life was so full of exhausting conflict: catching criminals at work, at home I had addiction, exclusion, expectation and responsibility. How could nature be so *peaceful*? What was it about the landscape, about the environment, that was gentle in a way people were not?

I couldn't stay here. I needed to go back, needed to face all the shit in my life.

Or what if I didn't?

I looked up at the broad oak tree, its thick branches stretching, reaching across the stream.

I had investigated hangings before. They were the worst type of death to deal with. Now I studied the branches in this quiet place and contemplated what it would be like.

The pain would stop.

Who would notice? Who would care?

So, this is what it felt like to be suicidal.

If I had been sane, perhaps I would have felt shocked. But I was just numb. I had never sunk to these depths before.

I looked again at the branch: it seemed like such an obvious and peaceful answer. Staring up, it seemed simple, easy. It would all go, I could just be with nature.

But what about my children?

I had to be responsible, I had to be there for them.

I picked up my phone and found a helpline number attached to a police email.

'Hello, this is CareCrew.'

'Hello,' I said. 'I need some help. I get this service through work and I'm starting to get low, I mean, really, really low.'

'Why's that?' asked the woman.

'Well, I've just had this operation, a major thing, really. And no one's taking it seriously, everyone expects me to just carry on.'

'Ohh, oh no,' she said.

'And I've got a massive job to get back to when I've recovered. I mean, a huge job. I can't make the slightest mistake. If I do, well, it's not worth thinking about. The responsibility is overwhelming.'

I started walking away from the stream, started climbing the fields back towards the house.

'I've got one child who's on drugs, the other's always suspended from school. And a third who's not in the country. I've got no idea what she's up to or if she's safe …'

I stopped to breathe.

'But the biggest thing's my relationship. I'm trapped, I am fucking trapped. This man despises me, he certainly doesn't do anything for me. I'm at the end of my tether.'

'Well, you need to get out then, don't you?'

I looked at my phone.

'How the fuck am I going to do that? We have a fuck-off massive mortgage, I'm financially committed beyond anything I can afford. I don't have the money to rent anywhere and I've got no one to stay with.'

'Oh, that is a bad situation. Well, the only thing you can do is get out of it.'

'Didn't you hear me? I've just explained, I can't get out of it.'

I hit the red button on my phone, terminating the call.

'Stupid fucking bitch!' I yelled.

Nobody heard.

CHAPTER 40

NOVEMBER 2015

Kate Brunner QC's offices were behind a wrought-iron gate, down an ancient alley in a hidden corner of one of the oldest parts of Bristol.

I had put back my return by an extra week. I hadn't felt ready to deal with the challenges of live murder inquiries while I was so physically and mentally tender, but now it was good to have the prospect of finalising the case against Christopher Hampton.

'The case is shaping up well,' said Kate.

'Yes, 80 per cent disclosure. Not far to go.'

Kate had questioned everything: every line, every fact, every assumption and we were able either to answer her questions or to verify our point quickly.

'I don't think we should call Ben to give evidence,' she added.

I'd assumed that our key witness would appear in court.

'Why not?'

'He couldn't identify Hampton from the line-up. And I'm not sure how well he will come across, giving live evidence.'

He was our star witness.

'The defence will tear him apart. He's clearly a very nice man, but Hampton's barrister will be able to sow enough doubt about him that we should rely just on his written statement.

'Did you do a video interview with him at the time?'

'No.'

'Why not?'

The truth was we hadn't thought to. I wished I could go back in time six years and tell Alan Andrews to get Ben's testimony on tape.

'And there's also the chance the defence might call him,' said Kate.

'And rip him to shreds anyway?'

Christ.

Back in the Inquiry Room the forensic results were coming back. Scientists could link Hampton's DNA to four marks found on Melanie's clothing.

'What defence could he have?' Gary asked.

'Well, there was a case in London, wasn't there? A girl was found raped and murdered, they got the guy through DNA. And in court he stood up and claimed he was walking back from the pub, stumbled across the corpse of a woman. He said she'd been murdered by someone else but he had an urge to commit necrophilia.'

'Did the jury believe him?'

'No. People will say anything to get off a murder charge.'

'What more have we found out about Hampton?' I asked Meader.

'We've tried at the cricket club and looked for people who were members of the Red House Snooker Club, to see if he was a member at either, but no luck.'

'Have we tracked down his brothers?'

'Yes, they've had no contact with him for years. They know nothing. But we found the woman he had an affair with in Plymouth, back in the late seventies.'

'Does she say he's a killer?'

'No, but he was highly sexed, she said.'

'Hmmm …'

'Anything from Julie Hampton?'

'Well, she's not playing ball. The defence don't want her to engage with us.

'We could call her to give evidence, but we had no way of getting her to cooperate with the inquiry. We had to respect her wishes. The only thing of any interest is that he's always so calm, never gets angry, except one night in May he came home from work furious, said the police had been in touch.'

'Gary has that effect on people.'

'And we found an old work colleague who decorated a school in Weston-super-Mare in the summer holidays in 2003. He found Hampton wanking over a copy of the *Daily Sport* at lunchtime.'

'In a school?'

'The kids were away for the summer.'

'Still pretty seedy.'

'Another colleague describes him as "a thief, liar and pervert" and said they did a private job together. Hampton took all the money and told him to fuck off.'

A thief, liar and a pervert. We put Hampton through the matrix and realised he would have got more than fifty points, had he been in our system.

By now, I was sleeping in the barn, the annexe Matt and I had converted for our children to live as one big, happy, blended family. He was in the main house.

I was staring at the ceiling. It wasn't late but I spent a lot of time there, my mind wandering between the case progression, all the ways the defence might try to tear it to shreds, the breakdown of my relationship with Matt, money – or lack of it.

What was happening inside me?

And then my phone rang.

'Callum, are you okay?'

'I've had a bit of a crash, Mum.'

'What?'

Callum had booked flights to go to Australia and was on a last night out. I had a pang as I saw him leave the house on his motorbike, revving up the road in an uncertain way. I'd never wanted his dad to get him the bike.

'Where are you?'

He said he was at the Royal United Hospital, nothing broken.

'What happened?'

'A car had stopped at the zebra crossing in front of me, I didn't realise and it was wet and I went through the rear windscreen. I landed in the back seat.'

'Fucking hell, Callum! What were you doing? You could have been killed, you could have killed someone else.'

'I didn't and I haven't.'

'Have you been smoking weed? For fuck's sake, Callum! You can't do this. It's illegal, you'll hurt someone. And I'm a fucking detective, I'm the bloody law.'

Callum left for Australia two days later. Within a week, he called, saying he'd been arrested. Bouncers had picked on his friends and he'd got into a fight. Police had taken his passport. He wouldn't be able to work out there as planned.

'I told you to be careful out there. Aussie cops aren't nicey-nicey like me and the English police. And they don't like gobby backpackers.'

'Mrs Mackay, we really don't know what to do about Toby. He is simply so *disruptive*.'

I had been in this schoolroom the week before and the week before that. This time he had stormed out of the class, shouting at the teacher.

I had had the day planned out: more preparations for the Hampton prosecution.

And I had a board for a chief inspector's position looming.

But then came that call from school and I found myself on the M4, driving to hear what the latest drama was about.

'Well, I am really sorry for the other pupils,' I sighed at the teacher when I reached school, 'but what can I do? He's sixteen. All I know is that when Toby's at home he is the loveliest, kindest boy. Respectful and thoughtful. But when he comes into school, he kicks off. It only ever happens here. If I'm the problem, or our home life is, I'll do whatever it takes. But I'm not sure we're the problem.'

'Well, we're putting him in isolation again.'

When would they realise this wasn't helping him?

Could I just have a week when I dealt with normal issues? Why did my life have to be so... mad?

A storm was breaking as I started driving out of Chippenham, heading back to work. Wipers flicked fat teardrops of rain from the windscreen. But I couldn't see the road ahead, everything was blurred.

It wasn't the weather, I realised: I was crying.

For fuck's sake. What am I doing? What has my life become? I'm in my mid-forties, I've got a good job, I love my family, but everything is out of control. I'm just bouncing from crisis to crisis and no one has my back. Who is there for me?

I turned on to the M4 and started heading west, but I couldn't keep driving. Through my tears, I saw the slip road for the service station. I pulled into the car park, finding a space away from the big saloons driven by businessmen, trucks parked by delivery guys and young, smiling families with children skipping happily in puddles, off to get their lunch.

The rain was pounding the car now. I turned up the radio to drown out my sobbing. I glimpsed the rear-view mirror and saw my wet, burning eyes and tear-streaked make-up.

Why had things come to this? Why did things always happen to me? Everyone around me seemed to float through life in states of marital bliss, packed lunches prepared by caring spouses, financial security, children at university. At my age, most of my friends were healthy, comfortable and together. Getting promoted, finding success. At ease. I was spiralling. Just spiralling. And I couldn't get a grip on anything. I had never felt more desperate in my life.

I picked up my phone and called the care helpline – I hoped that woman wouldn't answer.

This time it was a man's voice.

'I don't know what I'm going to do,' I said. 'I've rung you before. I can't sort things out, I genuinely don't know what to do. I'm trapped in a home we can't sell, I'm financially committed. I don't have any fucking money to get out.

'My kids are rampant, or two of them are. And I have all this pressure. Pressure from work, from the school, from my ex.

'I am dealing with drug-taking, a child who is always being expelled, I don't sleep and I am *broken*.

'And nobody helps. I'm there for everyone and no one's there for me.

'If I didn't have my children, I would seriously think about taking my life.

'Listen to me … I am fucking *demented*.'

There was a silence.

'Okay,' he said. 'I'm going to get you some help.'

What? Had someone actually listened to the words I was saying? It took me a moment to understand what he'd said.

'You need emergency counselling and I'm going to arrange that for you straight away.'

He checked that I wasn't going to do anything stupid, then he rang off and called back with the contact details for a counsellor in Bath.

I took down the details and we said goodbye.

I was too upset to thank him.

I looked down at the number, scribbled on a receipt.

I don't know who you are, I thought about the man on the end of the line, *but you've just saved my life*.

CHAPTER 41

I was still trying for promotion. The worst board had been the previous year. It had been on the same day as a hard-fought trial. We had charged five men after a forty-nine-year-old was found dead in his home in Bristol. He'd had forty-nine separate injuries. One of the accused had even cut off part of the victim's ear. But we were struggling to prove they'd killed him because he had died of renal failure. The forensics were dubious. Somehow the pathologist had managed to miss a couple of stab wounds on the body.

The defence was dogged, but late in the day the jury had returned its verdicts for a mix of crimes, including robbery and assault.

Within an hour, I was in my Chief Inspector's board. This was the second in a few months. I had passed the previous one, but a colleague had beaten me by a point to get the job. He had then been promoted within six weeks to a superintendent's position. But Avon and Somerset Police had decided they didn't want to give the job to me, even though I had passed the board. I would have to try again. And I arrived at Portishead headquarters with my mind still on the five-handed case back at Bristol Crown Court.

I have always struggled with boards and this was the worst.

As I left, the Assistant Chief Constable thanked me.

'Have you had a busy day?' she asked.

I told her about the case.

Her face fell.

'Why didn't you tell us? We'd have rescheduled.'

'I didn't think I could.'

And now I found myself in another room with two senior officers and a woman from human resources, trying to prove once again why I should be made a chief inspector.

I left the room with the same lack of hope. I had been burned too many times.

We were making our final preparations for the case, going through our lists of things to do, ticking things off, when CPS lawyer Huw Rogers called me. It was a week before trial.

'Julie?'

'Yes.'

'You sitting down?'

'Why?'

'Christopher Hampton. He's going to plead guilty.'

'What makes you say that?'

'His solicitor's written to me.'

'What the actual f—?'

'Yes. Well done, Julie.'

'Well, does that mean he has to plead guilty in court? Can he change his mind? Is that a legal document?'

'No, yes and no. Nothing's confirmed until he stands up in court and pleads guilty. But his lawyer has copied in Bristol Crown Court, so the judge will know.'

'Well, we'll prepare as if the case will go ahead. Just in case it's a tactic.'

'Very wise, Julie.'

He hung up.

I don't believe it, I said to myself. *I just don't believe it. What if he doesn't enter that plea on the day?*

I had called Jean, Adrian and Karen Road and told them that I needed to see them. I said I would have to break some big news which was exciting, important, but I would also have to have a difficult conversation too.

I made an appointment to see Karen later, but went to Jean's first. Adrian was there.

Jean made tea, pulled out a packet of biscuits and we sat down in the lounge.

'We've got some incredible news. We've received an indication that Christopher Hampton's going to plead guilty.'

'Really?'

'But nothing's set in stone until he actually stands up and says it. He could change his mind, the whole thing's down to him.

'We'll prepare as if it's a "not guilty".

'Although you're witnesses, your testimony is unlikely to be challenged. You'll be in court and you will hear the details.

'This is heartbreaking. What happened to Melanie will be talked about in court in forensic detail. And it's horrific.

347

But I want you to be prepared. I don't want you to suddenly hear all of this while you're surrounded by reporters and lawyers. I've got the opening speech which sets it all out. I can do this now, or I can tell you another time. But you should listen to it before court to be prepared.'

Jean said that she wanted to hear it now. And she sat in her front room – in the same room where, thirty-one years earlier, she had learnt about her daughter's murder – while I read the opening speech our prosecuting barrister Kate Brunner had drafted. Brutal details of Melanie's final moments.

If I have had harder conversations in my life, I can't remember them.

Jean knew everything that I had told her, but she had buried the details deep. Perhaps, over the years, the ghastly forensic facts of what her youngest daughter had gone through had been covered by kinder, warmer thoughts of what Melanie had been like. It was as though I was informing Jean of Melanie's murder again. I thought for a moment that what I was saying to Jean would be the death of her. She was, after all, eighty-one years old: how could any mother of any age cope hearing these details again?

'If he does plead guilty, you have the option of writing victim impact statements. You can ask a police officer to read them out in court or you can do it yourself.'

They said they would think about it.

As we said goodbye, all three of us were in tears.

CHAPTER 42

9 MAY 2016

I woke early. Truth was, I hadn't slept. At 5.30 a.m. I opened the door and, with the dog, made my way down the footpath at the side of the house and into the fields.

I had been going to counselling. I still had little idea of how I would get out of my mess. The property market had stagnated during the lead up to the Brexit referendum and no one wanted ours. But this morning there was a freshness in the air, a sense of promise. I felt a sense of destiny; I felt something was changing.

I had spent the weekend preparing for today. I had spent the last seven years preparing for today. If Hampton pleaded guilty, I had a press statement in my folder. I had written it over the weekend. If he denied the charge and we went to trial, we had a prosecution case: arguments, witnesses, exhibits and evidence and we would unleash thirty-two years of work in his direction.

I had seen a pile of papers on Friday: Jean, Karen and Adrian's victim impact statements had been taken by my sergeant, John Dowding. He'd left them on my desk with a note on top: 'This is why we come to work'.

I made my way to the edge of the valley. The sun was rising across the brow, casting great beams of gold from the horizon as the dog ran free. I was excited, but was emboldened by a peace I could feel. I couldn't remember the last time I had felt this.

In my mind, preparation was beating apprehension.

I was ready.

I had stood next to the Queen before. I'd been responsible for her safety during a royal visit to Bath, years before. I'm only 5'4" and I'd towered over this tiny figure. She had been amazing, the way she held herself, the way she kept her composure with the cameras, the crowds and the craziness all around her.

Smiling impenetrably.

And something about watching Jean Road arrive at Bristol Crown Court on the morning of Christopher Hampton's trial reminded me of the Queen. The throng of news crews out front, the click-click-click of their cameras.

I had arrived twenty minutes earlier. No one had snapped me as I entered. None of the photographers knew who I was. A juror perhaps? Just anonymous.

And when Jean appeared, she walked slowly, quietly and graciously into the court building. Gently leaning on her stick, her face impassive. Adrian and Karen were with her. Neither shared their mother's serenity.

Adrian looked nervous, Karen was flustered.

It was only when Jean opened her mouth to she revealed what she was thinking: 'I want to look this monster in the eye ...'

'How are you doing, Jean?'

'I'll be better when this is over.'

I nodded to Adrian and Karen.

'Shall we do this?' I asked. I opened the door. Jean moved slowly through the doorway. Karen and Adrian followed. A group of reporters waited quietly behind as Jean tap-tapped her way into court.

Jean, Adrian and Karen had never been in this courtroom before. Their last hearing had been Hampton's first appearance before Bath Magistrates nearly a year before. This was a grander stage, intimidating, imposing. The press bench was full. Journalists whispering, laughing, comparing notes.

Kate Brunner QC was looking through her papers. Hampton's barrister sidled over to her and said something in a low voice. She nodded.

To the left was a block of twenty seats in four rows of five. The front row had laminated signs saying 'Reserved' on each of the seats.

'These are yours.'

I looked up at the public balcony above and saw Pauline, Hampton's first wife. She gave me a little wave.

I sat directly behind the Road family. Huw Rogers was behind Kate Brunner. Gary found a place near me. This was the day we had both worked so hard to get to, waited so long for. So much had happened since I'd joined him in the Review Team, since those days when the inquiry lay disorganised in a cold case storehouse and a man called Gallagher was the killer, for sure. We exchanged a look – a glance acknowledging the seven years of effort we had both made.

There was a knock at the judge's door. The room fell silent and everyone stood up. In walked Mr Justice Popplewell, a tall figure in a wig and red robes. A pale, authoritative, bespectacled man with a jutting chin and a serious face.

'Sit down, please.'

He looked around the room, at the bench, at the public gallery. His eyes rested for a moment on Jean, Adrian and Karen Road.

'The case of Hampton,' said the court clerk.

'Yes. Bring him up.'

The judge looked down at his notes. He had a laptop on one side and a set of legal books to the other.

There was a clink at the custody door behind and a young blonde security officer walked in. Hampton shuffled silently into the dock behind her. Seeing this old, colourless man in a cheap suit next to a young woman made him seem ever greyer, somehow.

Jean glanced at Hampton but was now looking back at the judge. Adrian gazed ahead. Karen had turned and was staring directly at her sister's killer.

Kate Brunner stood.

'Yes, My Lord, the case of Hampton, the murder of Melanie Road in 1984. We need to arraign first.'

'Yes, carry on standing, Mr Hampton.'

The court clerk stood up.

'Christopher John Hampton, you are charged with the murder of Melanie Road on the 8th to 9th of June 1984. How do you plead?'

I looked at Hampton.

It was a moment for which I had waited seven years. A moment for which Jean, Karen and Adrian had waited nearly thirty-two years. But there was no dramatic pause, no moment of glory for the accused. The answer came quicker than I'd anticipated.

In the end, it was a mumble. A quiet murmur from an insignificant man.

Barely audible.

'Guilty.'

I swung my head round and saw Adrian putting his arms around his mother and sister. They weren't crying, they were keeping it together.

Well done, Jean.

'Yes, we'll move on to sentencing. You may sit.' It was the judge.

Hampton sat as Kate Brunner returned to her feet.

'Yes, this was a murder which happened in the early hours of June 9th 1984.

'At 5.30 a.m. a milkman on his rounds and his son discovered the body of Melanie Road in St Stephen's Court. She'd been stabbed and was deceased. The post-mortem showed Melanie had died from her stab wounds. In total, she was stabbed twenty-six times.

'Melanie was a seventeen-year-old A-level student, the youngest of three children to Anthony and Jean Road,' Kate Brunner continued.

I noticed a sound coming from the dock. I looked around and saw the young blonde dock officer starting to cry. Hampton was looking straight ahead, but this security officer next to him had a tissue at her eyes, her face was reddening.

'… Christopher Hampton moved to Bristol in the 1990s, where he remarried and had another child. He continued working as a painter and decorator. He carried on living his life. In total, he had three daughters and a son. All of them completely unaware of their father's murderous past.

'Christopher Hampton has no other convictions. He never came to the police's attention for any reason. He led a completely ordinary life.'

Kate Brunner was now talking about how many years she thought Hampton should serve in prison, according to case law.

I looked at the dock. Hampton continued to stare blankly, his face like granite. Emotionless.

'... May I assist your lordship further?'

A nod from the judge.

'The family of Melanie Road have prepared victim impact statements, which they would like to read to the court, with your permission.'

The judge nodded and Kate Brunner sat down.

Adrian got up. I watched him move across the courtroom and into the witness box.

Every set of eyes in the courtroom was on him.

Except for Hampton's.

'My name is Adrian Road and I am the brother of Melanie Road.' Adrian spoke quietly, steadily. 'Saturday, June the 9th 1984. A day I had planned out as I had my final Navy exams on the Monday. A day Melanie had planned out as she had final A level exams on the Monday. We'd both spoken earlier in the week about our exams and how we were going to get really good marks.

'Her last comments to me, as I called her from the Nautical College in Glasgow, were: "Best of luck in your exams. I love you."

'Saturday, June 9th 1984, my uncomplicated world as a twenty-two-year-old student collides catastrophically with yours. Melanie didn't get to sit her exams on Monday. And neither did I.

'Because you murdered Melanie. You snuffed out her life and altered my life forever.

'I have spent the last thirty-two years worrying about every man that ever walked down the street, asking myself, "Did you kill our little sister Melanie?"

'Every man that sat near to me in a restaurant, "Did you kill my little sister Melanie?" Every man that I have ever met, "Could you have killed my little sister Melanie?"

'Even my friends, "Did they kill my little sister Melanie?" But now I know, thankfully, none of them killed Melanie.

'You did, you killed Melanie, you mutilated her, and you chose to abandon her. You abandoned her when she was dying, my little sister Melanie.'

Adrian's voice was still gentle and he didn't look up from his papers. I noticed the journalists in the press bench behind him were leaning in, trying to catch every word.

'You took away a very special person who was so close to me you wouldn't be able to understand or comprehend what she meant.

'She was a lovely girl and I loved her. We all loved her. You couldn't possibly understand how it feels to love another human.'

The dock officer was still sobbing. I noticed Adrian was raising his voice now.

'You couldn't possibly understand how it feels to show compassion to another person as you chose to murder a defenceless child. A child, only seventeen. You have no compassion, you have no right.

'*You killed a child*.

'A child who posed no threat to you, a child who was more interested in whether she would get three A levels which would enable her the choice of university. Thirty-two years I have patiently waited for the telephone call to say, "Adrian, we have him."

'Thirty-two years I have listened to dozens of police officers assure me, "Adrian, we will find him." They were right, they did find you and when they told me, I cried, uncontrollably. I cried.

'My six-year-old daughter asked me, "Daddy, why are you crying?" I had to tell her the man who killed Auntie Melanie, my little sister, a long time ago, has now been caught. So we are all safe. She didn't quite understand, but her innocent face looked up at me and started to think it over and even at her young age her moral compass points in the right direction. Her words to me were: "That is so sad, he needs to be punished."

'Your capture will not bring me closure. It never will. But I now feel safer that you will be locked away for a very long time.

'I take little comfort from the thought of you killing someone else's daughter but you are paradoxically caught by your own daughter's DNA.

'As you start your new life of being a convicted child murderer, I will start my new life of freedom. Freedom of the thirty-two years of not knowing.'

Adrian stopped talking. It felt as if no one was breathing in the courtroom. He was looking at Hampton. Just looking. Silent. Then Adrian nodded. He thanked the judge. He looked back at his family and walked back to his seat.

He passed Karen as she made her way to the witness box. Karen was going to cry. She wasn't in tears yet but I could feel them brewing. She clutched the papers as if her life depended on them.

Karen made it to the witness box, looked down at her papers, then started: 'My name is Karen Road and I am the sister of Melanie Road.'

It was striking, hearing Karen's voice. So loud, so clear after Adrian's quieter, measured delivery. The journalists on the press bench sat back as they scribbled their shorthand.

'People often tell me what a beautiful or safe place Bath is. When they tell me this, I just keep quiet. I think about my sister Melanie. I'd always longed for a baby sister, and when she was born in 1966, I thought all my prayers had been answered. She was pretty, sweet and clever. We used to call her a "little duckling" with her NHS glasses, with a patch over one eye. I knew she was going to turn into a beautiful swan one day, and she did.'

'Aaagh!'

I looked across at the dock. The security officer was leaning back, sobbing. Simply sobbing. Hampton's grey face hadn't moved. He stared ahead. Not looking at the woman in convulsions next to him. Not looking at Karen Road in the witness box.

Karen continued.

'You would think nothing could be worse than being told your little sister had been sexually assaulted and murdered in the most brutal way. But it did get worse. No one was brought to justice for her murder. At the time, we were told that Melanie had been stabbed twenty-six times, that she had suffered some kind of sexual assault, that she had been attacked, and left – as it turned out – heartbreakingly close to her home. In the absence of any more information, my imagination filled in the gaps.

'I've had thirty-two years to fill in the gaps. Melanie has died hundreds of times, in hundreds of different ways in my mind. While I'm awake, while I'm asleep. I could tell you that it's like being in a nightmare, but you wake from a nightmare and life returns to normal. This is a nightmare I can't ever wake up from.'

Karen paused for a moment, looking at her words. The room seemed frozen: journalists, police, lawyers staring at the witness box, the judge looked pale.

'I haven't wanted my whole life to be defined by murder. But it has been. Melanie's death has consumed my life and it's been frightening. For thirty-two years I've felt as if I'm living in a horror film, one where the perpetrator has not been caught. Not knowing who is responsible for Melanie's death has been torture. I can't explain the impact of not knowing who the murderer is, where he is. Is he nearby? Is it someone we know? Does he know who we are?

'My body and mind have been on red alert since 9th June 1984. It's exhausting. It's affected every aspect of my life: physically, emotionally, financially, relationships, work, my family, my girls, this nightmare has been their life; there's not a single thing that has not suffered as a consequence of Melanie's death and my suffering has been magnified by the horrific nature of her death.

'Grief is a lonely place. Grief caused by murder is lonelier. Having a sister is a special bond. Losing the sister I had longed for – and in such a violent, callous way – has left me traumatised.

'For years I was unable to retrieve any happy memories of Melanie and was constantly reliving her death. Her death has been all-encompassing and has defined her life as well as mine. I want to be able to remember her life, rather than the focus being forever on her horrific last hours. Melanie has disappeared. Since her death she's been a statistic, a crime to be solved, a court case. But she's my sister. She's a person, she deserves to be remembered for herself – caring, kind, sensible and intelligent; she was applying for university. She had dreams and wishes – about being married, having children – we'd talked about that during our last week together.

'She was due to go to the Greek islands on holiday. She was excited about life, about going travelling, about her little nieces. That last morning she'd bathed and dressed her youngest niece, a baby of just six weeks at the time. And that's the point at which her life, her future, was brutally taken away. If you want to know what it's like to lose a sister in this way, it's impossible to tell you. There's not a cell in my body unaffected. Not a single day passes without me thinking about her. For me, after Melanie's death, everything has been frozen in time, or buried.'

Karen's voice was starting to break now, she wiped a tear from her eye.

Come on, Karen, come on.

'Since 9th June 1984, I've hoped, desperately, for her killer to be brought to justice. For thirty-one years no one was charged for Melanie's murder. It's called a "cold case". To me, it has never been cold. It occupies all my thoughts and the police have continued to investigate leads and to re-examine evidence using new technologies. The impact on me of Melanie's murder not being solved is huge. I have wanted to do anything I can to help find and identify the person who killed my sister but this inevitably has come at a cost. The physical and emotional effort of trying to maintain a normal life while waiting for my sister's killer to be found is immeasurable.

'There is no "getting over" such a loss, such a death. I've longed for someone to be caught, but even the news of someone being charged has been very difficult. I've been catapulted emotionally back in time to day one of Melanie's death and I am reliving it all again. I'm glad I didn't know at the time of Melanie's death it would take thirty-one years for someone to be charged. It's hard to believe that, for thirty-two years, this evil person has not owned up to his horrific crime, has been willing to let us go on suffering the consequences of his terrible actions.'

Karen was looking directly at Hampton now. He continued looking at the judge.

'All I have ever wanted is justice for Melanie. My wish is that Hampton spends the rest of his life in prison and that I will be able to remember my happy memories of Melanie and for her memory not to be defined by her horrific last hour.'

The whole court seemed to breathe out as Karen stepped from the witness box.

Jean stood up. She hugged Karen – I couldn't remember seeing them having any type of physical contact before. Jean started across the courtroom floor. I noticed she'd left her walking stick propped against her chair. She was walking without her cane in front of the entire court and her daughter's killer.

Be strong, Jean. Don't fall. There's nothing to help you.

It was about five metres between the public gallery and the witness box. Adrian and Karen had covered that distance in seconds. Jean was taking ages. She looked good, but I realised I was holding my breath.

There's a step up, Jean. Watch. A step up.

Jean took that step and emerged, standing in the witness box.

I looked back to Hampton. He was still looking ahead. Maybe he was still looking at the judge, maybe he was looking at the wall behind the judge – he was paying no attention to Jean.

The custody officer next to him had calmed down and was dabbing her swollen eyes.

'My name is Jean Road and I am the mother of Melanie Road.'

Jean's voice cut through the court.

'On the 9th June 1984 at 9.15 a.m. our world fell apart. As we heard and saw a police car by the window, the officer was calling out Melanie's name. I ran out of the house, caught up with the car, frantically banging on the boot, "Stop, please stop!" The police officer escorted me back to the house and that's when all hell let loose as our lives were taken over by the tragedy and horror when hearing of our daughter's death.

'As we waded through the questions, identification and all that follows after a death such as Melanie's, the impact it had on our individual lives was and still is devastating.

'We forgot to eat, sleep was interrupted with constant nightmares. We lost weight.

'I wandered aimlessly through the streets of Bath, hoping to see a glimpse of Melanie. Searching the places we had visited together.

'Where Melanie's blood was spilled, I prayed that it would not rain to wash it away, and when it did, I cursed the rain for finally taking it away. I felt even the weather was against Melanie and the family.'

I looked at the press bench: a couple of the journalists were looking at each other as they took down Jean's words.

'We sat for hours traumatised by the horror of knowing Melanie was gone forever. To never see her beautiful smile and girlish laughter hurts beyond repair. We were not functioning properly.

'We constantly had no energy. My husband refused to talk to me about Melanie. I never knew if he discussed his feelings with anyone else in the family or at work. Therefore, it was inevitable that we drifted apart.'

The sobbing had started again in the dock.

Jean, you are amazing, I thought.

I had read these words over the weekend, but seeing them on paper was scant preparation for this spine-tingling moment: Jean in a courtroom, delivering an insight into the thirty-one and a half years of pain she had endured. Delivering these words to her daughter's killer in her beautiful crisp, calm, warm voice.

'My husband returned to work, not sure if he was functioning properly there because he certainly was not functioning when at home,' she continued. 'It was suggested I go back to work teaching, but I could not have borne the responsibilities of other people's children after what had happened to Melanie.

'We put on a face for the outside world. Once asleep, I hoped I would never wake up so that I could be with Melanie and comfort her.

'I couldn't and wouldn't speak to the few people I had got to know in Bath, for fear that they would tell me how to cope. I mistrusted everyone. I wanted to gather my other children and family together and disappear forever.'

I noticed the judge was wiping his eye.

'Yes, people were kind in sending letters, cards and flowers for which I was thankful, but I wanted Melanie, not these gifts. But that wasn't going to happen.

'The thought of what our lovely daughter had to endure on that fateful night still sucks the energy from within me. The horror of the way our daughter died hangs over us like a heavy lead weight which never moves away.

'Some days I think I have moved on with my life but energy forsakes me and the weight presses further and further down.

'Sadly, Melanie's father, my husband, now lives in a haze of dementia hastened by our daughter's death. When will this pain stop? The horror of that sunny day in June will never leave us.

'Our patience has been tested but we have survived these thirty-one and a half years, not without heartache and sorrow, whilst we have waited for justice to take its course to hopefully allow Melanie to rest in peace.

'I was forty-nine years old in 1984 when all this happened. Now in my eighty-first year, I pray that the family will find some peace. Over the past thirty years we have gradually been torn apart by this evil deed.

'Nothing will bring Melanie back, but I pray that the rest of the family can again be reunited.'

Jean looked at the judge. She nodded to him. She looked at Hampton, her face impassive. She folded her paper, went down the step and walked slowly back to her seat.

In the dock, the security officer was no longer visible. I could hear her crying – she must have been doubled up.

Meanwhile Christopher Hampton stared straight ahead. His face grey, like stone.

CHAPTER 43

Mr Justice Popplewell sentenced Christopher Hampton to life in prison with a minimum tariff of twenty-two years.

'You will very likely die in prison,' he told Hampton before instructing the tearful dock officer to take him down. Hampton's ex-wife Pauline watched as he exited through the security door. I noticed that his wife and daughter had stayed away.

I understood why the judge gave that sentence. He was tied by the sentencing guidelines from 1984. Had Hampton committed the murder today, the term of imprisonment would have been much heavier: a thirty-one-year tariff. And Hampton had lived a life of liberty for thirty-one years after killing Melanie.

There was no sense of jubilation from the Road family nor anyone else.

Kate Brunner said: 'I would ask that Detective Chief Inspector Julie Mackay be commended for her leadership over many years to ensure this case has been brought before the court.'

The judge agreed. A judge's commendation is a true honour.

Mr Justice Popplewell rose, exited and we started to leave the court.

I walked behind Jean, Karen and Adrian and was just passing through the double doors when I felt a tap on my back.

It was Huw Rogers.

'Julie, you were right, and you were right to bamboozle me into making the charge.'

'Thanks, Huw. We did the right thing.'

I embraced the Road family and said goodbye.

Avon and Somerset Police had provided a press officer for the day.

'Are you ready to do the court steps?' he said.

I nodded. He went outside to tell the assembled pack of camera crews and reporters that I would be a couple of minutes and to stand by.

It was dark in the court atrium and I quickly read through my notes, the words I had written over the weekend. I would have one chance to deliver this statement. A statement I had been waiting seven years to read.

I waited a moment, then stepped from the darkness of the court building into the bright May morning.

Clicks from the cameras, lights from the video crews ... I walked across the road to a cluster of microphones.

'Firstly, I want to pay tribute to Melanie's family who have been searching for the truth since 1984. They've conducted themselves with the utmost dignity and composure and their faith in us to find the person who murdered Melanie has given us the extra drive to keep going.

'The key to solving this case has been a combination of traditional police inquiries, advances in forensic science and the tenacity of a small group of officers and police staff.

'They've been supported by the wider constabulary and our forensic providers.

'Although Hampton has admitted murdering Melanie, he has spent more than thirty years living a lie, able to conceal his dark secret from all those around him.

'Aside from the devastating impact this has had on Melanie's friends and family, the after-effects of this case have been felt by many in Bath.

'I'd like to take the opportunity to thank them and everyone who has assisted in our investigations since the mid-1980s.

'Without the hard work of the police officers from that very first morning, the 9th of June 1984, and the support of the public today, the progress we've achieved would never be possible.

'I hope that this case sends out a strong message. It doesn't matter how long ago an offence took place, we'll never give up trying to find those responsible and bring them to justice.'

I went back to the court entrance, where I saw Gary Mason. For the first time that day, I noticed that he was wearing a tie.

I gave him a hug, I knew it would annoy him.

Then we returned to work.

Reports of Hampton's plea and sentencing made the lunch-time and evening news slots on national TV, as well as local, regional, national and international newspapers.

'*Well done, Mum,*' Toby wrote in a text.

Back in the office there were a few messages in my inbox. A lovely email from a PC I'd never met before, down in Somerset. But apart from a note from an assistant chief constable, there was silence from the wider chief officer group.

Then came the email from human resources:

> To Det Insp Julie Mackay,
> We regret to inform you that you have failed to pass
> the Chief Inspector's Board …

Within the space of two hours I had received a judge's commendation for my leadership of one of the biggest cold case investigations in British history and a job rejection for a position I already held.

That night, I went to Liz's house for a glass of wine. I didn't want to spend the evening at home. The following morning, I was up early at Kenneth Steele House. I was being interviewed by Piers Morgan and Susanna Reid for ITV's breakfast show *Good Morning Britain*.

'How did you do it?' asked Susanna.

'The way it came about was through tenacity and determination and using every investigative tool in our box to try to find out who was responsible,' I told her.

Piers Morgan: 'The incident involving his daughter was so minor, but because she got cautioned, she then entered the DNA Database.'

'It's often the smaller things in the investigation that complete the jigsaw puzzle. People have a concept that there's one big piece of evidence that leads us to finding the person responsible but actually, it's not. This case is like that. It's like doing a thousand-piece jigsaw of blue sky and you just have to put together the pieces and eventually you get the little bird in the middle,' I said.

Piers Morgan: 'The police get a tough time. I have to say this is one of those examples of outstanding police work. Talking to you, you look and sound a little like Helen Mirren, DCI Tennison. Are you getting movie offers?'

'Not just yet, I'm afraid I focus on my day job.'

Later that day, there were more television appearances and more interviews. I also saw that Gloucestershire Police, the neighbouring force, was recruiting for detective chief inspectors. I decided at that moment to apply. They needed the right qualifications and experience – I had both. And doors started to open.

CHAPTER 44

Had Christopher Hampton killed more than once? Was there evidence connecting him to any of the other high-profile unsolved murders?

After thirty-two years, we had still not identified the killer of the young mother Shelley Morgan, who vanished on 11 June 1984 and was raped, stabbed and left in a copse in a Somerset village. The psychiatrist in 1984 said her killer and Melanie Road's was likely to be the same man. Even in the early 1980s, knife-wielding rapists were a rarity. Could two men have struck twice within two days, ten miles apart? Christopher Hampton had been working in Clevedon at that time and would have driven near the deposition site on the Monday after he murdered Melanie on the Saturday.

We reviewed everything to do with the Shelley Morgan case. As I write, her killer has still not been identified.

Was Hampton anything to do with the disappearance and death of Melanie Hall, the hospital clerical officer whose killing had been on the same date as her namesake twelve years earlier? Her remains were discovered dumped in black bin bags on that motorway verge in 2009.

The parallels were haunting but also doubtful. Our inquiries into Melanie Hall's killing took us to other men, other names. We always kept an open mind about Hampton but we were unconvinced about his involvement in Operation Denmark.

And was Christopher Hampton the Bath rapist? The sex attacker who struck so many times in the 1990s? The Bath attacker fitted a similar profile to Hampton. The rapist knew Bath as a local man would; he had links with the eastern fringes of Bristol, as Hampton did. And one of the rapist's victims was convinced the court sketch of Hampton showed the man who tried to assault her. We did not proceed with that in court – there was no forensic evidence and identification wasn't strong enough – but the victim was convinced. The inquiries were always linked.

Hampton had married in 1997, around the time the bulk of the rape attacks stopped. There were just two more afterwards: in 1999 and 2000.

So far, we have been unable to prove a connection.

And there are other cases: Linda Guest was a thirty-five-year-old sex worker who had been picked up in St Paul's in central Bristol, driven away, probably in a van, and was found stabbed and sexually assaulted on a bridleway in a village north of Bristol. That was ten months after Melanie Road and Shelley Morgan were killed.

The same modus operandi.

And Helen Fleet, a sixty-six-year-old, was found stabbed in Weston-super-Mare in 1987. Neither of these murders have been solved.

Christopher Hampton has said nothing to anyone about his murder. He could do the decent thing and talk to cold case detectives to either confirm that he is responsible or allow us to eliminate him from the inquiries. I have written to Hampton in prison. After decades of investigating murders, I now work on homicide prevention. Why did he kill Melanie? What could anyone have done to prevent this murder? What could anyone do to stop another family suffering the same fate as Melanie Road and her mother, father, sister and brother?

Months later, at a golf club in Bath, we held a ceremony marking the conclusion of Operation Rhodium. Gary and I made a presentation showing how, over thirty-one years, we had each contributed to solving the case. Which part of that blue-sky jigsaw puzzle had we put in?

There were investigators and officers from the original inquiry. There were the two PCs who had arrested Clare Hampton and done the right thing, followed the guidelines and taken a swab in a report of domestic abuse. There were MCIT detectives and cold case investigators.

Original investigators from the inquiry were there. Lovely old detectives, true gentlemen. But all men, I noticed. Some had died; their relatives came in their place. Melanie's friends were there. Adrian came later in the day, Karen Road couldn't make it. And although she didn't attend, one person was there in spirit: Jean Road.

I have learnt so much from Jean. About resilience. About dignity. That sometimes it is all right to not be all right.

I was just a few months younger than Melanie when Hampton murdered her in 1984. When he appeared in court, I was a few months younger than Jean had been in 1984. And my daughter, Connie, was Melanie's age.

A lifetime had passed between crime and punishment.

It takes a certain type of officer to want to solve cold cases. To have that hunger and drive. I was lucky, I was in the Review Team when it was filled with investigators who were dedicated to achieving justice for the victims of unsolved crimes.

Not everybody has that bug. You need people like Gary Mason, Andy Mott, Claire Nelson, Kath Synott or me. People who have that determination, that attention to detail, that bloody-mindedness, that willingness not to accept the facts as they are presented. People who are dogmatic, open-minded, problem-solvers. People who are willing to think their way around an obstacle when it presents itself. But we were also helped because this was a good case, from that very first moment of the awful discovery of Melanie's body.

No corners were cut. All the investigators were ethical, nothing was compromised. We had complete faith that the detectives who had come before us had done the right thing.

In a way, it had felt like a relay race. Others had been running with the baton before us, it had been passed from one generation of detectives to another, and then finally to Gary and me. We had no idea that our journey to the finish line would be as long and as gruelling as it proved, but every step of the way was worth it – for Melanie.

Months later, Gary and I were invited to a ceremony in Rome, where we won the International DNA Hit of the Year award. Gary's sense of direction had not improved.

Afterwards, clutching the trophy, he got us lost as we went through the city centre, ending up in the red-light district.

Soon after returning to the UK, I passed my Chief Inspector's board at Gloucestershire Police with straight As. After failing so many boards over so many years, it was both exciting and liberating to do so well just by being myself. On my first day there was a murder and I ordered the arrest of fourteen people.

Things happened to me.

Within a year, I was a superintendent in charge of investigations in Gloucestershire.

I managed to sell the house I had bought with Matt. I left that relationship with some equity, two beds, a small table and a chest of drawers.

I found myself a cottage in the countryside and started building a new life. And a little while later, I applied for and became the head of the MCIT, the three-force regional murder squad.

As a young detective, I had dreamt of working on murder teams. Then I managed to get in, spending four challenging but rewarding years on MCIT. I had thought that becoming the head of the department would always be just beyond my grasp, but I achieved it and that was thrilling.

I learnt what it was like to lead a homicide investigation. I understood what it took to hunt a killer.

I thought back to my first exposure to a murder enquiry, my attachments to CID, my application to become a detective constable, interviews, exams, lying in bed late studying criminal law with a young baby who never slept. I thought of my promotions, the teams I had worked with, the resilience

374

and humour of the detectives. Balancing swimming lessons and pony club with rapes, GBH and drug dealers.

Looking after life's most vulnerable.

It had taken thirty years. Nothing about it was fast-tracked or accelerated, but I made it in the end.

I retired in April 2020. These days I work on homicide reviews and am asked to give talks and make television appearances discussing my experiences and offering analysis of ongoing crime cases.

Despite a few teenage wobbles, my children have all turned into well-rounded grown-ups. Connie rides for an international eventer, Cal lives abroad, Toby is a tree surgeon. The irony wasn't lost on me when his former school invited him back to give a talk to pupils about how to make a life for yourself after struggling in class.

We are a close family, my children and I. And I am so proud of them all.

Even though I seem to be busier than ever, I always make time for someone special.

I still see Jean Road.

Jean has taught me the true meaning of resilience. Alongside laughter, some tears and great inner strength, we have found in each other a very special relationship. Sometimes I'll just pop in to say hello and raid her biscuit barrel. Or we'll go to garden centres or the pub for lunch. Always starters and puddings, never mains. We check how we're both doing, catch up with each other's news, she'll chat about gardening, I'll talk about horses. But the conversation will always return to the person who brought us together.

We still talk about Melanie.

PHOTO CREDITS